KETO
Gatherings

Festive Low-Carb
Recipes for Every Occasion

KRISTIE H. SULLIVAN, PhD

VICTORY BELT PUBLISHING

Las Vegas

This book is dedicated to my friends and family with whom
I love to find any excuse to gather. Much love!

First Published in 2019 by Victory Belt Publishing Inc.

Copyright © 2019 Kristie H. Sullivan, PhD

ISBN-13: 978-1-628603-49-1

Front and back cover photos by Hayley Mason and Bill Staley

Recipe photos by Kim and John Varga of Berly's Kitchen, Jenny Lowder, and Kristie Sullivan

Cover design by Justin-Aaron Velasco

Interior design by Yordan Terziev and Boryana Yordanova

Printed in Canada

TC 0118

contents

Introduction

Keto Gatherings features some of my favorite recipes. These are the foods that my family has enjoyed as we have celebrated birthdays, holidays, milestones, and accomplishments and stayed on plan. Many of these recipes were developed for a specific loved one to replace a high-carb favorite or simply to combine preferred ingredients into a healthy low-carb dish.

Creating healthy versions of family favorites has been important to me for several reasons. For most of us, celebrations and holidays revolve around food—high-carb food that has caused years of compromised health. The challenge of navigating celebrations is often our emotional connection to those celebrations. The foods we eat to celebrate are frequently steeped in tradition. Moreover, food is often our way of expressing love in a tangible way. When we no longer eat those old high-carb favorites, it can be a challenge to feel like part of the celebration. At times, we might even feel somewhat resentful that we can no longer enjoy those foods. Others find that they end up going completely off plan in social settings simply because they feel deprived or won't refuse traditional celebratory fare.

Whether you commit to facing social situations 100 percent on plan or you find yourself wavering at the buffet table, navigating social situations is one of the hardest challenges to long-term success. If you're following a ketogenic diet for health reasons, you likely need to stay on plan all day, every day. This book is designed to support you through a year of celebrations. Regardless of the gathering, you can still participate by sharing foods you love with the people you love. It is my hope that this book gives you options that you can enjoy, and that when you serve these dishes, your friends and loved ones will accept and enjoy your "keto food" simply as a delicious option and not consider it "special diet food."

When I started creating this book, before anything was written, I envisioned it as a guide to the holidays. Too often, I've seen people go off plan and never recover from "just one day off." Sadly, diabetes doesn't take a day off. Neither does epilepsy, metabolic syndrome, or any of the other conditions that keto seems to help. Still, those of us for whom keto isn't optional need and want to celebrate. We still want to connect with others—to gather! Hence the title of this book.

I've organized this book by months of the calendar year instead of following the traditional recipe layout by appetizers, salads, main dishes, and so on. I invite you

to join me month by month as we celebrate with delicious foods and stay healthy. In addition to suggesting recipes for holidays and other special occasions, I've included four standard recipes for each month. First, you will find a muffin recipe. Muffins are a favorite of mine because they can be eaten for breakfast or as a dessert. I always feel that I'm spoiling the children a little when they can enjoy a homemade muffin for breakfast. These flavors are classics and are intended to add a seasonal option to each month. Second, I have included a birthday treat to give you ideas about how to spoil the birthday girl or boy with foods that just might give them many more happy years. Third, I have included a recipe for ice cream, because ice cream cannot be bound by season! Also, I wanted to show you how versatile and delicious a low-carb lifestyle can be. Lastly, I've included a celebratory cocktail. Our gatherings often do include adult beverages, and no one wants to be left out. Not only can you enjoy a low-carb cocktail on occasion, but you should probably plan on having enough to share, as even carbivores enjoy these! A long-term ketogenic lifestyle does not mean that you can't enjoy special foods. In my house, at my gatherings, deprivation is not on the menu!

Keep in mind that just because I've organized the recipes by month doesn't mean that you can't enjoy them any time of the year. You can use the index to find dishes to make whenever you want. Regardless of the month or season, I love the recipes in this book more than most of my other recipes simply because these are the foods that I have prepared for my loved ones. Christmas 2016? Yes, we had French Toast Casserole for breakfast! Thanksgiving 2017? I created a Cherry Yum-Yum recipe just for my mom, who didn't think I could, and it was a hit with everyone at the table! Since November 2013, my birthday, every birthday celebrated by Grace and David, every Christmas, every Thanksgiving, every Easter, and every other gathering that you can imagine has featured a low-carb menu. These foods have become a part of our traditions. Now these special family recipes can be part of your holidays and celebrations, too!

My Food Is a Love Story

Like many of you, and like generations before me have done, I have used food as a currency for compassion, care, and even love. God blessed me with a wonderful extended family that included two grandmothers who loved to cook. While they were very different in personality, they both, without any culinary training or even a high school diploma, could whip up a feast that not only fed loved ones, but kept them lingering at the table long after a meal and kept each of us looking forward to the next meal they prepared.

KRISTIE H. SULLIVAN, PhD

My maternal grandmother, Alice Burleson, was known simply as Grandmother. She was the most natural of cooks. She never baked much unless it was a holiday or birthday, but she cooked frequently. Grandmother's specialties were big pots of soup, dumplings, fried meats, pans of cornbread, and lots of fresh vegetables from the garden. Her two most "famous" desserts were fried jack pies (handmade apple turnovers) and a moist, decadent coconut cream cake, which she made only, and always, at Christmas. One of the reasons I love this book so very much is that I managed to make a truly low-carb version of her recipe—a version that her children and grandchildren have vowed is delicious!

Grandmother loved from the depths of her toes to the top of her curly head that only bumped against a measure of four-foot-nothing. She was fun and funny. Grandmother was passionate and possessed a sharp tongue that kept all of us in line. By all, I mean all six of her children, their spouses, and all fifteen-plus grandchildren with whom I grew up. She secretly told each of us that we were her favorite, but I knew I was because I was the only one with brown eyes. Each of her children had brown eyes like her, but I was the only grandchild with her brown eyes, which was evidence enough of my special status. Grandmother was a renegade in the kitchen. She rarely looked at a recipe, and when she did, it was merely a suggestion. She cooked using all five senses and whatever ingredients she had on hand.

My paternal grandmother, Ruth Huneycutt, was called Mamaw (pronounced "ma'am-aw"). In spite of her less-formal moniker, she was the more formal of my two grandmothers. While Grandmother expected us to be in the kitchen helping, Mamaw would say, "Too many cooks in the kitchen spoil the broth!" There was a stool designated for me to sit, watch, and talk while she cooked. I could ask questions and chatter all afternoon if I liked, but I was directed to stay away from the pots and mixing bowls unless it was time to "help my plate." Mamaw had several dozen cookbooks and hundreds of recipes clipped from newspapers and magazines. Although she had thousands of recipes, she insisted, "Ain't no recipe gonna tell me how to cook!"

She loved baking and served a dessert or two with nearly every meal. Her chocolate and vanilla pound cakes were staples in her kitchen. While they were good, her persimmon pudding was legendary. Maybe that's why fall is one of my favorite seasons. I still take note of the persimmon yield each year, even though the fruit is too high in carbs for me to enjoy. The entire dessert was surrounded by heightened anticipation as we waited for the first frost, which was supposed to make the fruit less bitter. We placed sheets under the trees and then shook them. Only the fallen fruit was sweet enough to eat; the rest was so bitter that it would pucker your lips up to the back of your head until Christmas day! We used the sheets to gather the ripe fruit, which was sorted into bowls. The skin and seeds had to be removed, and the fruit was strained to yield the precious pulp that would later become persimmon pudding. The long, laborious process of getting the pulp was a tremendous labor of love even before the cooking began. Besides persimmon pudding, Mamaw made the very best pumpkin and sweet potato pies you might ever beg to eat. My Pumpkin Pie Cheesecake (page 292) uses the base of her version for the pumpkin part.

If food is love, and it is, then I grew up immersed in it, with Grandmother being the cook who shined at cooking main dishes, sides, biscuits, and cornbread and Mamaw baking the cakes, pies, puddings, and casseroles. Both matriarchs lured family to their homes with a subtle, "I've got a big pot of vegetable beef soup and a cake of cornbread fixing to come out of the oven!" or a more direct, "I baked a pound cake for you." Or, "Y'all come on and eat with us; we got plenty!" And we went. And we were fed. We frequently left with storage containers full of leftovers.

My Mamaw died in 1992, and my Grandmother died in 2003, just a few months after Grace was born, but they are still a core part of who I am. They taught me that I was loved, and they taught me how to love. I grew up at their feet, watching them cook and serve. They both adored their families, and they were both fiercely independent in different ways. In this book, in my home, and in my life, they are still close by, whispering to me that there "ain't no recipe gonna tell me how to cook!"

In my own fiercely independent way, I aim to show you with this book that you can stay true to your health goals and enjoy delicious low-carb foods on nearly any occasion. Month by month, I share some of my family's and friends' favorite dishes. We use these foods both to celebrate and to stay healthy. Even more important, my extended family and friends love many of these recipes. Instead of thinking of our foods as "diet foods," they simply think of them as delicious. I never tire of sharing keto recipes with others, and I'm always thrilled when others enjoy the foods I make.

More than one person has told me that a ketogenic diet is "too restrictive" and that it "can't be sustained long-term." This book proves those notions wrong by offering up an extra-special serving of hospitality and asking, "Would you prefer a Pumpkin Spice Coffee or a Pumpkin Spice Margarita?" The recipes range from holiday classics like Green Bean Casserole to outrageous creations such as the Epic Banana Split Ice Cream Cake that I made for Grace's thirteenth birthday.

I also want to note that since going low-carb, my family has been intentional about creating new, nonfood traditions. I've included some of those new traditions at the beginning of each month's chapter. As we have become healthier and more active, we enjoy doing more together. We also spend less time hovering around the food table and focus more on spending time with the people we love.

Since I've begun sharing my recipes through YouTube, books, and blogs, I now get the joy of not only serving these new "old" recipes to my loved ones, but also watching as others enjoy making the recipes, sharing them with their loved ones, and then sharing with me on social media. It is truly a privilege to be included in your holidays and other special celebrations. I hope that if you make these dishes, your loved ones enjoy them as much as mine do.

KRISTIE H. SULLIVAN, PhD

Ingredients Guide

Before you begin tracking down ingredients at your local grocery store or ordering them online, you may find it useful to familiarize yourself with the ingredients frequently used throughout this book. While many of these ingredients are now widely available, some of them may need to be ordered online. As you stock your keto kitchen, please note some important information about the key ingredients used to make many of these recipes.

KRISTIE H. SULLIVAN, PhD

Fats and Oils

Butter. Butter definitely makes my life better. I use it for low-carb baking and to season foods. I don't often use it for frying because butter burns at high temperatures. For these recipes, use unsalted butter unless a recipe specifically calls for salted butter. Using unsalted butter allows you to adjust the amount of salt in the dish to your taste.

Ghee. With the casein—or milk solids—removed, ghee is a good option for most people who avoid dairy. In addition, ghee doesn't burn like butter and can be an excellent fat for roasting or frying.

Coconut Oil. Refined coconut oil is another good option for cooking at high heat. I use it when baking, roasting, and frying. The two basic types you will find in stores are refined and unrefined. Although some people swear by the additional health benefits of unrefined coconut oil, I tend to use refined because it has little or no coconut flavor, which my family prefers. If I want the end product to have a coconut flavor, then I defer to unrefined coconut oil. Coconut oil is often a good option for those who are dairy-free.

Bacon Fat. A personal favorite of mine, bacon fat works well for baking, roasting, and frying because it holds up to higher temperatures. Unfortunately, rendered bacon fat is not available commercially. To get it, you have to cook bacon and render the fat. It's a win-win, actually, because you're left with bacon to eat! If you avoid pork, you often can use butter, ghee, or coconut oil in place of bacon fat.

Avocado Oil. Avocado oil can be used for both hot and cold applications. I keep some on hand to use on cold salads and to make mayonnaise. It has a very mild flavor, so it works well in a variety of dishes.

Olive Oil. While there are many types of olive oil, I tend to use a light-tasting variety for most applications. If you like a heartier, more robust olive oil flavor, you can use extra-virgin olive oil. Manzanilla is a very mild-flavored olive oil. I enjoy using it in ice cream for an extra rich and creamy result.

Sesame Oil, Toasted. Most sesame oil is intended as a finishing oil and is not meant for cooking. Just a tablespoon adds great flavor to Asian-inspired dishes.

Dairy

Heavy Cream. My fridge is rarely devoid of at least a pint or two of heavy cream. I use it in coffee as well as in many different dishes. An excellent source of fat, heavy cream gives dishes a fantastic creamy texture. When possible, I prefer to use heavy cream because it has a higher fat content than heavy whipping cream, but heavy cream can be more difficult to find. You can always ask your favorite store to stock it. Another tip regarding heavy cream relates to carb counts. Despite nutrition labels saying that cream has zero carbs, it actually has 0.6 gram of carbs per tablespoon, meaning that ¼ cup contains 2.4 grams, which can quickly put you over your carb limit if you aren't careful. Just be sure to count all the carbs!

Sour Cream. Sour cream is a great thickener and a wonderful base for dips, sauces, and casseroles. Be sure to buy the full-fat version and to check the ingredients. Some brands have added food starches, which increase the carb count.

Crème Fraîche. Though pricey, crème fraîche is worth every penny. Similar to sour cream in texture, crème fraîche has a much higher fat content, is lower in carbs, and has a moderate amount of protein. You can use it in place of sour cream or use it to make a healthy full-fat alternative to yogurt; see my Yogurt recipe on page 344.

Cream Cheese. Cream cheese is another staple in my house. We eat it with deli meat and pickles or olives for quick lunches, and we add it to dishes to create a creamy gravy. When you shop for cream cheese, be sure to read the label and select a brand that has 1 gram of carbs per serving; avoid those with 2 grams of carbs per serving.

Mascarpone. Mascarpone is similar to a soft cream cheese but has a higher fat content and less protein than cream cheese. It can be used in sweet or savory dishes and pairs well with crème fraîche to make a high-fat, low-carb faux yogurt (see page 344).

Ricotta. Ricotta is another example in which the nutritional values vary greatly among brands. When buying ricotta, search for full-fat versions and check the ingredients for food starches. Always compare labels to find the brand with the lowest carbs and highest fat. Interestingly, store brands are often the best nutritional option because they contain the fewest additives.

Other Cheeses. After decades of searching for low-fat cheese options, keto lets me enjoy the fattiest versions! Double-cream Brie, Gouda, Gruyère, and fresh goat cheese are just a few of my family's favorites. Be aware that you generally want to avoid processed cheese such as American cheese, as well as anything labeled "cheese product." Most brands of American cheese include vegetable oils in their ingredients. You want to avoid anything that contains food starches or added oils, so be sure to check the labels.

General Pantry Items

Almond Milk. Almond milk is a popular dairy-free option. Be sure to purchase unsweetened almond milk and be vigilant about finding brands without added ingredients.

Coconut Milk. If you're dairy-free, coconut milk is an excellent choice, but again, you must be vigilant about reading labels. Too often, sugar and thickeners are added to coconut milk.

Coconut Cream. Like coconut milk, coconut cream often is adulterated with sugar and thickeners. In particular, you want to avoid the coconut cream used to make cocktails and other beverages, as they almost always contain added sugars. If you can't find pure coconut cream, you can place a can of coconut milk upside down in the refrigerator overnight. When you remove it from the refrigerator, turn the can right side up, use a can opener to remove the top, pour off the coconut water, and use the fattier cream that remains.

Ketchup. As someone who doesn't care for ketchup, I never dreamed that I would make my own. Who does that? After reading the carb counts and seeing the ingredients in commercial ketchup, I hope you do, too! Homemade ketchup (see page 338) is super quick to make and actually tastes better than the high-carb commercial options. Be careful about using "sugar-free" commercial brands, as many contain undesirable sweeteners and are higher in carbs than homemade.

Mayonnaise. Mayo is my favorite condiment by far; however, commercial brands can be problematic because they are often made with canola oil or vegetable oils, which are known to be inflammatory and are suspected of contributing to cardiovascular disease. In addition, many brands have added sugars. With the exception of Primal Kitchen brand mayo, which is made with olive oil and which I purchase when pressed for time, I prefer to make my own mayonnaise. You can find my recipe in my previous book, *Keto Living Day by Day.*

Mustard (Dijon, Spicy, Prepared Yellow). Low in carbs, mustard is a good keto condiment. I keep prepared yellow mustard on hand for burgers and deli meats, and I keep Dijon and spicy mustard in the fridge for salad dressings and other sauces and condiments. Just read the labels to avoid added sugars.

Pickles. As long as there is no sugar in the ingredients list, pickles are a great low-carb staple. The salt often helps with keto flu, and some people swear that pickles are perfect for combating food cravings.

Pork rinds. Don't underestimate the humble, inexpensive pork rind. I've used pork rinds to make everything from desserts (such as the Classic Keto No-Nana Pudding on page 130 and the Chocolate Éclair Cake on page 228) to casseroles (like my Best of Summer Seafood Casserole on page 210). Ground pork rinds make a great substitute for breadcrumbs and can even be used as a "breading" for fried meats. When one of my recipes calls for "pork dust," you can make your own by pulverizing pork rinds into a fine powder in a blender. Furthermore, you can use pork dust as a low-carb, high-fat flour substitute. My husband refuses to eat pork rinds straight out of the bag, but he has never refused them in a cooked dish. Don't be afraid to try them in alternative ways. Also, pork rinds vary by type. There are fluffy, crisp versions and smaller, harder, crunchy types. I tend to use the fluffy versions for cooking. These are also the ones that I pulverize to make pork dust.

Balsamic Vinegar. Just a splash provides a lot of flavor. Like other pantry options, carb counts vary greatly from brand to brand because of the sugar content. Buy with caution and use balsamic vinegar sparingly.

Rice Wine Vinegar, Unseasoned. Some brands are sweetened, so use caution and check the labels when buying rice wine vinegar. A few brands are very low in carbs.

Salt. I use basic table salt in the recipes throughout this book; however, you may choose to use sea salt in its various forms if you prefer.

Seasoning Salt. Many brands of seasoning salt contain added sugars or starches. Jane's Krazy Original Mixed-Up Salt is one brand that does not, which is why I sometimes refer to it by brand name in my recipes. You may use your preferred seasoning salt instead, but be aware of variations in ingredients and carb counts.

Coconut Aminos. An excellent alternative to soy sauce. My favorite brand is Coconut Secret, as it has a lower carb count than other brands. Coconut aminos are slightly sweet and not as salty as soy sauce or tamari. Reduce the amount of salt in recipes that call for coconut aminos if you choose to use soy sauce instead.

Fish Sauce. Fish sauce provides an excellent flavor to Asian dishes, but some brands have added sugars. Red Boat is one brand that does not, so I prefer it.

Tomato Products. All tomato products are not created equal. Many contain added sugars or sweeteners. The best advice I can offer is to read every label and to compare nutritional values among brands. I tend to use diced tomatoes or tomato sauce, as each is less concentrated and provides flavor without adding too many carbs.

Glucomannan. Made from the konjac root, glucomannan is an excellent thickener. Not only has it been shown to be safe for diabetics, but there is some evidence that it might even lower blood glucose. When using glucomannan, be sure to sprinkle it into the other ingredients, stirring as you do, so that it doesn't clump. Glucomannan thickens further as the dish cools, so take care to add only a little at a time.

Hemp Seeds. Hulled hemp seeds, or hemp hearts, contain great omega-3 fatty acids and offer protein to boot. Although hemp seeds come from the hemp plant, they contain little or no THC, which is the active drug in marijuana.

Alternative Ingredients for Low-Carb Baking

Without traditional wheat flours, creating baked goods can be a challenge. If you're new to using low-carb ingredients, you can learn a lot by following recipes and paying attention to how the texture and taste vary. I like to use a combination of almond flour, whey protein isolate, and oat fiber for most of my baked goods. This trifecta creates a finished product that closely resembles traditional wheat-based goodies. The key to consistently good results is to replace the gluten, which gives high-carb baked goods structure, with a protein that also provides structure when baked. For this reason, you will find that low-carb baked goods often use eggs, protein powders, pork rinds, and cheeses.

Remember that although many of these ingredients are called "flours," many of them are not flour and will not behave similarly. For example, neither almond flour nor coconut flour will thicken a gravy, and both will burn before they can ever be used as a reasonably good "breading."

Almond Flour. Basically just finely ground almonds. I prefer blanched almond flour rather than almond meal, which is more coarsely ground and includes bits of the almond skin. Finely ground almond flour produces baked goods with a finer crumb.

Coconut Flour. Although, ounce for ounce, coconut flour is much higher in carbs than almond flour, recipes call for far less of it. Coconut flour requires more moisture and more eggs (for structure) than other flour substitutes. I like to combine it with other ingredients to mask the coconut flavor, as my husband objects to anything that tastes remotely like coconut.

Hazelnut Flour. Although not as easy to find in stores as almond flour, hazelnut flour is lower in carbs than almond flour and has a rich, earthy taste. It works well in crusts and in some cookie recipes.

Oat Fiber. Oat fiber is probably the least well known and most poorly understood ingredient in the low-carb world. It must be ordered online. Oat fiber is not oat bran, nor can it be made from oatmeal. Oat fiber is the pure insoluble fiber from the outer husk of the oat. It cannot be digested or absorbed. Some brands have a very strong flavor that some people find off-putting. I strongly suggest that you use only LifeSource or Trim Healthy Mama brand, both of which are certified gluten-free. LifeSource is available from Netrition and Amazon. Trim

Healthy Mama is available from Amazon. Personally, I do not count the carbs from oat fiber because it is indigestible. Unlike other ingredients that include soluble fiber, oat fiber passes through the body in the same form in which it enters.

Psyllium Husk Powder. While my favorite brand, Source Naturals, is available primarily online, you often can find psyllium husk powder in the laxative aisle of the grocery store. Look for an unflavored version with no sweeteners or additives. Psyllium husk powder has a gel-like quality and adds a chewy texture to baked goods. It includes both soluble and insoluble fiber.

Whey Protein Isolate. Of all the ingredients you will use to make the recipes in this book, whey protein isolate is probably the most important to choose with caution. Whey protein isolate is different from whey protein. The isolate form has the lactose and casein removed. Whey is highly insulinogenic; whey protein isolate is not. Look for a brand that has zero carbs and no added sweeteners. There are only two brands that I recommend: Isopure Zero Carb Whey Protein Isolate (Unflavored) and Jay Robb. These brands are more expensive than the whey protein powders you are likely to find in many stores; however, those other products are full of really bad ingredients. Please use caution and good judgment when purchasing whey protein isolate.

Meats and Eggs

Beef, Ground. Not only is ground beef relatively inexpensive, but it's also easy to cook quickly, making it a staple in my kitchen. Often, I use 93 percent lean ground beef in recipes that have a lot of added fat so that the beef fat isn't simply drained away.

Chorizo, Mexican-Style Fresh (Raw). Mexican chorizo is high in fat and high in flavor! We love it in anything with a Southwestern flavor. Supremo brand is easy to find and does not contain added sugar and fillers, which you must be careful to check for when sourcing chorizo.

Meat, Deli. Deli meat often contains added fillers and sugars. When I buy deli meat for my family, I check the ingredients and purchase brands that have less than 2 percent dextrose.

Sausage. For some reason, manufacturers like to add fillers and sweeteners, particularly corn syrup, to sausage. You can easily make your own breakfast sausage with ground pork or look for brands that do not have added ingredients. Jimmy Dean Naturals is a relatively clean commercial option that I favor.

Bone Broth or Bouillon. Homemade broth is super easy to make and easy to keep stocked in the freezer. If you have difficulty sourcing ingredients to make broth, use caution when buying commercial brands. Look for products that have no added sugars or corn syrup solids. Not only do manufacturers tend to add these ingredients, but they also remove the fat, so store-bought versions are low in fat compared to homemade broth. If you buy broth that is low in fat, you can add some butter or your favorite fat to make it more ketogenic.

Eggs. I have used standard large eggs throughout this book. I prefer to buy pastured eggs, but if I can't find those, then I buy whatever is on sale.

KRISTIE H. SULLIVAN, PhD

Sweeteners and Flavorings

There are many different options for ketogenic sweeteners and many different opinions about which ones are best. As a general rule, I prefer to use the natural sweeteners erythritol, monk fruit, and stevia. I have also used, and like, xylitol. Artificial sweeteners such as aspartame, phenylalanine, and acesulfame potassium (Ace K) often raise blood glucose and keep cravings high, so I avoid them. In addition, some sugar alcohols that are ubiquitous in sugar-free products not only raise blood glucose but also can cause intestinal distress. Those include maltitol, sorbitol, and mannitol. Sucralose is an artificial sweetener that I do use from time to time; however, pure sucralose, which is 600 times sweeter than sugar, is not the same as Splenda. Splenda uses maltodextrin to provide bulk to sucralose; this bulk makes Splenda easier to use in conventional recipes because it measures cup for cup like sugar. The problem is that maltodextrin is a food starch and has a higher glycemic index than pure sugar! I do not recommend Splenda for that reason.

For the purpose of determining which sweetener to use, I'll describe their use by texture, form (liquid, powder, granulated, and so on), and intensity. Regardless of which, if any, sweetener you choose to use, be mindful that these sweeteners affect each of us differently. If you are diabetic, please use your meter to monitor your blood glucose to see whether a sweetener affects you adversely.

Liquid Sweeteners. Besides taste, the form that sweeteners take can be important. Most liquid sweeteners are very intense, with just a few drops providing the equivalent sweetness of ¼ to ½ cup of sugar. The liquid sweeteners with which I am most familiar are sucralose and stevia. The intensity of liquid stevia seems greater than that of liquid sucralose and varies widely by brand. Start with just a drop or two of either and add only a drop at a time until the taste is sweet enough for you.

Granulated Sweeteners. In addition to sweetness, granulated sweeteners can add bulk, which can be important in baked goods. Granulated erythritol and xylitol are examples of bulk sweeteners. Pure sucralose and powdered stevia are other non-liquid options, but they do not provide bulk. When I need bulk, I often use some erythritol or xylitol and then add powdered pure sucralose or stevia to achieve the desired sweetness. If you're using stevia, look for brands with 90 percent or higher steviosides to avoid the bitter aftertaste that is common in stevia products.

Powdered Sweeteners. Sometimes recipes call for powdered sweeteners. Using a powdered form can be important when you need a smooth texture, as in a ganache, a "buttercream" frosting, a creamy chilled dessert, or a sauce. If a recipe calls for powdered sweetener, you can simply run your preferred granulated sweetener through a blender or clean coffee grinder until it is powdery. You can also purchase powdered sweetener. Sukrin Melis is my preferred brand of sweetener. The powdered Melis variety is perfect for making icings and sauces. I use it to avoid the grittiness of granulated sweetener.

Brown Sugar Substitute. While there are a few good commercial brown sugar substitutes, you want to avoid anything that contains cane sugar, maple syrup, molasses, or other high-carb ingredients. If you can't source a good low-carb brown sugar substitute, you can add ½ teaspoon of maple extract to ½ cup of granulated sweetener to make a reasonably good, and inexpensive, version.

Extracts. Throughout this book, I use a variety of flavored extracts. Note that I use extracts and not "flavorings," which often contain questionable ingredients. I also avoid extracts with propylene glycol in them. Two excellent retailers of quality extracts are Silver Cloud Estates and OliveNation.

Chocolate, Cocoa Powder, and Cocoa Butter. When a recipe calls for chopped chocolate or chocolate chips, I often use a sugar-free chocolate bar such as Lily's, Cavalier, or Coco Polo, which are sweetened primarily with stevia and erythritol. I avoid sugar-free chocolate sweetened with maltitol, sorbitol, or other undesirable sweeteners (see page 19). Depending on the recipe, you may be able to use a chocolate bar that is 90 percent cacao or higher. The chocolate flavor will be richer and the chocolate will be darker; whether that is suitable or not is a purely personal preference. Some recipes call for unsweetened baking chocolate, which is simply the block of chocolate that you find in the baking aisle. Be sure to select bars that have no sugar or other sweeteners in them.

Many of these recipes also use cocoa powder, which acts a bit like an alternative flour. Be sure to buy unsweetened cocoa powder. One recipe calls for special dark cocoa powder, which should be found in the baking aisle. Special dark cocoa powder lends a deep, rich chocolate flavor for us die-hard chocolate lovers.

Lastly, there is one recipe that calls for cocoa butter. Be sure to purchase food-grade cocoa butter. While it is available in large chunks or chips, the chips are often easier to use. Again, check to make sure that you are purchasing pure cocoa butter with no other ingredients.

KRISTIE H. SULLIVAN, PhD

Making Substitutions

Some of these creations involve ingredients with which you may be unfamiliar. If you are just learning how to cook or bake with low-carb ingredients, you likely will be most successful if you follow the recipes exactly as written until you feel more comfortable adding a pinch of this or a dab of that. If you find that you need to make a substitution, consider whether you are varying the carb, fat, or protein content.

In addition to thinking about macros, consider whether a substitution will affect the moisture content, texture, or yield of the finished product. For example, if you use coconut milk instead of heavy cream, remember that coconut milk has a thinner consistency and less fat; therefore, the texture and moisture content will be different, as will the macros.

Finally, while I wish I was aware of a good substitute for oat fiber or whey protein isolate, I know of none that is consistently reliable. Egg white protein powder often can be used in place of whey protein isolate, but I have not tried it in each of these recipes. When I have tried using coconut flour in place of oat fiber, I have included that option in the recipe; however, please note that using coconut flour raises the total carb count of the finished product.

Tips and Tricks for Those
with Baking Trepidation

Baking Times. Among my most treasured possessions from my Mamaw are her handwritten recipes. She jotted them down on scraps of paper, listing each ingredient and then providing written directions for the preparation. Nearly all of her recipe instructions end with "Bake until done." That's it. "Bake until done." No baking times or other guidelines, such as, "Bake until the center is set." Due to variations in ingredients, oven temperatures, pan sizes, altitude, and so on, baking times may vary from my house to yours. For these reasons, I offer a range of baking times as well as guidelines for how the finished product should look or feel. I hope you find this guidance helpful so that over time, you can learn how to intuitively "bake until done."

Following Multiple Steps. Some of the more complicated desserts in this book involve several steps or multiple components. If you think of each component as a separate product and then combine all the parts at the end, the recipe will seem much easier.

Handling Baked Goods. If the idea of slicing a cake horizontally or removing an intact loaf of bread from a pan intimidates you, I completely understand. One never-fail tip is to line each baking pan with parchment paper, greasing the pan liberally before lining it. You can then use the parchment paper to lift the baked good out of the pan and place it on a serving plate. Baked goods also are easier to handle when they are completely cool, especially if they need to be sliced. For layer cakes, I often freeze the layers before slicing them, and I use a serrated knife to cut evenly through the layers. Just remember that a creamy icing hides a multitude of sins in a layer cake gone wrong. If all else fails, crumble or cube the cake into a trifle bowl and top it with dollops of icing as if to say, "I meant to do that!" No one will be the wiser.

KRISTIE H. SULLIVAN, PhD

Cooking Tools and Equipment

Cookware. A basic set of pots and pans is essential. I prefer stainless steel because it holds up well over time. The essential pieces include a 2-quart saucepan with a lid, a 9-inch sauté pan, a 10-inch skillet, and a 5-quart pot. While I use a variety of skillets, I am partial to cast iron and enameled cast iron, both of which easily transition from cooktop to oven. Oven-safe skillets provide flexibility and allow you to finish a dish in the oven without dirtying an extra pan.

Bakeware. In addition to oven-safe skillets, a couple of baking sheets (or cookie sheets) and rimmed baking sheets (or sheet pans) are essential. The baking sheets that I use measure 13 by 18 inches, 11 by 17 inches, and 9 by 13 inches. Also useful are sets of glass or ceramic baking dishes and ramekins that can be placed in the oven or microwave to serve multiple functions. Specialty baking may require one or more of the following:

- **Muffin Pan**—Most of my recipes call for a standard-size 12-well muffin pan. Even if the pan is nonstick, using parchment paper liners is a good idea.

- **Muffin Top Pan**—This is useful for single-serving desserts, as well as for making low-carb buns and cookies.

- **Donut Pan**—These come in varying sizes and are useful for donuts and low-carb bagels. The one I used for the recipes in this book makes a standard 3½-inch donut. Some donut pans accommodate a smaller 3-inch-diameter donut.

- **9-Inch Springform Pan**—This is a necessity for making cheesecakes. I always line the bottom with parchment paper so that I can remove the bottom of the pan and place the cheesecake on a cake plate or tray just before serving it.

- **Cooling Rack**—A wire cooling rack allows baked goods like cookies, donuts, and bagels to cool without getting soggy. It helps cookies crisp up a bit as well.

- **Ramekins**—These often come in sets and may hold 4, 6, or 8 ounces. The 6-ounce ramekins are generally the perfect size for my needs.

- **Broiler Pan**—A broiler pan enables you to crisp up meats or roast veggies while the fat drips away to be collected or discarded.

- **9-Inch Pie Plate**—This can be deep-dish or standard. I like having one of each.

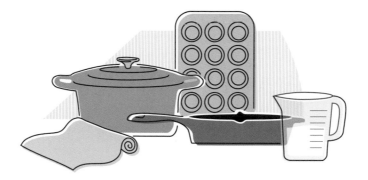

Cutting Boards. While I use wooden cutting boards for serving, I prefer to cut on a glass cutting board to avoid potential food contamination. Unlike wood or plastic, glass doesn't get cuts and therefore is safer to use.

Mason Jars. I enjoy using both pint and quart jars for storing salad dressings and condiments. Jars also work well for storing dry mixes for rubs, dressings, and other seasonings.

Measuring Cups. I'll admit to being a little obsessed with measuring cups. I prefer glass and stainless-steel measuring cups because they are easier to clean. Another important feature is the measurement being stamped into the glass or metal as opposed to being printed on, because the print often wears off with use.

Measuring Spoons. For those of us who do a lot of cooking, multiple sets of measuring spoons are a necessity. In addition to the standard sets that include ¼ teaspoon up to 1 full tablespoon, I have a set that includes a "tad," "dash," "pinch," and "smidgen," which are ¼ teaspoon, $^{1}/_{8}$ teaspoon, $^{1}/_{16}$ teaspoon, and $^{1}/_{32}$ teaspoon, respectively.

Mixing Bowls. Glass or stainless-steel mixing bowls are often the easiest to use and work well for hot and cold dishes. Glass bowls provide the additional advantage of being able to see whether the ingredients inside are thoroughly combined.

Strainer/Colander. These are useful for rinsing vegetables and shirataki noodles. I also use a strainer to strain the solids from bone broth and sauces.

Parchment Paper. I wouldn't want to bake without parchment paper! Thankfully, it is inexpensive and easy to find. I use it to line baking sheets, cake pans, springform pans, bread pans—anything you don't want food to stick to.

Wax Paper. Don't mistake wax paper for parchment paper. Wax paper has a waxy side and is good for allowing cookies to cool or for separating foods such as pancakes before freezing.

Kitchen Tools and Utensils

Cheese Grater. Whether it is with a box grater, a rotary grater, or a hand grater, I much prefer to grate my own cheese. While a box or rotary grater is easier for shredding more than ¼ cup of cheese, a hand grater is perfect for small amounts, such as for topping a dish with just a sprinkling of cheese. For large amounts, I use an attachment on my stand mixer that shreds several pounds of cheese quickly with little effort or cleanup.

Food Scale. This tool comes in handy not only for monitoring portions but also for weighing ingredients such as cheese, cream cheese, and meats.

Garlic Press. The flavor of fresh garlic is hard to replicate. I appreciate a garlic press that gives me finely minced garlic with little effort.

Kitchen Shears. My first set of kitchen shears was given to me as a wedding present. Since then, I have bought three more sets! I use them to cut open food packages, portion and trim meat, snip herbs, and trim shirataki noodles. My kitchen shears are exclusively used for food preparation and get washed frequently, so it is important that the blades come apart easily.

Quality Knives. I've cooked with dull, sharp, cheap, and expensive knives. Sharp knives make cooking much easier and more efficient. Invest in a good set and keep them sharpened.

Rubber Spatulas. I'm not sure how anyone can cook without rubber spatulas. They are perfect for mixing batters and doughs and scraping mixing bowls clean.

Thermometer. A quick-read thermometer is inexpensive and is indispensable for knowing when meats are cooked to a safe internal temperature.

Tongs. If you've ever used your fingers to flip frying meats, then you need a pair of tongs. I like those that are no more than 8 to 10 inches long for stovetop cooking. Longer tongs are useful for grilling and for turning foods in the oven.

Vegetable Peeler. This tool works well for removing the peels from vegetables like cucumbers, which are lower in carbs when peeled.

Whisk. A small whisk is ideal for mixing dry ingredients before incorporating them into a batter or dough. I also use a whisk when making a smooth cheese sauce or Alfredo sauce. Using a whisk seems to make the sauce a bit lighter.

Wooden Spoons. I really love cooking with wooden spoons. I use them primarily for making sauces, when I need to scrape the sides of pots and pans.

Zester. This small tool removes the outer layer of skin (or zest) from citrus fruits such as lemons, limes, and oranges. There are no carbs in the zest, but lots of flavor. For this reason, a zester is a necessity for low-carb cooking.

Appliances

Blender. Quick batters like pancakes or anything that uses eggs (such as the French Toast Casserole on page 312) can be made quickly in a blender. You also can use a blender to pulverize pork rinds.

Food Processor. While you can grate cheese and slice vegetables in a food processor, I enjoy using my food processor to make cookie dough. The dough seems to form better and to be more thoroughly mixed when I process it with the plastic mixer attachment.

Hand Mixer. A hand mixer is inexpensive and is easy to use to whip cream or make baked goods when you need more power than elbow grease can provide.

Ice Cream Maker. I received my compressor ice cream freezer as a Mother's Day gift in 2014, when I wanted to start making low-carb ice cream. We use it at least two dozen times a year to make small batches. Because of the compressor, one batch takes only about 45 minutes, which leaves plenty of time to make several different flavors. Other models are less expensive and work really well, so don't feel you need a compressor freezer to make great ice cream. Many models do require freezing the ice cream bowl for 24 hours before making ice cream, so having an extra bowl is handy if you want to make more than one batch at a time.

Immersion Blender. Also called a stick blender, this tool is useful for making mayonnaise and can be used to cream soups.

Stand Mixer. In case of fire, please grab my stand mixer first. A stand mixer is really useful for making cakes, cheesecakes, and muffins. I especially appreciate the attachment that whips cream while I pour in extracts and ingredients and keeps the whipped cream from spattering all over the kitchen. Stand mixers often come with attachments that make ice cream or grate cheese, which are especially helpful.

Slow Cooker. This working mom's best friend is a slow cooker that I can fill and set in the morning and trust to have dinner hot and ready when I return home. Even though it takes a while to cook foods in a slow cooker, it's an appliance that requires little hands-on time.

Guide to Using the Recipes

Many of the recipes in this book involve multiple steps. Even when a recipe appears complicated, I've provided simple instructions to make it manageable.

Don't fear ingredients that are unfamiliar to you. Many of them were once unfamiliar to me as well! I've included notes in the "Ingredients Guide" section about some ingredients that may not yet be staples in your kitchen. Also, the preceding section includes a list of kitchen tools to make cooking and baking these recipes much easier. If you're still feeling uncertain, remember that I'm a home cook with no formal training. If I can make these recipes, I know that you can, too!

Key Recipe Components

Yield

Because these recipes were developed for entertaining, most of them yield a large number of servings. You can easily halve many of the recipes to feed fewer people. With a few exceptions, the cocktail recipes yield one serving but can easily be doubled or tripled as needed. The muffin and bagel recipes all make one dozen, but most of these baked goods can easily be frozen, which makes them ideal for travel, for brown-bag lunches, or simply to satisfy a sweet tooth.

Icons

Icons are provided at the top of each recipe to give you at-a-glance guidance for avoiding allergens or knowing how quickly a recipe can be made. Look for the following icons to help guide your meal planning:

Dairy-Free. Recipes that are marked as dairy-free may include ghee, which is often safe for those who are lactose intolerant. If you don't tolerate ghee, you can often substitute another fat, such as coconut oil or bacon fat. Whenever possible, I noted whether almond milk, coconut milk, or coconut cream can be used in place of dairy; however, I have not personally tried many of these dairy-free substitutions in many of these recipes. If you are accustomed to cooking or baking dairy-free, then you may be able to make more substitutions than I have suggested.

Egg-Free. If you are sensitive to eggs or have allergies, use this icon to identify recipes that do not include eggs.

Nut-Free. While many baked goods are made with nut flours, I have included several recipes for muffins and other baked goods that are nut-free. This icon helps you find those recipes easily. For the purpose of this allergen icon, I do not consider coconut to be a nut because most people with nut allergies can tolerate coconut.

Carbivore-Friendly. The recipes marked with this icon are those that I've served to carb-loving family members, friends, coworkers, and complete strangers—and they have loved them! Carbivores need love, too, and these recipes will allow you to express your love with food that just might convince them that your way of eating is delicious enough for them to try it, too.

Make Ahead. Celebrations often happen at the busiest times of life, and an event or holiday often requires not only cooking, but decorating, socializing, and travel as well. Recipes that can be made in advance can help alleviate the stress of preparing a huge meal or buffet all at once. Also, because most keto-friendly baked goods taste better a day or two after they are made, many of these recipes should be made at least a day in advance. This icon guides you to those recipes.

30 Minutes or Less. Recipes marked with this icon can be made from start to finish in 30 minutes or less. This includes prep and cook time. When I entertain, I generally leave these recipes to be made last.

Freezes Well. Just in case your celebrations are cozier than a gathering of several dozen people balancing plates on their knees, I've included this icon to reassure you that any leftovers should freeze easily. Some people find that freezing desserts in individual portions helps them manage portion control better and leaves them with ready options when they want a keto-friendly dessert.

Nutritional Information

I have provided nutritional information for each recipe. The information I have included is based on the ingredients that I used. The macronutrients in an ingredient can vary widely from brand to brand. For example, brands of cream cheese vary from 1 gram of carbs per 1-ounce serving to 2 grams of carbs per 1-ounce serving. Because I use the brands that have 1 gram of carbs per ounce, when a recipe calls for 8 ounces of cream cheese, I count it as 8 grams of carbs. If you are using one of the higher-carb brands of cream cheese, you would count it as 16 grams of carbs.

Likewise, different brands of sausage, tomato sauce, dairy products, and coconut products are more likely to have widely varying nutritional information. Do use the nutritional information that I have provided as a guide, but know that it is not intended to be a substitute for calculating your own nutritional information based on the specific ingredients you use and the serving sizes you consume.

I do not count the sugar alcohols from erythritol in the total carbohydrate number, as they do not raise blood glucose for most people; you will find a separate listing for erythritol in those recipes that use it. If you are diabetic or have other health concerns, please test your blood glucose to know whether erythritol affects you negatively.

Also notice that I have provided a separate count for oat fiber. Oat fiber is the pure insoluble fiber made from the outside of the oat. It is completely indigestible and has been tested as safe for diabetics. Just as with any sweetener, you should monitor your blood glucose to know whether oat fiber impacts you.

Several good online recipe calculators enable you to select the brands of products you buy. I encourage you to use those calculators if you have any questions about the nutritional content of these recipes.

01
january

JANUARY has the distinction of being the first month of the year. For many of us, it brings some of the harshest winter weather. The grass is brown or covered in snow and the trees are bare, yet we ring in the new year well before the birth of spring. Perhaps the timing is to remind us that new beginnings start when we say they do.

For me, the first month of the year is a favorite. Not only is it my birthday month, but it is also the month in which we are most likely to get snow—a rare treat here in the South. In January, we celebrate New Year's Day, enjoy football bowl games, and try to stay warm as we resolve to do better in the coming year.

We make sure that our holiday decorations are put away before January 1 so that we don't go into the new year with that chore hanging over our heads. Our New Year's Day menu used to be filled with peas for change, collards for cash, pork for luck, and cornbread because we liked it! Our new keto traditions still include **Lucky New Year's Day Collards, Simple Roasted Pork,** and **Kristie's Keto Cornbread,** and I've added a hearty **Steamy Seafood Chowder** because seafood is associated with swimming into the new year. I've chosen a **Bloody Mary** for the January cocktail recipe because it pairs beautifully with a New Year's Day brunch menu. The muffin of the month is **Quick Banana Nut Muffins** because the flavors are warm and comforting, and the muffins are as perfect for breakfast on a cold weekday morning as they are for a leisurely weekend brunch.

Even though January is typically a cold month, the time is always right for ice cream. I chose cookie dough as the flavor of the month because Grace and David like it, and because I like to bake cookies in winter, so the dough can do double duty. When I make a batch of cookie dough, a third of the dough generally disappears before I can shape it into cookies and pop them into the oven. Yes, my family shamelessly snatches and eats my cookie dough from the mixing bowl. Some of the dough that survives is reserved and stashed in the freezer. I do this for two reasons: to keep it from being eaten before I can bake it, and to make **Cookie Dough Ice Cream.** Chocolatey cookie dough and creamy vanilla custard make January a little less gloomy. This frozen treat tastes even better when two or more of us enjoy it while snuggled in under a quilt on the sofa.

While our family doesn't follow football like many other families do, we occasionally take the time to watch, and I know that others love to throw football parties. I've included a versatile and hearty **Winning White Chicken Chili** recipe that can be made quickly in a pressure cooker or simmered slowly on the stovetop. For another winter classic, try Grace's absolute favorite meal, a **Chopped Hoagie Bowl,** which includes nearly every goodness included in a hoagie without the high-carb bread. The sauce has made this dish a hit with everyone who has tried it, and I love sharing it at parties because it is so simple to make. **Italian Meatballs with Tomato Sauce** is another great main dish to share, and no one would ever think of these options as "diet" food. For the tensest plays of the game, you can crunch on a snack that my family has unceremoniously labeled **Trash Mix.** This crunchy mix is bursting with great flavor but surprisingly contains no wheat or other grains.

Finally, I've included a **Chocolate Chip Cookie Pizza**—because warm chocolate chip cookies are delicious in every season!

Quick Banana Nut Muffins

makes
12 muffins
(1 per serving)

Banana nut is a warm flavor, which is why I've chosen it for one of the coldest months of the year. Whether you enjoy these muffins for New Year's Day brunch or make up a batch for quick weekday breakfasts, you will find that they are easy to prepare and tasty warm or cold. And no, bananas are not low-carb, but no bananas were harmed in the making of these satisfying muffins.

⅓ cup blanched almond flour

⅓ cup whey protein isolate

⅓ cup oat fiber, or 2 tablespoons coconut flour

1 teaspoon baking powder

¼ teaspoon salt

½ cup (1 stick) unsalted butter, cold

½ cup granulated sweetener, or more to taste

4 ounces cream cheese (½ cup), cold

3 large eggs

1 tablespoon sour cream

1 teaspoon banana extract

1 teaspoon vanilla extract

½ cup chopped raw pecans, toasted

Preheat the oven to 350°F. Line a standard-size 12-well muffin pan with parchment paper liners.

In a large bowl, whisk together the almond flour, protein isolate, oat fiber, baking powder, and salt; set aside.

In a separate bowl, use a hand mixer or stand mixer to cream the butter and sweetener. When the butter has lightened in color, add the cream cheese and continue blending until everything is smooth and well incorporated.

Add the eggs one at a time, mixing well after each addition. Mix in the sour cream and extracts.

When the wet ingredients are well blended, stir the dry ingredients into the wet ingredients by hand. Taste for sweetness and add more sweetener if needed. Add the toasted pecans and stir to combine.

Divide the batter evenly among the wells of the prepared muffin pan, filling each well about two-thirds full. Bake for 24 to 28 minutes, until lightly browned and just firm to the touch. Let cool in the pan for 5 to 10 minutes before serving.

Store leftovers in the refrigerator for up to 5 days.

CALORIES: 186 | FAT: 17.4g | PROTEIN: 6.1g | CARBS: 1.9g | FIBER: 4.2g | ERYTHRITOL: 12g | OAT FIBER: 5g

Decadent Chocolate Candy Bar Cake

makes
20 servings

Since I've known her, David's mother has always made a Hershey Bar Cake. It's a rich and creamy layered chocolate concoction with chopped bits of candy bar in the icing. The chocolate cake and the creamy, crunchy icing come together to make an amazing dessert—delicious, but decidedly not keto. I don't remember when I decided to try making this cake low-carb, but at some point I asked David's mother for her recipe. She eyed me suspiciously. I knew I could make the frosting low-carb, but I wasn't confident about the cake! Months later, I was attempting to make muffins and ended up with a batter that had a great cakelike texture. I grabbed a low-carb milk chocolate bar made by Sukrin and started making my very own low-carb Chocolate Candy Bar Cake. This healthier version is one of those cakes that makes keto sustainable for me for a lifetime. I love making it and sharing it because this is not deprivation. I've chosen it as my birthday cake because of the life I have now thanks to keto. January is also my mother-in-law's birthday month, so happy birthday to us!

CAKE:

½ cup unsweetened cocoa powder

⅓ cup blanched almond flour

⅓ cup oat fiber

⅓ cup whey protein isolate

1½ teaspoons baking powder

1 teaspoon instant coffee granules

¼ teaspoon ground cinnamon

½ cup (1 stick) unsalted butter, softened

1 cup granulated sweetener

2 ounces cream cheese (¼ cup), room temperature

3 large eggs

½ cup sour cream

3 ounces low-carb milk chocolate, chopped, or low-carb milk chocolate chips (see Tip)

Preheat the oven to 350°F. Butter two 8-inch round cake pans and line with parchment paper.

Make the cake: In a large bowl, whisk together the cocoa powder, almond flour, oat fiber, protein isolate, baking powder, coffee, and cinnamon; set aside.

In a separate bowl, use a hand mixer or stand mixer to cream the butter. Add the granulated sweetener and mix for 1 to 2 minutes; the color of the mixture should lighten slightly.

Add the cream cheese and mix well. Add the eggs one at a time, beating well after each addition. Scrape the sides of the bowl with a spatula and blend in the sour cream by hand.

Add the dry ingredients to the wet ingredients and mix lightly. Do not overmix. Gently stir in the chocolate, vanilla extract, and liquid sweetener.

Divide the batter evenly between the prepared pans. Bake for 20 to 22 minutes, until the tops of the cakes are lightly springy when touched gently. Do not overbake. Allow to cool completely.

While the cakes are cooling, make the icing: In a large bowl, use a hand mixer or stand mixer to whip the heavy cream until peaks just begin to form; set aside.

CALORIES: 214 | FAT: 19.8g | PROTEIN: 5.3g | CARBS: 5.3g | FIBER: 3g | ERYTHRITOL: 18.2g | OAT FIBER: 3g

1 tablespoon vanilla extract

4 to 6 drops liquid sweetener, to taste

ICING:

2 cups heavy cream, cold

1 (8-ounce) package cream cheese, room temperature

1 cup powdered sweetener

2 teaspoons vanilla extract

6 drops liquid sweetener

4½ ounces low-carb milk chocolate, finely chopped

In another large bowl, use the mixer to blend the cream cheese with the powdered sweetener. Beat in the vanilla extract and liquid sweetener. Use the mixer to blend the whipped heavy cream into the cream cheese mixture. Stir in the chocolate by hand.

To assemble, slice each cake in half horizontally to create four thin layers. Place one layer on a cake plate or serving platter and top with some of the icing. Continue stacking the cake layers with a layer of icing between them. Use the remaining icing to cover the entire cake. Place in the refrigerator to chill overnight or for at least 4 hours before serving. Store leftover cake in the refrigerator.

tip

Be choosy when picking chocolate for this cake. Some brands are sweetened with maltitol, which you want to avoid because it can raise blood glucose and/or cause gastric distress. For this reason, I prefer Lily's or Sukrin brand chocolate for this recipe.

Cookie Dough Ice Cream

makes
6 servings

Even though January is a cold winter month, you can still enjoy ice cream. Cookie dough mixed into creamy vanilla custard makes January a little less gloomy! If you prefer, you can add a large egg and ½ teaspoon of baking powder to the cookie dough, shape the dough into cookies, and bake them at 350°F for 6 to 8 minutes. Let them cool before crumbling and adding them to the ice cream.

1¾ cups heavy cream

1 cup unsweetened almond milk

5 large egg yolks

¾ cup powdered sweetener (see Tip)

2½ teaspoons vanilla extract

½ teaspoon salt

COOKIE DOUGH BITS:

½ cup blanched almond flour

2 tablespoons powdered sweetener

1 tablespoon oat fiber, or 2 teaspoons coconut flour

1 tablespoon whey protein isolate

2 tablespoons unsalted butter, softened

1 tablespoon finely chopped low-carb milk chocolate or chocolate chips

½ teaspoon vanilla extract

SPECIAL EQUIPMENT:

Ice cream maker

Heat the heavy cream and almond milk in a heavy saucepan over low heat, stirring with a whisk. Add the egg yolks and continue whisking until the custard begins to thicken.

Add the sweetener and whisk until completely dissolved. Continue heating, whisking constantly, until the custard thickens, about 10 minutes. When the custard coats the back of a wooden spoon or reaches 140°F on a candy thermometer, remove the pan from the heat. Do not allow it to warm to over 140°F or the eggs will begin to cook.

Stir in the vanilla and salt. Transfer the mixture to a bowl and place in the refrigerator to cool.

Make the cookie dough bits: Combine all the ingredients in a small bowl. Mix with a rubber spatula until the ingredients are well combined and a thick dough forms. Crumble the dough into pieces the size of small pebbles. Place the cookie dough bits in a single layer on a baking sheet and place in the freezer until ready to add to the ice cream.

When the ice cream mixture is cool, churn in an ice cream maker following the manufacturer's directions. Add the cookie dough bits to the ice cream while it is churning and after it has begun to freeze, but while it is still soft. Continue churning until it reaches your desired consistency.

Store leftovers in the freezer. When frozen, this ice cream will harden to a solid state. Allow to thaw at room temperature for about 10 minutes before enjoying.

tip

The type of sweetener used makes a huge difference in the texture of the ice cream. For the best texture, use allulose or xylitol; remember that each sweetener has different characteristics (see pages 19 and 20 for details). Use the sweetener that you prefer and that does not impact your blood glucose.

New Year's Brunch Bloody Mary

makes
2 servings

Even though I've never been a Bloody Mary drinker, I'm quite proud of this recipe! I love that I was able to create a version that tastes fantastic yet is low enough in carbs to be keto. The key to reducing the carbs was to use less tomato juice than is traditional, replacing the flavor with beef bone broth. (Yes, that was my idea!) When I discovered that this substitution worked, I immediately wanted to share this delicious drink with others—especially those who are fond of the classic cocktail. Each time, I got nearly the same response: "How did you do that?" Cheers!

½ cup tomato juice

3 ounces beef bone broth (see Note)

2 jiggers (3 ounces) vodka

1 tablespoon lemon juice

½ teaspoon Worcestershire sauce

3 dashes Tabasco sauce

1 teaspoon freshly grated horseradish

¼ teaspoon salt

¼ teaspoon celery salt

⅛ teaspoon ground black pepper

2 stalks celery, for garnish (optional)

2 lemon or lime wedges, for garnish (optional)

Mix all the ingredients in a pitcher and set aside. Fill two cocktail glasses with ice and strain the drink over the ice. Garnish with celery stalks and/or lemon wedges, if desired.

note ——————————————————
If using homemade broth, skim the fat before using it in this drink.

tip ———————————
To make this drink look really special, before filling the glasses, rub the rim of each glass with lemon juice, then dip it in celery salt, creating a thin coating of celery salt around the entire rim.

CALORIES: 120 | FAT: 0.5g | PROTEIN: 0.9g | CARBS: 3.7g | FIBER: 0.3g

New Year's Day

Kristie's Keto Cornbread

makes
8 servings

As I have done many times, I stumbled onto this recipe while trying to create something entirely different. This is one of my favorite low-carb breads that I have created. The bacon fat and corn extract set it apart (although my husband is less fond of the bacon fat than I am, so I've given you the option to use coconut oil if you prefer). Don't you let me catch you making this bread in anything but a cast-iron skillet. This recipe is too authentic not to use cast iron. I'd serve this to my grandfather if he were here to eat it, and I think he'd be proud!

⅓ cup whey protein isolate

⅓ cup oat fiber

¼ cup coconut flour

1½ teaspoons baking powder

¼ teaspoon salt

½ cup (1 stick) salted butter, melted but not hot

⅓ cup bacon fat or refined coconut oil, melted

4 large eggs

¼ cup water

¼ teaspoon corn extract

Preheat the oven to 350°F. Place a greased 10-inch cast-iron skillet in the oven to heat while you make the cornbread batter.

In a large bowl, combine the protein isolate, oat fiber, coconut flour, baking powder, and salt.

Add the melted butter, bacon fat, eggs, and water to the dry ingredients. Beat with a hand mixer or stand mixer until combined. Stir in the corn extract.

Pour the batter into the hot skillet and bake for 22 to 26 minutes, until lightly browned and firm to the touch.

CALORIES: 253 | FAT: 24.1g | PROTEIN: 7.4g | CARBS: 4.4g | FIBER: 2g | OAT FIBER: 7.5g

Steamy Seafood Chowder

makes
8 servings

Did you know that there's a tradition of eating seafood for New Year's so that we can swim into the new year? There's also a tradition of eating round foods to symbolize the continuous circle of new beginnings, which is why I chose to use shrimp and scallops in this soup. You can substitute other seafood, such as pieces of a hearty fish like cod, if you prefer. This chowder is relatively quick to prepare, which I think makes it even more perfect.

¼ cup (½ stick) unsalted butter

½ medium onion, chopped

2 cups chopped cauliflower, including stem

1 tablespoon dried parsley

1 teaspoon minced fresh garlic

2 cups chicken bone broth or seafood stock

⅓ cup white wine

3 ounces cream cheese (¼ cup plus 2 tablespoons), room temperature

¼ cup finely chopped sun-dried tomatoes (optional)

¼ teaspoon salt

1 cup heavy cream

1 pound medium shrimp, peeled, deveined, and patted dry

8 ounces clams, shelled and drained

8 ounces crab claw meat

8 ounces sea scallops

¼ cup grated Parmesan cheese, for garnish

⅓ cup chopped cooked bacon, for garnish

Melt the butter in a stockpot over medium heat. Add the onion and cook for 4 to 6 minutes, stirring often, until the onion is translucent and just beginning to brown.

Stir in the cauliflower, parsley, and garlic. When the onion is fully browned, add the broth, wine, cream cheese, sun-dried tomatoes (if using), and salt. Simmer for 5 to 7 minutes, until the cream cheese is melted and everything is well combined. The cauliflower should be just tender.

Pour in the heavy cream and return to a simmer.

Stir in the shrimp, clams, crab claw meat, and scallops and return to a low simmer for 6 to 8 minutes, until the seafood is cooked through. Remove from the heat and garnish with the grated Parmesan and bacon pieces.

CALORIES: 337 | FAT: 27.2g | PROTEIN: 16.3g | CARBS: 6.6g | FIBER: 1.4g

Lucky New Year's Day Collards

makes
8 servings

At the risk of embarrassing my ancestors, this Southern gal does not love collards. There. I said it. Because we have to eat them on New Year's for luck, I've found a way to make them taste better. The secret ingredients are salt pork, onion, beef bone broth, and apple cider vinegar. Bring on the good luck!

4 ounces salt pork, chopped

⅓ small onion, sliced

2 cloves garlic, chopped

2 pounds fresh collard greens, trimmed and chopped

1 cup beef bone broth

1 tablespoon apple cider vinegar

½ teaspoon ground black pepper

In a stockpot or Dutch oven over medium heat, cook the salt pork until it is browned and just barely crisp. Add the onion and garlic, reduce the heat to medium-low, and sauté for 8 to 10 minutes, until the onion is caramelized.

Add the collards and sauté until the greens are wilted and coated in the fat from the pork, 8 to 10 minutes.

Stir in the broth and vinegar, scraping the delicious bits from the bottom and sides of the pan. Cover and simmer over low heat for 1 hour, stirring occasionally. Remove the lid and continue to simmer for an additional 30 to 45 minutes, stirring occasionally, until the collards are tender. If the collards are getting too dry, add more broth as needed.

When the collards are tender, remove from the heat. Season with the pepper before serving.

CALORIES: 123 | FAT: 12.5g | PROTEIN: 1.8g | CARBS: 1.9g | FIBER: 0.9g

Simple Roasted Pork

makes
8 servings

When it comes to roasted meats, I think that simple is usually better. Forgoing a lot of spices or seasonings lets the flavor of the meat shine through, especially with a fatty cut like pork butt. Roasted meats like this are a protein palette for fatty sides.

1 (3-pound) pork butt or pork shoulder

1 tablespoon salt

2 teaspoons ground black pepper

Preheat the oven to 300°F.

Pat the pork roast dry with a clean kitchen towel and sprinkle with the salt and pepper. Place the roast on a wire baking rack set inside a roasting pan, fatty side up, so that the fat runs down into the roast as it cooks. Roast the pork for about 2 hours, until the internal temperature reaches 180°F. Because roasts vary in thickness, using a meat thermometer is the most accurate way to test for doneness.

Remove the pork from the oven and let it rest, uncovered. Increase the oven temperature to 425°F. When it reaches temperature, return the pork to the oven and roast for 12 to 15 minutes, until the outside is browned and the fat on top is crispy. Cut into slices to serve.

CALORIES: 316 | FAT: **19.5g** | PROTEIN: **31.5g** | CARBS: 0g | FIBER: 0g

Football Party

Game-Day Sausage Dip · 50

Winning White Chicken Chili · 52

Chopped Hoagie Bowl · 54

Italian Meatballs with Tomato Sauce · 56

Chocolate Chip Cookie Pizza · 58

Trash Mix · 60

Game-Day Sausage Dip

makes
8 servings

This thick, rich sausage dip is very similar to a dip I used to make years ago. The primary difference is that I don't serve this one with bread. While I might provide carby dippers for others, I enjoy this savory dip with sliced celery or pork rinds— or just a spoon! I think you will love it, too. This dip is excellent to serve in a small slow cooker to keep it warm. Just stir it occasionally to keep the bottom from cooking too much.

1 pound ground beef

1 pound bulk Italian sausage

2 tablespoons dried minced onions

1 tablespoon Italian seasoning

1 tablespoon Worcestershire sauce

1 teaspoon garlic powder

1 (8-ounce) package cream cheese, cubed

½ cup beef bone broth

½ cup heavy cream

1 pound cheddar cheese, shredded (about 4 cups)

Sliced green onions, for garnish (optional)

In a large skillet or Dutch oven over medium heat, cook the ground beef and sausage until well browned, 5 to 7 minutes. Drain the fat, if desired.

Add the onions, Italian seasoning, Worcestershire sauce, and garlic powder and mix thoroughly. Add the cream cheese and broth and stir until the cheese is melted.

Stir in the heavy cream and reduce the heat to a simmer. Simmer for at least 15 minutes, until the dip thickens. Remove from the heat.

Wait 10 minutes, then stir in the cheddar cheese; letting the dip cool a bit helps ensure that it will be creamy and the cheddar cheese will not become stringy. Garnish with sliced green onions, if desired.

tip

For a fun variation, use 1 pound of mild Italian sausage and 1 pound of hot Italian sausage, or use all ground beef for a milder flavor.

CALORIES: 632 | FAT: 51.2g | PROTEIN: 38g | CARBS: 4.1g | FIBER: 0g

Winning White Chicken Chili

makes
8 servings

White chicken chili is an easy yet flavorful recipe made even easier with the use of an electric pressure cooker. You can have this chili on the table in less than 30 minutes, and the leftovers taste even better the next day. Without tomatoes, this chili is very low in carbs. The extra dairy adds satiating fat, while the chicken provides perfect protein.

2 tablespoons bacon fat

2 pounds boneless, skinless chicken thighs

⅓ cup chopped onions

2 cloves garlic, minced

1 cup chicken bone broth

1½ cups chopped cauliflower florets

1 (4-ounce) can diced green chilies

1 tablespoon ground cumin

2 teaspoons chili powder

1 teaspoon dried oregano

¼ teaspoon salt

¼ teaspoon red pepper flakes (optional)

4 ounces cream cheese (½ cup), cubed

⅓ cup heavy cream

4 ounces white cheddar cheese, shredded (about 1 cup)

FOR GARNISH (OPTIONAL):

Sliced green onions

Chopped fresh cilantro

Sour cream

Place the bacon fat, chicken, onions, and garlic in an electric pressure cooker such as an Instant Pot; use the Sauté function to cook, stirring constantly, until the chicken is browned and the onions are translucent, 10 to 15 minutes. Pour in the broth.

Seal the lid and, following the manufacturer's instructions, cook on high pressure for 15 minutes; once finished, allow the pressure to release naturally.

Remove and shred the chicken, then return it to the pot.

Add the cauliflower, chilies, cumin, chili powder, oregano, salt, and red pepper flakes, if using. Cook on high pressure for an additional 5 minutes; release the pressure manually.

Add the cream cheese and heavy cream and stir until melted.

Sprinkle the cheddar cheese over the chili just before serving. Garnish with green onions, cilantro, and/or a dollop of sour cream, as desired.

note —————

You can also make this chili on the stovetop. Heat the bacon fat in a Dutch oven. Add the chicken, onions, and garlic and cook over medium heat until the chicken is browned and the onions are translucent. Add the broth and seasonings, increasing the amount of broth to 2 cups. Reduce the heat and simmer, uncovered, for 20 to 30 minutes, until the chicken is tender. Remove and shred the chicken, then return it to the pot. Add the cream cheese and stir until melted. Add the heavy cream, increasing the amount to ½ cup, along with the cauliflower and chilies. Simmer until the cauliflower is tender. Remove from the heat and wait 10 minutes before sprinkling the cheddar cheese over the chili and serving.

CALORIES: 318 | FAT: 18.9g | PROTEIN: 27.6g | CARBS: 3.8g | FIBER: 5.9g

Chopped Hoagie Bowl

makes
8 servings

Grace eats this delicious bowl for breakfast, lunch, and dinner! I can't seem to chop the ingredients fast enough for her. I use whole grape tomatoes rather than chopped tomatoes in this recipe so that the dish stays fresher longer and so that those who don't enjoy tomatoes can easily avoid them. If you want to lower the carb count, you can skip the tomatoes altogether, but don't omit the cucumbers, banana peppers, or red onions. Along with the sauce, those ingredients give the bowl just the right punch of flavor and texture. One bite and you will say, "Ask me if I miss bread!"

BOWL:

8 ounces Genoa salami, chopped

8 ounces ham, chopped

8 ounces roasted turkey, chopped

8 ounces provolone cheese, chopped (optional)

4 ounces mild cheddar cheese, chopped

2 cups shredded lettuce

1 cup grape tomatoes

½ cup peeled and chopped cucumbers

¼ cup chopped pickled banana pepper rings

2 tablespoons finely diced red onions

SAUCE:

¾ cup mayonnaise

¼ cup red wine vinegar

2 tablespoons olive oil

1 teaspoon dried basil

½ teaspoon Italian seasoning

½ teaspoon dried oregano

Place all the bowl ingredients in a large serving bowl and set aside.

In a separate bowl, whisk together the ingredients for the sauce.

Pour the sauce over the meats, cheeses, and vegetables in the serving bowl and toss to combine.

CALORIES: 454 | FAT: 36.9g | PROTEIN: 28.2g | CARBS: 5.2g | FIBER: 0.6g

Italian Meatballs with Tomato Sauce

makes
24 meatballs
(6 per serving)

These meatballs can be served in a large skillet, from a slow cooker, or on slices of mozzarella with tomato sauce spooned over them, as shown here. They are a hit with kids, teens, and adults because they are full of flavor. I love that I can whip up a batch quickly and freeze them either raw or cooked, giving me a quick option for a meal or gathering.

1 pound ground beef

1 pound ground pork

1 large egg, beaten

2 tablespoons dried minced onions

2 teaspoons Italian seasoning

1 teaspoon salt

1 teaspoon dried basil

1 teaspoon garlic powder

½ teaspoon dried oregano

2 tablespoons heavy cream (optional; see Note)

1 pound fresh mozzarella cheese, cut into 24 slices

2 (8-ounce) cans tomato sauce, warmed

Chopped fresh basil, for garnish (optional)

Preheat the oven to 375°F.

Place the beef, pork, egg, onions, seasonings, and heavy cream, if using, in a large bowl and use your hands or a large rubber spatula to mix thoroughly. Shape the mixture into twenty-four 1½-inch balls.

Place the meatballs on a rimmed baking sheet, spacing them at least ½ inch apart. Bake for 15 to 18 minutes, until browned and cooked through.

Before serving, place each meatball on slice of mozzarella. Spoon the tomato sauce over the meatballs. Garnish with chopped basil, if desired.

note

The heavy cream is optional, but it adds fat and gives the meatballs a softer texture.

CALORIES: 571 | FAT: 38.9g | PROTEIN: 43g | CARBS: 6.7g | FIBER: 0g

Chocolate Chip Cookie Pizza

makes
12 servings

My son doesn't always love my low-carb desserts, but he loves a large chocolate chip pan cookie. This recipe comes together quickly because you don't have to worry about refrigerating the dough or shaping it into individual cookies. You simply press the dough into a pizza pan, and off it goes into the oven. There is plenty to share with friends.

1 cup blanched almond flour

½ cup oat fiber, or ¼ cup coconut flour

½ cup unsweetened shredded coconut

1 tablespoon unflavored gelatin

1 teaspoon baking powder

½ teaspoon baking soda

1 teaspoon salt

¾ cup (1½ sticks) unsalted butter, softened

¾ cup granulated sweetener

2 large eggs

2 teaspoons vanilla extract

1 teaspoon ground cinnamon

4½ ounces low-carb milk chocolate, chopped, or chocolate chips

½ cup chopped raw pecans (optional)

Preheat the oven to 350°F. Grease a 16-inch pizza pan with coconut oil or butter.

In a large bowl, use a hand mixer or stand mixer to mix together the almond flour, oat fiber, coconut, gelatin, baking powder, baking soda, and salt, making sure that there are no clumps of gelatin.

Add the butter, sweetener, eggs, vanilla extract, and cinnamon; mix until a thick dough forms.

Stir in the chocolate and pecans, if using, by hand.

Spread the dough in the prepared pan and smooth the top. Bake for 15 to 18 minutes, until lightly browned and set. Let cool on the pan for at least 10 minutes, or the cookie will be crumbly. When the cookie has cooled somewhat but is still warm, slice and serve.

Trash Mix

makes
8 servings

I developed this recipe for my brother Stewart. Every year I would make a batch of classic Chex Mix to share at a family gathering and a second batch for him to take home. When I went low-carb, I worried about what to do. I didn't want to stop making his favorite snack, but I didn't want that high-carb version in my house. After a day or two of thinking, I decided to try mixing different textures of pork rinds to mimic the textures of the different cereals used in the carbivore version. I'm not sure who was happier that it worked, him or me! The only downside to this recipe is that it is just as addictive as the original version, which means I don't make it often, and I don't make it unless I have someone to enjoy it with me.

3½ ounces raw peanuts

3½ ounces raw pecan pieces

3 ounces crunchy pork rinds, broken into bite-sized pieces

3 ounces fluffy pork rinds, broken into bite-sized pieces

7 tablespoons unsalted butter

2 tablespoons Worcestershire sauce

2 teaspoons seasoning salt

1 teaspoon garlic powder

½ teaspoon onion powder

Preheat the oven to 300°F.

In a large bowl, mix together the peanuts, pecans, and pork rinds.

In a separate microwave-safe bowl, melt the butter in the microwave. Add the remaining ingredients to the melted butter and mix well.

Pour the melted butter mixture over the pork rind mixture and toss well to coat. Spread on a rimmed baking sheet and bake for about 45 minutes, stirring every 7 to 8 minutes, until lightly browned and toasted. Let cool and enjoy!

tip

If you don't have different types of pork rinds available, use whatever you have. I like to omit the peanuts to keep the carbs very low, but you can experiment with other nuts or low-carb kibbles.

CALORIES: 381 | FAT: 33.8g | PROTEIN: 17.1g | CARBS: 4.4g | FIBER: 2.4g

02

february

FEBRUARY brings the hearts and flowers associated with Valentine's Day, along with the hope for spring. While it's usually the last of the cold-weather months here in the South, we sometimes enjoy milder days—especially by the end of February when the daffodils begin to bloom. Influenced by Valentine's Day, I tend to think of February as a month for raspberries, chocolate, and white chocolate. Any combination of those, or a trifecta of all three (as in the **White Chocolate Raspberry Cheesecake**), is nirvana. I also associate February with comfort foods, which is why I included a recipe for **Asiago Rosemary Bagels.** Sometimes comfort food is necessary even at breakfast! These bagels are great way to spoil your Valentine while keeping him or her healthy, and rosemary stands for remembrance, so it is perfect for this season of love.

I'm not a huge fan of the Valentine's Day frenzy, but because I think of food as one of the many ways in which we show our love for others (or at least that I show my love for others), I've included some of my favorite recipes here. I like flowers because someone is thinking of me and wants to surprise me, not because they are trying to fulfill an obligation. Nonetheless, I'm not above spoiling my loved ones with **Bacon-Wrapped Stuffed Chicken Breasts with Asiago Gravy.** In fact, our family tradition for Valentine's Day is to stay in, dress up, and make a nice meal together. The children set the dining room table with our fine china. They are responsible for the centerpieces and for making sure the place settings are perfect. It's the one time each year that we eat in the dining room! We look forward to creating the menu together, and we especially enjoy the dessert after the dinner dishes are cleared and cleaned. **Keto Cherry Chocolate Ice Cream** is a great Valentine's Day dessert, or the kids could help toss together a batch of **Mud Pie Brownies** if you want to start your own Valentine's Day cooking tradition.

While no one in my immediate family has a February birthday, February 5 happens to be the birthdate of both my maternal and my paternal grandmothers. I always thought it was special that they shared a birthday. Although they both passed away more than a decade ago, they were important parts of my life. Each had a love of flowers and plants and loved to work outside. One grandmother insisted that you should never cut flowers and bring them inside. The other insisted that you must cut them and bring them inside to enjoy. They both loved peonies and grew them in their yards, which is one reason I wanted to feature peonies on the cover of this book.

My grandmothers passed on to me a love for plants and flowers as well as a love for feeding others. They cooked differently. One followed and collected every recipe she could find, yet declared, "Ain't no recipe gonna tell me how to cook!" I don't recall ever seeing the other grandmother follow a recipe, but that woman could make dirt taste good. She, like me, also loved to eat!

Both women loved to call the family to the table, and I'm convinced that they cooked primarily to encourage visits. I can still hear my maternal grandmother holler, "Y'all come fix your plates. Hurry up! It's getting cold!" My paternal grandmother, when thanked for a meal, would always answer, "I'm just glad you could eat it." I suspect that phrase had multiple meanings, acknowledging both that she was glad we were there to eat and that she was grateful the food was edible! You'll catch me smiling and using that same phrase with dual intent—glad you're here and glad you can enjoy it.

I'll confess that I, too, have been guilty of making food just to gain time with a loved one. I can only imagine my future self calling adult Grace and Jonathan and telling them that I've made something special just for them. I'm sure I'll just be happy that they can eat it with me.

One-Bowl Raspberry Muffins

makes
12 muffins
(1 per serving)

Inspired by Valentine's Day, these muffins get a lot of flavor from a few fresh red raspberries. The first time I made them, I had a TV news crew ask me for an on-camera interview. With less than three hours' notice before we went on camera, I was glad I had been experimenting with this slightly sweet muffin recipe—which the TV crew loved, by the way! I like to top them with a little crème fraîche or freshly whipped cream when I enjoy them for breakfast. Straight out of the oven, they are especially delicious smeared with butter.

6 ounces mozzarella cheese, shredded (about 1½ cups)

4 ounces cream cheese (½ cup), cold

6 tablespoons (¾ stick) unsalted butter, cold

½ cup granulated sweetener

½ cup whey protein isolate

⅓ cup oat fiber

1 teaspoon baking powder

¼ teaspoon salt

1 teaspoon vanilla extract

1 teaspoon raspberry extract

2 large eggs

6 ounces fresh raspberries

Preheat the oven to 350°F. Line a standard-size 12-well muffin pan with parchment paper liners.

In a large bowl, use a hand mixer or stand mixer to mix the mozzarella, cream cheese, and butter until well blended. Add the sweetener, protein isolate, oat fiber, baking powder, salt, and extracts and mix well.

Add the eggs one at a time, mixing well with the mixer after each addition. Gently stir in the raspberries by hand.

Divide the batter evenly among the wells of the prepared muffin pan, filling each well about two-thirds full. Bake for 24 to 28 minutes, until browned and just firm to the touch. Let cool in the pan for 5 to 10 minutes before serving.

Store leftovers in the refrigerator for up to 5 days.

CALORIES: 149 | FAT: 12.6g | PROTEIN: 8.8g | CARBS: 1.7g | FIBER: 9.1g | ERYTHRITOL: 8g | OAT FIBER: 5g

White Chocolate Raspberry Cheesecake

makes
16 servings

White chocolate raspberry is David's favorite flavor of cheesecake. I created this recipe because he enjoys the flavor so much, and it has since become one of my favorites, too. From the dark chocolate crust to the rich, velvety cheesecake to the burst of raspberry flavor in the sauce, it is a perfect dessert. It seemed fitting to make this cheesecake the birthday treat for February because of the combination of dark chocolate, white chocolate, and raspberries. If you don't have a birthday in February, I'd find someone who does and bake this cheesecake in his or her honor! Serve it with a few fresh raspberries and/or some freshly whipped cream.

CRUST:

5 tablespoons unsalted butter, softened

⅓ cup blanched almond flour

⅓ cup hazelnut flour

⅓ cup oat fiber

3 tablespoons unsweetened cocoa powder

2 tablespoons granulated sweetener

½ teaspoon vanilla extract

⅛ teaspoon ground cinnamon

6 drops liquid sweetener

RASPBERRY SAUCE:

6 ounces fresh raspberries

½ cup plus 2 tablespoons water, divided

2 tablespoons powdered sweetener

1 tablespoon unflavored gelatin

1½ teaspoons raspberry extract

½ teaspoon vanilla extract

Preheat the oven to 325°F. Line a 9-inch springform pan with parchment paper.

Make the crust: Mix together all the crust ingredients by hand in a large bowl, or combine the ingredients in a food processor. Press the crust into the prepared pan, making sure it goes about ½ inch up the sides. Set the crust aside.

Make the raspberry sauce: Place the raspberries, ½ cup of the water, and the sweetener in a small saucepan. Simmer over low heat until the raspberries are soft and begin to break down, 5 to 7 minutes.

Meanwhile, in a small bowl, dissolve the gelatin in the remaining 2 tablespoons of water. Add the gelatin mixture to the raspberry mixture, stirring as you add the gelatin.

Remove the sauce from the heat and stir in the extracts. Set aside to cool and thicken, about 1 hour.

While the sauce is cooling, make the cheesecake filling: In a large bowl, use a hand mixer or stand mixer to beat the cream cheese until creamy. Add the eggs one at a time, mixing well after each addition. Beat in the granulated sweetener until smooth. With the mixer running, pour in the melted cocoa butter. Add the heavy cream, extracts, and liquid sweetener and blend well.

To assemble, pour half of the cheesecake filling into the prepared crust. Top with the raspberry sauce, then the remaining cheesecake filling.

CALORIES: 359 | FAT: 36.5g | PROTEIN: 5.8g | CARBS: 3.5g | FIBER: 1g | ERYTHRITOL: 8.6g | OAT FIBER: 3.8g

CHEESECAKE FILLING:

3 (8-ounce) packages cream cheese, room temperature

5 large eggs

½ cup granulated sweetener

3 ounces cocoa butter, melted but not hot

⅓ cup heavy cream

1½ teaspoons vanilla extract

1 teaspoon raspberry extract

4 drops liquid sweetener

Bake the cheesecake for 1 hour 15 minutes to 1 hour 25 minutes, until mostly set with no jiggle. Turn off the oven, leave the oven door ajar, and let the cheesecake cool in the oven for about 1 hour before removing it from the oven to cool completely. When cooled to room temperature, place the cheesecake in the refrigerator to chill overnight or for at least 6 hours before slicing and serving.

Keto Cherry Chocolate Ice Cream

makes
6 servings

Cherries and chocolate are truly a dream flavor combination. The first time I made this ice cream, Grace and I were blown away. She kept saying, "Mom, it's so creamy!" I'd read that adding avocado oil to a custard base adds to the richness of the ice cream, but I'd never tried it until I created this recipe. Not only is the texture perfect, but the flavor is spot on as well. If you don't want to use oil, you can substitute an equal amount of heavy cream, but I encourage you to try making it with the oil.

6 large egg yolks

1¼ cups unsweetened almond milk

1 cup heavy cream

⅓ cup avocado oil or mild-flavored olive oil, such as Manzanilla

⅓ cup powdered sweetener (see Tip)

2 teaspoons cherry extract

1 teaspoon vanilla extract

4 fresh Bing cherries, pitted and finely chopped

2 ounces dark chocolate (90% cacao), finely chopped

SPECIAL EQUIPMENT:

Ice cream maker

Use a blender or hand mixer to mix together all the ingredients except the cherries and chocolate. Transfer the mixture to a small saucepan.

Heat the ice cream mixture over low heat, stirring constantly, until it reaches between 120°F and 140°F on a candy thermometer, 4 to 6 minutes. Do not heat the mixture to above 140°F or the egg yolks will cook. The mixture will begin to thicken and will coat the back of a wooden spoon. Take the pan off the heat and let the mixture cool.

When cool, churn the ice cream mixture in an ice cream maker following the manufacturer's directions. Add the chopped cherries and chocolate to the ice cream mixture while it is churning and after it has begun to freeze, but while it is still soft. Continue churning until it reaches your desired consistency.

Store leftovers in the freezer. When frozen, this ice cream will harden to a solid state. Allow to thaw at room temperature for about 10 minutes before enjoying.

tip

The type of sweetener used makes a huge difference in the texture of the ice cream. For the best texture, use allulose or xylitol; remember that each sweetener has different characteristics (see pages 19 and 20 for details). Use the sweetener that you prefer and that does not impact your blood glucose.

CALORIES: 291 | FAT: 27.4g | PROTEIN: 6.3g | CARBS: 5.2g | FIBER: 1.5g | ERYTHRITOL: 8g

White Russian

makes
1 serving

A dessert or a cocktail? How about a cocktail dessert? A White Russian makes an excellent finish to a Valentine's celebration, or makes an ordinary February day more special. Use espresso powder instead of instant coffee granules for a more intense coffee flavor.

2 tablespoons unsweetened cocoa powder

2 tablespoons powdered sweetener

2 tablespoons warm water

3 ounces heavy cream

1 jigger (1½ ounces) vodka

½ teaspoon instant coffee granules or espresso powder, or 2 tablespoons strong brewed coffee (such as espresso)

¼ teaspoon vanilla extract

Whipped cream, for garnish (optional)

Mix the cocoa powder and sweetener with the water to dissolve. Add the heavy cream, vodka, coffee, and vanilla extract and mix well.

Pour over ice in an Old-Fashioned glass. Garnish with freshly whipped cream, if desired.

CALORIES: 273 | FAT: 16.4g | PROTEIN: 3.1g | CARBS: 5.1g | FIBER: 2g | ERYTHRITOL: 24g

Valentine's Day

Asiago Rosemary Bagels · 72

Raspberry Vinaigrette · 74

Pan-Seared Scallops · 76

Lemon-Herb Compound Butter · 78

Bacon-Wrapped Stuffed Chicken Breasts with Asiago Gravy · 80

Mud Pie Brownies · 82

Asiago Rosemary Bagels

makes
12 bagels
(1 per serving)

Bagels on a ketogenic diet? I promise, these are good and very low-carb. We enjoy them for breakfast, including as bagel sandwiches eaten on the go. The Asiago cheese and rosemary add a nice savory flavor that combines well with bacon, sausage, or eggs. You can surprise your Valentine with a healthy but delicious breakfast sandwich and send him or her out the door with a smile. Rosemary, after all, is for remembrance. These bagels also are excellent toasted and served plain with butter or cream cheese.

5 ounces part-skim mozzarella cheese, shredded (about 1¼ cups)

2 ounces Parmesan cheese, grated (about ⅔ cup)

2 ounces cream cheese (¼ cup), room temperature

½ cup egg whites (about 4 large eggs)

3 tablespoons ghee or bacon fat, melted but not hot

¾ cup whey protein isolate

3 tablespoons psyllium husk powder

1½ teaspoons baking powder

½ teaspoon salt

¼ teaspoon garlic powder

½ cup very hot water

9 ounces Asiago cheese, finely shredded (about 2¼ cups), divided

1 tablespoon finely chopped fresh rosemary

SPECIAL EQUIPMENT:

2 (6-well) donut pans

Preheat the oven to 350°F. Grease two 6-well donut pans.

In a large bowl, use a hand mixer or stand mixer to mix the mozzarella, Parmesan, cream cheese, eggs, and ghee; set aside.

In a separate bowl, whisk together the protein isolate, psyllium husk powder, baking powder, salt, and garlic powder. Add the hot water to the dry ingredients, stirring constantly so that the psyllium powder doesn't clump. When the mixture is thoroughly combined, stir in the cheese mixture. The batter will be runny.

Add 7 ounces of the Asiago cheese and the rosemary to the batter and mix well.

Divide the batter evenly among the wells of the prepared pans. Bake for 15 to 18 minutes, until just browned and set. Remove from the oven, sprinkle the bagels with the remaining 2 ounces of Asiago cheese, and return to the oven for 6 to 9 minutes, until the cheese is melted and lightly browned.

Let cool in the pans for at least 10 minutes before serving. The texture of these bagels is even better when they are cooled, sliced, and toasted.

CALORIES: 137 | FAT: 7.7g | PROTEIN: 11.2g | CARBS: 1.4g | FIBER: 1g

Raspberry Vinaigrette

makes
about ½ cup
(2 tablespoons
per serving)

Although fruit is limited on a ketogenic diet, small amounts can be used occasionally. Unlike commercial versions of raspberry vinaigrette, this one has no added sugar and uses good fats to boost the flavor. This is an excellent dressing for mixed greens and is especially good on a grilled chicken salad.

⅓ **cup walnut oil or mild-flavored olive oil, such as Manzanilla**

¼ **cup balsamic vinegar**

2 **tablespoons freeze-dried raspberries**

1 **teaspoon powdered sweetener (optional)**

¼ **teaspoon salt**

Place all the ingredients in a blender and blend well. Store in the refrigerator for up to a week. Stir well before serving.

tip

You can also make this vinaigrette with fresh raspberries. Puree ¼ cup of fresh raspberries in a blender, then strain to remove the seeds. If you use fresh raspberries, you should use the vinaigrette immediately; it will not store as well as a vinaigrette made with freeze-dried raspberries.

CALORIES: 284 | FAT: 12.8g | PROTEIN: 27g | CARBS: 0.6g | FIBER: 0.3g

Pan-Seared Scallops

makes
4 servings

Scallops—I love just saying that word! Buttery and tender on their own, scallops that are pan-seared and then topped with crispy bacon and a touch of freshly grated Parmesan cheese are outrageously delicious. Because scallops are expensive, they seem fitting for celebrating a special occasion such as Valentine's Day.

1½ pounds large sea scallops (16 to 20)

1 tablespoon ghee

3 tablespoons finely chopped cooked bacon

1 ounce Parmesan cheese, grated (about ⅓ cup)

⅓ cup white wine

3 tablespoons unsalted butter

Rinse the scallops and place in a single layer on a dry kitchen towel. Press gently with a second dry towel to remove the moisture.

Heat the ghee in a large skillet over high heat. When melted and hot, add the scallops in a single layer. Sear for 1 to 1½ minutes on each side. Do not overcook.

Remove the scallops from the skillet and place in a single layer on a serving dish. Sprinkle the bacon and Parmesan over the scallops.

In the same skillet, combine the wine and butter. Simmer for 5 to 6 minutes to melt the butter and reduce the wine. Use a wooden spoon to scrape the sides and bottom of the pan so that any browned bits are incorporated into the sauce.

Spoon the pan sauce over the scallops and serve immediately.

CALORIES: 350 | FAT: 13.4g | PROTEIN: 40.4g | CARBS: 1.8g | FIBER: 0g

Lemon-Herb Compound Butter

makes
about 1 cup
(2 tablespoons
per serving)

Compound butter is deceptively simple to make, but it looks impressive on a table and tastes even better! I love that I can make a large batch, divide it into smaller portions, and pull one from the freezer whenever I need it. For Valentine's Day, serve a pat of compound butter over a perfectly seared steak for a festive and flavorful addition to a romantic dinner.

1 cup (2 sticks) unsalted butter, softened

1 tablespoon chopped fresh oregano

1 tablespoon chopped fresh thyme

1½ teaspoons finely chopped fresh rosemary

1 teaspoon salt

½ teaspoon pepper

1 teaspoon lemon juice

2 teaspoons olive oil (optional; see Note)

Use a fork to combine the butter, herbs, salt, and pepper in a medium mixing bowl. When well blended, add the lemon juice and olive oil, if using, and stir to combine.

Place the butter mixture on a sheet of parchment paper and shape into a log about 1½ inches in diameter. Wrap tightly and refrigerate until firm, then slice crosswise into rounds to serve. You can store the butter, wrapped tightly, in the refrigerator for up to a week or in the freezer for up to a month. If you like, store the butter in the freezer unsliced and slice it after you thaw it.

note

The olive oil is optional, but it makes the butter softer as it sits at room temperature, which makes it easier to spread.

CALORIES: 211 | FAT: 24.9g | PROTEIN: 0.2g | CARBS: 0.3g | FIBER: 0.2g

Bacon-Wrapped Stuffed Chicken Breasts with Asiago Gravy

makes
8 servings

This dish might look difficult to make, but it isn't. Filleting and flattening the chicken may be the hardest parts of this recipe—and these aren't challenging steps. After you remove the skillet from the oven, you use the pan drippings and some Asiago cheese to make a rich but thin gravy to pour over the chicken just before serving. Make sure that the cheese is at room temperature and add it gradually while stirring so that the sauce doesn't break.

4 large boneless, skinless chicken breasts (about 2½ pounds total)

½ teaspoon salt

½ teaspoon pepper

4 ounces smoked Gouda cheese, sliced

½ red bell pepper, cut into 16 strips

1 cup fresh spinach leaves

8 slices bacon

About ½ cup chicken bone broth

⅓ cup grated Asiago cheese, room temperature

Preheat the oven to 375°F.

Use a sharp knife to butterfly the chicken breasts. Pound each breast with a meat mallet to a ½-inch to ¾-inch thickness. Sprinkle the salt and pepper all over the chicken.

Place an ounce of Gouda on one half of each filleted breast. Top the cheese with 4 red bell pepper strips. Divide the spinach leaves evenly among the breasts and place on top of the bell peppers.

Beginning on the side with the toppings, roll up each breast, tucking the toppings inside as you roll. Wrap 2 slices of bacon around each rolled chicken breast.

Place the chicken in an oven-safe skillet and bake for 30 to 35 minutes, until the meat is tender and the juices run clear.

Increase the oven temperature to 425°F and bake the chicken for an additional 12 to 15 minutes, until the bacon is crispy and the chicken is browned. Remove the skillet from the oven and place the bacon-wrapped breasts on a serving plate.

Add enough broth to the pan drippings to make about 1 cup of liquid in the pan. Use a wooden spoon to deglaze the skillet, scraping the drippings from the bottom into the liquid. Whisk in the Asiago cheese, adding just a bit at a time and stirring constantly so that the sauce does not break.

To serve, spoon the gravy over the stuffed chicken breasts. Cut each breast in half to make 8 servings.

CALORIES: 284.4 | FAT: 12.8g | PROTEIN: 27g | CARBS: 0.6g | FIBER: 0.3g

Mud Pie Brownies

makes
24 brownies
(1 per serving)

We were vacationing at the beach when I made up this batch of brownies. (Why yes, I do travel with oat fiber and almond flour!) As I poured the thick batter into a baking dish, I thought, "These look like mud pies!" Images of thick dark "cakes" made of mud on barefoot summer days in the rural area where I grew up made me smile. From toes to nose, I would end up covered in dirt, which my grandmother always said was a sign of a good day. I decided that if those experimental brownies turned out well, I would call them Mud Pie Brownies. Unlike a lot of low-carb baked goods, we loved these right out of the oven because they were soft and light. The next day, they were dense and fudgy, like brownies should be. Whether you gobble them straight from the oven or savor them later, these brownies are a sign of a good day.

1 cup blanched almond flour

½ cup oat fiber, or ¼ cup coconut flour

½ cup unsweetened cocoa powder

1 teaspoon instant coffee granules

½ teaspoon salt

⅛ teaspoon ground cinnamon

½ cup (1 stick) salted butter, softened

1 cup granulated sweetener

5 ounces cream cheese (½ cup plus 2 tablespoons), room temperature

2 large eggs

¾ cup heavy cream

½ cup sour cream

1 teaspoon vanilla extract

10 drops liquid sweetener

3½ ounces dark chocolate (90% cacao), melted

Preheat the oven to 350°F. Grease a 9 by 13-inch glass baking dish.

In a large bowl, whisk together the almond flour, oat fiber, cocoa powder, coffee granules, salt, and cinnamon; set aside.

In another large bowl, use a hand mixer or stand mixer to cream the butter and sweetener. Add the cream cheese and mix well. Add the eggs and continue blending.

Add the dry ingredients to the cream cheese mixture and mix by hand. Add the heavy cream, sour cream, vanilla extract, and liquid sweetener and stir to combine well. Stir in the melted chocolate. The batter will be very thick, like mud.

Scoop the batter into the greased baking dish and smooth the top. Bake for 42 to 45 minutes, until the brownies have risen slightly and are just firm to the touch. Let cool in the pan for at least 10 minutes before slicing and serving.

CALORIES: 138 | FAT: 11.8g | PROTEIN: 4.1g | CARBS: 3.1g | FIBER: 1.3g | ERYTHRITOL: 8g | OAT FIBER: 3.8g

03

march

MARCH is a busy month with birthdays, St. Patrick's Day (we are Sullivans, ya know!), and the arrival of spring. Of course, St. Patrick's Day foods are good any time of the year, but **Homemade Corned Beef** and **Delicious Faux-tato Cakes** are an excellent reason to celebrate. Truthfully, we enjoy the **Easy Weeknight Reuben Casserole,** made with leftover corned beef, as much as we enjoy the corned beef itself. It's one of those times when no one minds eating leftovers!

March is also my wedding anniversary month. David and I were married on March 2, 2002, at 2 p.m. in the Village Chapel in Pinehurst, North Carolina. It rained the entire day. Not a sprinkle, but full rains from the time the wedding party ate breakfast until after we left the reception in the evening. They say that rain on a wedding day is good luck, and I believe that's true given the many blessings bestowed on us and our family.

We celebrate several family birthdays in March, including David's father and two of my nephews. Gene Sullivan was known as a peanut doctor. A professor at North Carolina State University, he dedicated his career to the peanut plant and the diseases that affect it. The first time I made **Peanut Butter Bundt Cake** was to take to his birthday party. It was a popular option on the dessert table that day! Many of the peanut butter desserts I've made over the years were created with Gene in mind.

As spring nudges winter aside, I like to prepare foods that include lemon, like **Taste of Summer Lemon Curd,** and what better way to enjoy that than with **Traditional Angel Food Cake**? The combination reminds me so much of spring—light, fresh, and springy! We also like being outdoors more, dining al fresco on the back porch, riding bikes, and planting flowers near the end of the month.

I'll confess to being one of those people who loads up the car at the garden center and then returns home with far more plants than I can reasonably tend. Even when I think I've bought a reasonable number of annuals and "just a few more" perennials, getting everything potted or planted seems to take several days. David just looks at me, amused. He has learned that chastising me generally doesn't make either of us feel good, so he sets to work alongside me. By early summer, we enjoy seeing how the plants have filled in.

I especially enjoy growing herbs. There's something about walking outside to gather herbs for cooking that makes me feel accomplished and self-sustaining. The flavor of fresh herbs is worth the effort, but more than that, it's satisfying to know that my "work" of growing the herbs is useful. Rosemary and mint grow year-round here, but my favorite herb, basil, must be planted each spring. Growing basil is worth every effort when I get to combine it with fresh tomato and mozzarella cheese. I also grow thyme and oregano, although those herbs never seem to flourish like the others do. While I love fresh cilantro, I find that I simply have to buy it at the store because I've never been able to grow it for longer than a brief two-week season.

I'm sure that growing your own vegetables must be equally rewarding, but we've never had more than a few pepper and tomato plants, and they never seem to produce much. In fact, just last year David told me that I'd be better off using my tomato and pepper plant money to simply buy the produce, as our property doesn't have a great sunny spot for those plants to thrive, and we have critters who seem to eat more of the harvest than we do. Each year, I plant a few token tomato and pepper plants, but I head to the local farmer's market for fresh, local produce.

Savory Breakfast Muffins

makes
12 muffins
(1 per serving)

When I developed this recipe, I was searching for a savory breakfast option that could be eaten on the run. I started by making a crust and then filled it with fat and protein. My picky son, Jonathan, took a hesitant bite and said, "Yep, I'd eat that for breakfast!" That's when I knew this was a recipe worth sharing.

CRUST:

3 ounces sharp cheddar cheese, shredded (about ¾ cup)

2 ounces cream cheese (¼ cup), cold

¼ cup (½ stick) unsalted butter, cold

¼ cup plus 1 tablespoon whey protein isolate

3 tablespoons oat fiber

½ teaspoon baking powder

¼ teaspoon garlic powder

¼ teaspoon onion powder

1 large egg

2 tablespoons sour cream

FILLING:

2 ounces chopped ham

2 ounces cooked crumbled breakfast sausage

5 slices bacon, cooked and chopped

1½ ounces cheddar cheese, shredded (about ⅓ cup)

6 large eggs

⅓ cup heavy cream

Preheat the oven to 350°F. Grease a standard-size 12-well muffin pan.

Make the "crust": In a large bowl, use a hand mixer or stand mixer to mix the cheddar cheese, cream cheese, and butter until thoroughly combined (or use a food processor).

Add the protein isolate, oat fiber, baking powder, garlic powder, onion powder, egg, and sour cream and continue mixing until a soft dough forms. Divide the batter evenly among the wells of the prepared muffin pan. Use a spoon to press the batter into the bottom and at least halfway up the sides of each well so that it serves as a "crust" for the filling.

Distribute the ham, sausage, bacon, and cheddar cheese evenly among the wells.

In a bowl, whisk together the eggs and heavy cream. Divide the egg mixture evenly among the wells of the muffin pan, filling each well just to the top.

Bake for 22 to 26 minutes, until the egg topping is puffy, lightly browned, and set. Let cool in the pan for 3 to 5 minutes before serving.

Store leftovers in the refrigerator for up to 5 days.

CALORIES: 198 | FAT: 17.3g | PROTEIN: 12.4g | CARBS: 1.1g | FIBER: 0g | OAT FIBER: 2.8g

Peanut Butter Bundt Cake

makes
16 servings

My father-in-law was the first in his family to go to college and the only one to earn a PhD. His work was in peanut crops and the diseases that affect peanuts. Given his life's work, it's safe to say that any dessert featuring peanuts is appropriate for Granddad's birthday month! In fact, I first made this cake for a birthday celebration for him. It was a hit with the extended family, too. I've only made it this way, as a Bundt cake covered with chocolate ganache, but you could also try baking it in a loaf pan and turning the slices into French toast.

½ cup peanut flour

⅓ cup blanched almond flour

⅓ cup oat fiber

⅓ cup whey protein isolate

2 teaspoons baking powder

¾ teaspoon salt

1 cup (2 sticks) unsalted butter, softened

1 cup granulated sweetener

4 ounces cream cheese (½ cup), room temperature

½ cup peanut butter, room temperature

4 large eggs

1 tablespoon vanilla extract

3 ounces low-carb milk chocolate, chopped, or chocolate chips (optional)

1 batch Chocolate Ganache (page 346)

Preheat the oven to 350°F. Grease a 9-cup Bundt pan.

In a large bowl, whisk together the peanut flour, almond flour, oat fiber, protein powder, baking powder, and salt; set aside.

In a separate mixing bowl, use a hand mixer or stand mixer to cream the butter and sweetener. After the butter has lightened in color, it is well mixed. If the butter becomes grainy-looking, it is too warm; place the bowl in the refrigerator to chill for a bit.

Add the cream cheese and peanut butter to the butter mixture and mix until smooth. Add the eggs one at a time, beating well after each addition. Add the vanilla extract and mix well.

Stir the dry ingredients into the butter mixture by hand. Stir in the chopped chocolate, if using.

Pour the batter into the prepared Bundt pan and bake for 40 to 50 minutes, until a toothpick inserted in the center comes out clean. Let cool in the pan.

Before serving, drizzle the ganache over the cake.

CALORIES: 273 | FAT: 24g | PROTEIN: 11.6g | CARBS: 3.9g | FIBER: 1.6g | ERYTHRITOL: 12g | OAT FIBER: 3.8g

Pistachio Ice Cream

makes
6 servings

Making pistachio ice cream was Grace's idea. I was hesitant, but I can assure you that girl has good taste! While this ice cream isn't green, it is delicious. Plus, as Grace says, "Real food isn't fluorescent." Green or not, this would make a great treat for a St. Patrick's Day celebration.

1½ cups heavy cream

1 cup unsweetened almond milk

6 large egg yolks

½ cup powdered sweetener (see Tip)

½ cup finely ground pistachios

2 teaspoons vanilla extract

⅛ teaspoon salt

2 tablespoons chopped pistachios

SPECIAL EQUIPMENT:

Ice cream maker

Heat the heavy cream and almond milk in a heavy saucepan over low heat, stirring with a whisk. Add the egg yolks and continue whisking until just warmed.

Add the sweetener and whisk until completely dissolved. Continue heating, whisking constantly, until the custard thickens, about 10 minutes. When the custard coats the back of a wooden spoon or reaches 140°F on a candy thermometer, remove the pan from the heat. Do not allow the mixture to warm to over 140°F or the eggs will begin to cook.

Stir in the finely ground pistachios, vanilla extract, and salt. Transfer the mixture to a bowl and place in the refrigerator to cool.

When cool, churn the ice cream mixture in an ice cream maker following the manufacturer's directions. Add the chopped pistachios to the ice cream while it is churning and after it has begun to freeze, but while it is still soft. Continue churning until it reaches your desired consistency.

Store leftovers in the freezer. When frozen, this ice cream will harden to a solid state. Allow to thaw at room temperature for about 10 minutes before enjoying.

tip ——————————————————————————

The type of sweetener used makes a huge difference in the texture of the ice cream. For the best texture, use allulose or xylitol; remember that each sweetener has different characteristics (see pages 19 and 20 for details). Use the sweetener that you prefer and that does not impact your blood glucose.

CALORIES: 236 | FAT: 19.6g | PROTEIN: 8g | CARBS: 5.1g | FIBER: 1.5g | ERYTHRITOL: 12g

Old-Fashioned Whiskey Sour

makes
1 serving

For some reason, I've always considered whiskey to be a man's drink and not very feminine. Now that I've made a whiskey sour, I'm okay with getting in touch with my masculine side!

2 ounces bourbon

1 ounce lemon juice

1 ounce water

3 drops liquid sweetener

Slice of lemon or twist of lemon peel, for garnish

Fresh mint leaves, for garnish

Combine the bourbon, lemon juice, water, and sweetener in a cocktail shaker. Fill the shaker with ice. Cover and shake vigorously for about 20 seconds.

Strain and pour into an ice-filled rocks glass. Garnish with a slice of lemon or twist of lemon zest and some fresh mint leaves.

CALORIES: 139 | FAT: 0g | PROTEIN: 0g | CARBS: 0g | FIBER: 0g

Saint Patrick's Day

Homemade Corned Beef

makes
10 to 14 servings

Commercial corned beef can contain sugar and inflammatory oils. Stock up on brisket when it's on sale, and you'll always have the start of a great keto meal. If you buy a very large roast, you can use the leftovers to make Easy Weeknight Reuben Casserole (page 96), a hearty dish that everyone in my family loves.

BRINE:

1 quart water

1 cup coarse sea salt

½ cup granulated sweetener

4 cloves garlic, crushed to a paste

1 tablespoon whole mustard seeds

2 teaspoons coriander seeds

1 teaspoon whole black peppercorns

½ teaspoon ginger powder

½ teaspoon dried thyme leaves

10 whole cloves

3 bay leaves

1 cinnamon stick, or ½ teaspoon ground cinnamon

2 cups ice cubes

1 (4- to 5-pound) brisket

3 cloves garlic, crushed to a paste

1 teaspoon ground black pepper

2 cups water

4 cups chopped green cabbage (optional)

In a large pot over medium heat, combine all the brine ingredients except the ice cubes. Stir well to dissolve the sweetener. Bring the ingredients to a boil, then remove from the heat and let cool.

Place the brisket in a large freezer-safe bag or glass container. Add the ice cubes to the brine. When the brine is cold, pour it into the bag with the brisket, making sure that the meat is completely submerged. Set the brisket in the refrigerator to brine for at least 3 days or up to 5 days.

When you are ready to cook the brisket, discard the brine. Rinse the brisket under cold water and place it in a large pot. Add the garlic, pepper, and water. Simmer, covered, for 3 to 4 hours, until the meat is fork-tender, adding water as needed so that the brisket does not dry out. If desired, add the chopped cabbage during the last hour of cooking. Leftover corned beef can be refrigerated for up to 4 days or frozen for up to 3 months.

note

You can also cook the brined brisket in a 6-quart slow cooker on low for 8 hours, adding the cabbage in the last 3 hours of cooking.

CALORIES: 285 | FAT: 13.4g | PROTEIN: 37.6g | CARBS: 2.1g | FIBER: 0g | ERYTHRITOL: 9.6g

Easy Weeknight Reuben Casserole

makes
8 servings

Who doesn't love a Reuben? Without a doubt, the very best part is not the bread, but the creamy mix of corned beef, sauerkraut, and that dreamy dressing that finishes it off. Baked into a casserole, the classic sandwich fillings make a satisfying meal. The caraway seeds in this comforting casserole really take the flavor up a few notches. Use leftover corned beef to make this dish or make it the centerpiece of your St. Patrick's Day celebration.

4 ounces cream cheese (½ cup), room temperature

½ cup mayonnaise

½ cup Kristie's Ketchup (page 338)

⅓ cup finely grated onions

2 tablespoons diced dill pickles

1 pound Homemade Corned Beef (page 94), chopped

8 ounces sauerkraut, drained

8 ounces Swiss cheese, shredded (about 2 cups)

1 teaspoon caraway seeds

Preheat the oven to 350°F. Grease a 9-inch square glass or ceramic baking dish.

In a large bowl, mix the cream cheese and mayonnaise until well combined. Add the ketchup, onions, and pickles and mix thoroughly. Stir in the corned beef, sauerkraut, Swiss cheese, and caraway seeds until uniformly mixed.

Spoon the mixture into the prepared dish and bake for 18 to 22 minutes, until browned and bubbly.

CALORIES: 457 | FAT: 39g | PROTEIN: 24.9g | CARBS: 4.7g | FIBER: 0.8g | ERYTHRITOL: 22g

Delicious Faux-tato Cakes (Cauli Fritters)

makes
8 cakes
(2 per serving)

My mother and grandmother (Mamaw) used to make fried tater cakes with leftover mashed potatoes. This is my version made with mashed cauliflower. Fry these cakes over low heat, flip them just before they burn, and enjoy them warm. They are excellent served with a dollop of sour cream and a few chopped green onion tops or chives. Chopped bacon and shredded cheese also make great toppings for these cakes.

2 cups cauliflower puree (see Tip)

3 ounces cheddar cheese, shredded (about ¾ cup)

⅓ cup pork dust (ground pork rinds)

2 tablespoons dried minced onions

2 tablespoons chopped cooked bacon

1 green onion, green part only, chopped

1 large egg, beaten

Dash of salt

Dash of ground black pepper

2 tablespoons bacon fat, for frying

Place all the ingredients except the bacon fat in a bowl and mix well. Place in the refrigerator to chill for at least 10 minutes.

Shape the chilled cauliflower mixture into patties that are 1½ to 2 inches in diameter.

Heat the bacon fat in a large skillet over medium-low heat. Fry the cauliflower patties in the fat until well browned on both sides, 5 to 7 minutes per side.

tip

To make the cauliflower puree, cook cauliflower florets until tender. (I steam them in the microwave.) Drain well, then use a clean kitchen towel to squeeze out any moisture. Puree the drained cauliflower.

CALORIES: 109 | FAT: 7.2g | PROTEIN: 6.9g | CARBS: 3.2g | FIBER: 0.8g

Traditional Angel Food Cake

makes
16 servings

Angel food cake was the low-fat dessert that my mom always served because she thought it was healthier. Of course, we smothered it with strawberries that had been macerated in white sugar. If we had only known about keto way back when! I never loved that low-fat confection, but one spring I got a hankering for angel food cake and set to work devising a low-carb version. This recipe is the result of those efforts, and it's a very good substitute. The hardest part of making this cake is getting it out of the tube-shaped angel food cake pan. To save yourself the trouble, you can bake it in a 9 by 13-inch baking dish and serve it as a sheet cake instead. If you do use a tube pan and disaster strikes, just cut the cake into cubes and use some Taste of Summer Lemon Curd (page 102) and a few fresh berries to make an impressive trifle that will convince your guests that you meant to make it that way all along!

1 cup vanilla-flavored whey protein isolate

⅓ cup oat fiber

1 teaspoon baking powder

12 large egg whites

1 teaspoon cream of tartar

1 cup powdered sweetener

1 teaspoon vanilla extract

6 drops liquid sweetener

note ————————————

You can use unflavored whey protein isolate instead of vanilla-flavored; simply increase the amount of vanilla extract to 2 teaspoons to give the cake more of a vanilla flavor.

Preheat the oven to 325°F.

Sift the protein isolate, oat fiber, and baking powder into a large bowl; set aside.

In a separate bowl, use a hand mixer or stand mixer to beat the egg whites. When the whites get foamy and start to thicken, add the cream of tartar and continue beating. Add the powdered sweetener in ⅓-cup increments while beating continuously. Mix in the vanilla extract and liquid sweetener. Keep beating until the whites form peaks but are still somewhat wet; don't overbeat them, as you want them to continue to expand while baking.

Use a spatula to gently fold the egg white mixture into the dry ingredients, being careful not to deflate them by folding too vigorously.

Pour the batter into an ungreased angel food cake pan. Bake for 35 to 40 minutes, until the top is brown and springy to the touch. Let cool slightly before removing the sides of the pan. The cake will deflate slightly as it cools.

CALORIES: 46 | FAT: 0g | PROTEIN: 10g | CARBS: 0.1g | FIBER: 3.8g | ERYTHRITOL: 9g | OAT FIBER: 3.8

Taste of Summer Lemon Curd

makes
about 1 cup
(2 tablespoons
per serving)

When winter seems to be dragging on forever, this sunny lemon curd is a taste of summer on a spoon. This recipe sincerely makes me want to learn how to can so that I can preserve it. When served with Traditional Angel Food Cake (page 100), it provides an especially bright pop of flavor. The ingredients are easy to source and it's quick to make, which makes it a favorite recipe of mine. This cake makes a great companion to any recipe that calls for only egg whites so that the yolks are put to good use!

6 large egg yolks

1 cup powdered sweetener

½ cup lemon juice (about 3 large lemons)

1 tablespoon finely grated lemon zest (about 1 large lemon)

6 tablespoons (¾ stick) unsalted butter, cubed

In a medium saucepan over low heat, whisk together the egg yolks, sweetener, lemon juice, and lemon zest. Whisk constantly until the mixture reaches 170°F on a candy thermometer and begins to thicken. If you don't have a candy thermometer, you will know that the curd is thick enough when it coats the back of a spoon and begins to cling to the whisk. Remove from the heat.

Add the butter one cube at a time, whisking constantly to melt the butter and incorporate it into the lemon curd.

When the butter is fully incorporated, strain the curd to remove any lumps or larger pieces of zest. Cover with plastic wrap, pushing the wrap gently onto the surface of the curd to prevent a skin from forming. Store in the refrigerator for up to a week.

tip

When zesting the lemons, be careful to include only the yellow zest; the white pith underneath is bitter-tasting and will alter the flavor of your curd.

CALORIES: 123 | FAT: 10.7g | PROTEIN: 3.5g | CARBS: 2g | FIBER: 0.1g | ERYTHRITOL: 18g

04

april

APRIL is a darling month! The end of the school year is near, the temperature outside is typically perfect (at least it is here in the South), and nearly everyone enjoys extended time off for the Easter holiday. When the kids were younger, David and I were always "busy," and we rarely took time for family vacations. Instead, when school was out, we sent them to camps or to their grandparents'. While I know that they enjoyed those things, as they have gotten older I've come to realize how quickly time goes. Determined not to miss any more of that precious time, two years ago we started a tradition of spending spring break on the North Carolina coast. While it is sometimes too cool to enjoy the ocean, we always enjoy the time away together. It's an opportunity to play games and test new recipes. In fact, many of the recipes in this book—such as the **Saucy Shrimp Scampi** featured this month, as well as **Shrimp Fra Diavolo** (page 168) and **Mud Pie Brownies** (page 82)—were devised during our spring break retreat!

The focus for April is dishes that you can share and enjoy for the Easter season, like a platter of **Miracle Ham Biscuits with Herbed Butter** or **Jalapeño Popper Deviled Eggs,** which make good use of dyed Easter eggs. I also like having a few simple sides for the holiday table, and my luscious and easy-to-make **Simple Hollandaise Sauce** goes well with nearly any vegetable or meat. One of my favorite recipes is **Kristie's Carrot Cake Cheesecake.** Not only has it appeared on our table at every

Easter celebration since 2015, but it was the very first low-carb dessert that I created on my own and shared with others. **Healthy Peanut Butter Cups** have become another Easter tradition for our family. It's my secret weapon against those store-bought peanut butter eggs that I used to hoard! Over the years that we've been keto, we have moved away from giving the kids candy in their Easter baskets. Instead, we opt to stuff their baskets with things such as sunglasses, flip-flops, hats, books, kites, and other toys to enjoy outside. We've learned the importance of *doing* more, not *having* (or eating!) more.

We always look forward to strawberry season, which begins locally in late April. I've included a **Strawberry Shortcake** recipe for those of you with April birthdays. Picking strawberries together is another fun family tradition that I treasure. When we go strawberry picking, we tend to get overzealous and pick far more than we could ever use. The kids compete to see who can pick the most or eat the most! I get caught up in finding the "perfect" berries and always end up with my bucket overflowing. Unfortunately, I know that each of those luscious berries packs about 1 gram of carbohydrate, so I have to be very careful about the amount I consume. While I might freeze a few to garnish bowls of **Old-Fashioned Strawberry Ice Cream,** we also tend to share them with neighbors, which makes the experience even more fun.

Lemon Poppyseed Muffins

makes
12 muffins
(1 per serving)

This classic muffin flavor is perfect for Easter brunch or an everyday breakfast. You can make 24 mini-muffins if you prefer. We enjoy them warm or cold. When warmed, a pat of butter or dollop of crème fraîche make this muffin a breakfast favorite for me.

⅓ cup blanched almond flour

⅓ cup whey protein isolate

⅓ cup oat fiber, or 2 tablespoons coconut flour

1 teaspoon baking powder

¼ teaspoon salt

½ cup (1 stick) unsalted butter, cold

¾ cup granulated sweetener

4 ounces cream cheese (½ cup), cold

3 large eggs

2 tablespoons lemon juice

2 teaspoons vanilla extract

1 teaspoon poppyseeds

Preheat the oven to 350°F. Line a standard-size 12-well muffin pan with parchment paper liners.

In a medium bowl, whisk together the almond flour, protein isolate, oat fiber, baking powder, and salt; set aside.

In a separate bowl, using a hand mixer or stand mixer, cream the butter and sweetener. When the butter has lightened in color, add the cream cheese and continue blending until everything is smooth and well incorporated.

Add the eggs one at a time, mixing well after each addition. Add the lemon juice and vanilla extract and mix until well blended.

Stir the dry ingredients into the wet ingredients by hand. Sprinkle in the poppyseeds and stir to distribute.

Divide the batter evenly among the wells of the prepared baking pan, filling each well about two-thirds full. Bake for 24 to 28 minutes, until browned on top and just firm to the touch. Let cool in the pan for 5 to 10 minutes before serving.

Store leftovers in the refrigerator for up to 5 days.

CALORIES: 152 | FAT: 13.8g | PROTEIN: 5.6g | CARBS: 1.3g | FIBER: 5.4g | ERYTHRITOL: 9g | OAT FIBER: 5g

Strawberry Shortcake

makes
6 servings

Fresh strawberries are plentiful in North Carolina as early as the end of April, and they usually last until mid- to late May, depending on when the hot weather arrives. One of my absolute favorite family outings is strawberry picking. The bright green leaves, the dark soil, and the beautiful red berries remind me of treasure hunting, and I nearly always pick more than I intend. Then we have to go around the neighborhood sharing with friends before the berries go bad. While I've used them to garnish a layer cake, a cream pie, and a crème roll, this recipe is my favorite way to enjoy fresh strawberries.

BISCUITS:

½ cup blanched almond flour

⅓ cup oat fiber, or 2 tablespoons coconut flour

3 tablespoons whey protein isolate

1 teaspoon baking powder

¼ teaspoon salt

2 large eggs, beaten

½ cup sour cream

½ cup granulated sweetener

¼ cup mayonnaise

3 tablespoons unsalted butter, melted

1 ounce cream cheese (2 tablespoons), room temperature

1 teaspoon finely grated lemon zest

1 teaspoon lemon juice

CREAM FILLING:

2 cups heavy cream

½ cup powdered sweetener

⅓ cup sour cream

1 teaspoon vanilla extract

1 teaspoon strawberry extract

2 cups Strawberry Sauce (page 345)

Preheat the oven to 350°F. Grease 6 wells of a standard-size muffin pan or line with parchment paper liners.

Make the biscuits: In a large bowl, mix all the biscuit ingredients until thoroughly combined. Divide the batter evenly among the prepared wells of the muffin pan, filling each well about two-thirds full. Bake for 15 to 18 minutes, until the tops are lightly browned and firm to the touch. Let cool in the pan for at least 5 minutes.

Make the cream filling: In a large bowl, use a hand mixer or stand mixer to whip the heavy cream until soft peaks form. Add the sweetener and continue whipping until it is dissolved. Beat in the sour cream and extracts until creamy and smooth. Chill until ready to serve.

To assemble the shortcakes, slice each biscuit in half. Top one half with ⅓ cup of the strawberry sauce and ⅓ cup of the cream filling, then place the other half of the biscuit on top. Top each biscuit with another tablespoon of the cream filling.

tip

To make the shortcakes extra pretty, garnish them with curls of lemon zest and sliced strawberries.

CALORIES: 430 | FAT: 39.7g | PROTEIN: 10.2g | CARBS: 9g | FIBER: 12g | ERYTHRITOL: 36g | OAT FIBER: 10g

Old-Fashioned Strawberry Ice Cream

makes
6 servings

Instead of fresh strawberries, this recipe uses unsweetened freeze-dried strawberries. I powder them and then add them to the ice cream mixture. Unlike fresh berries, the powdered freeze-dried berries do not add moisture to the ice cream, but they do add a nice punch of flavor and minimal carbs.

1½ cups heavy cream

1 cup unsweetened almond milk

5 large egg yolks

¾ cup powdered sweetener (see Tip)

2½ teaspoons vanilla extract

1 teaspoon strawberry extract

0.6 ounce (17 g) freeze-dried strawberries, powdered in a blender or clean coffee grinder (about ⅓ cup)

½ teaspoon salt

SPECIAL EQUIPMENT:

Ice cream maker

Heat the heavy cream and almond milk in a heavy saucepan over low heat, stirring with a whisk. Add the egg yolks and continue whisking until just warmed.

Add the sweetener and whisk until completely dissolved. Continue heating, whisking constantly, until the custard thickens, about 10 minutes. When the custard coats the back of a wooden spoon or reaches 140°F on a candy thermometer, remove the pan from the heat. Do not allow the mixture to warm to over 140°F or the eggs will begin to cook.

Stir in the extracts, strawberries, and salt. Place in the refrigerator to chill.

When cool, churn the ice cream mixture in an ice cream maker following the manufacturer's directions until it reaches your desired consistency.

Store leftovers in the freezer. When frozen, this ice cream will harden to a solid state. Allow to thaw at room temperature for about 10 minutes before enjoying.

tip

The type of sweetener used makes a huge difference in the texture of the ice cream. For the best texture, use allulose or xylitol; remember that each sweetener has different characteristics (see pages 19 and 20 for details). Use the sweetener that you prefer and that does not impact your blood glucose.

CALORIES: 169 | FAT: 13.6g | PROTEIN: 4.8g | CARBS: 4.1g | FIBER: 0.6g | ERYTHRITOL: 18g

Lemon Drop Martini

makes
1 serving

Just the name of this cocktail makes me smile. It reminds me of spring, and sunny days, and that bright citrus taste. As I've enjoyed a variety of low-carb cocktails, I'm frequently reminded that simple is better, which is certainly the case with this drink.

1 jigger (1½ ounces) vodka
1½ tablespoons lemon juice
⅛ teaspoon vanilla extract
4 drops liquid sweetener
4 to 6 ice cubes

Place all the ingredients in a cocktail shaker and shake vigorously for about 30 seconds. Strain into a chilled martini glass and serve.

tip

If you want to add a layer of fancy, before filling the glass, rub the rim with lemon juice, then dip it in granulated sweetener.

CALORIES: 102 | FAT: 0.6g | PROTEIN: 0.8g | CARBS: 1.6g | FIBER: 0g

Easter

Miracle Ham Biscuits with Herbed Butter

makes
12 biscuit
sandwiches
(1 per serving)

If you've ever enjoyed mini-biscuits with ham covered in herb butter, then you are sure to enjoy this low-carb version. I use three recipes for biscuits, and this is my favorite because it is most like a true Southern biscuit. You must use oat fiber for this recipe to be successful; you'll end up with gritty biscuits if you try to substitute coconut flour. While I love it with these ham biscuits, the Herbed Butter is also delicious on its own—and you will have leftover butter to enjoy. Try serving it on steak, vegetables, or Savory Breakfast Muffins (page 86).

HERBED BUTTER:

1 cup (2 sticks) salted butter, softened

1 teaspoon dried chives

1 teaspoon dried parsley

½ teaspoon garlic powder

BISCUITS:

½ cup blanched almond flour

½ cup oat fiber

1 teaspoon baking powder

½ teaspoon salt

5 ounces mozzarella cheese, shredded (about 1¼ cups)

2 ounces cream cheese (¼ cup), room temperature

¼ cup (½ stick) unsalted butter, softened

1 large egg

12 slices baked ham, cut to fit the biscuits

Preheat the oven to 350°F. Line a baking sheet with parchment paper.

Make the herbed butter: In a medium bowl, use a hand mixer or stand mixer to blend the butter, herbs, and garlic powder. Place the butter mixture on a sheet of parchment paper and shape into a log about 1½ inches in diameter. Wrap tightly and place in the refrigerator to chill for at least 2 hours, until firm.

Make the biscuits: Place all the biscuit ingredients in a large bowl. Use a hand mixer or stand mixer to thoroughly combine, being careful not to overmix or knead the dough. Use your hands to shape the dough into 12 biscuits about 2 inches in diameter and place the biscuits on the prepared baking sheet. Bake for 15 to 18 minutes, until lightly browned on the top and bottom.

To assemble, slice each biscuit in half. Top one half with a thin slice of herbed butter and the other half with a slice of ham, then bring the two halves together.

CALORIES: 115 | FAT: 10.6g | PROTEIN: 3.8g | CARBS: 1.6g | FIBER: 0.5g | OAT FIBER: 7.6g

Quick and Easy Sautéed Asparagus

makes
4 servings

Not every delicious recipe has to be complex; simple is sometimes better. Asparagus is an excellent example. We like it best when it's just tender (not overcooked) and served with hollandaise sauce.

2 tablespoons unsalted butter, softened

24 stalks asparagus, trimmed

Dash of salt

Grated lemon zest, for garnish

¾ cup Simple Hollandaise Sauce (recipe below), for serving

Melt the butter in a large skillet over low heat. Add the asparagus and increase the heat to medium-low. Cook for 5 to 7 minutes, turning the asparagus frequently to coat it in the butter, until the asparagus is just tender and bright green.

Season with the salt. Garnish with lemon zest, if desired, and serve with hollandaise.

Simple Hollandaise Sauce

makes
1½ cups

This simple sauce always intimidated me. Even though I enjoyed it in restaurants, I never attempted to make hollandaise myself until I started cooking keto. The only disappointment was that I hadn't tried making it earlier. It was perfect on the first try! Hollandaise reminds me a bit of mayonnaise—it's fantastic on everything, and it's an excellent way to add fat to a meal. We especially love it on asparagus, as shown here, as well as steak.

1 cup (2 sticks) salted butter, softened

5 large egg yolks

1 tablespoon lemon juice

1 tablespoon water

Dash of cayenne pepper

Dash of salt

Melt the butter in a small saucepan over low heat. Keep the heat low so that the butter does not get too hot. Set the pan aside.

Place the egg yolks, lemon juice, and water in a blender and blend well. Stream the melted butter into the blender while the blender is running. The sauce will begin to emulsify. Continue streaming in the butter until it is all added. Use only the liquid butter; do not include the solids clinging to the bottom of the pan.

Season the hollandaise with the cayenne pepper and salt and serve immediately. Store leftovers in the refrigerator for up to 3 days. Reheat over very low heat on the stovetop or on reduced power in the microwave.

CALORIES: 259 | FAT: 18.1g | PROTEIN: 3.6g | CARBS: 4g | FIBER: 2g

Jalapeño Popper Deviled Eggs

makes
12 servings

My husband doesn't care for deviled eggs, and while they've never been my favorite, either, they are an Easter tradition for many families. This is my unconventional twist on that classic. The cream cheese and bacon fat are the secrets to making these eggs taste so good. Adding bacon and sautéed jalapeños doesn't hurt, either!

1 dozen large eggs, hard-boiled, peeled, and cut in half lengthwise

2 tablespoons bacon fat

2 jalapeño peppers, seeded and chopped, plus more for garnish if desired

½ cup mayonnaise

2 ounces cream cheese (¼ cup), room temperature

1 tablespoon prepared yellow mustard

5 tablespoons chopped cooked bacon

¼ teaspoon salt

Paprika, for garnish (optional)

Scoop the egg yolks into a medium bowl. Place the whites on a serving tray and set aside.

Melt the bacon fat in a small saucepan over medium heat. Add the jalapeños and sauté until just tender and bright green, 5 to 7 minutes. Set aside to cool.

Add the mayonnaise, cream cheese, and mustard to the bowl with the egg yolks and mix until creamy. Stir in the bacon, salt, and cooled jalapeños; mix well.

Fill each egg white half with the yolk mixture. Sprinkle the tops with paprika and fresh jalapeños before serving, if desired.

note —————————————————————————
For safety, be sure to wear disposable gloves when chopping and seeding the peppers; the oil can cause painful skin irritation.

CALORIES: 162 | FAT: 14g | PROTEIN: 7.9g | CARBS: 1g | FIBER: 0.1g

Saucy Shrimp Scampi

makes
2 main dish or 4 appetizer servings

Any recipe that uses wine, lemon, garlic, and butter has to be good, especially when shrimp is added. As a main dish, this recipe makes only two servings; if I'm serving it on a buffet or with a second main dish, however, it typically serves four. As always, shrimp tastes best when it is not overcooked, so be sure to remove the shrimp from the skillet as soon as it turns pink and just begins to firm up.

6 tablespoons (¾ stick) unsalted butter, softened, divided

4 cloves garlic, minced

1 pound large shrimp, peeled, deveined, and patted dry

⅓ cup dry white wine

3 tablespoons lemon juice

1 teaspoon finely grated lemon zest

¼ teaspoon red pepper flakes (optional)

⅓ cup shredded Parmesan or Asiago cheese, for garnish

1 tablespoon chopped fresh parsley, for garnish

In a large skillet over medium heat, heat 4 tablespoons of the butter and the garlic. When the butter is melted, add the shrimp and sauté until just pink, 2 to 3 minutes. Use a slotted spoon to remove the shrimp from the skillet, leaving any pan juices in the skillet.

Add the white wine, lemon juice, and lemon zest to the pan and simmer until the liquid is reduced by half, 3 to 4 minutes. Stir in the remaining 2 tablespoons of butter and the red pepper flakes, if using.

Remove from the heat, return the shrimp to the skillet, and toss to coat with the pan sauce. Transfer to a serving dish and sprinkle with the cheese and parsley.

CALORIES: 667 | FAT: 39.7g | PROTEIN: 61.3g | CARBS: 3.5g | FIBER: 0g

Kristie's Carrot Cake Cheesecake

makes
16 servings

I love this recipe for many reasons. This cheesecake was the first recipe that I developed totally on my own. David wanted carrot cake for Easter, but I couldn't figure out how to make a version that was low-carb enough for us. That's when I decided to combine carrot cake and cheesecake. Because cheesecake is naturally lower in carbs, not to mention delicious, it made sense to stretch the carrot cake by adding a layer of cheesecake. I created a layer of carrot cake, topped it with a layer of cheesecake, and covered the top with a traditional cream cheese icing. The result was very well received—so much so that this cake has become a new Easter tradition for our extended family.

CARROT CAKE:

½ cup heavy cream

1 teaspoon apple cider vinegar

⅔ cup unsalted butter, softened

1½ cups granulated sweetener

3 large eggs

2 teaspoons vanilla extract

2 cups blanched almond flour

¼ cup plus 2 tablespoons whey protein isolate

1 teaspoon ground cinnamon

¾ teaspoon baking powder

½ teaspoon baking soda

¼ teaspoon salt

½ cup finely grated carrots

½ cup chopped raw walnuts (optional)

CHEESECAKE FILLING:

2 (8-ounce) packages cream cheese, room temperature

2 large eggs

½ cup granulated sweetener

4 drops liquid sweetener

1 tablespoon vanilla extract

Preheat the oven to 300°F. Grease a 9-inch springform pan with butter or coconut oil and line with parchment paper.

Make the carrot cake batter: Place the heavy cream in a small bowl and stir in the vinegar; set aside.

In a separate bowl, using a hand mixer or stand mixer, cream the butter and sweetener. When the butter has lightened in color, add the eggs one at a time, beating well after each addition. Mix in the vanilla extract and set aside.

In a third bowl, whisk together the almond flour, protein isolate, cinnamon, baking powder, baking soda, and salt.

Add the dry ingredients to the butter mixture and stir to combine. Stir in the heavy cream mixture. Add the carrots and walnuts, if using, and stir in by hand. The batter will be thick.

Scoop the batter into the prepared pan. Use the back of a spoon to push the batter against the sides of the pan, creating a well for the cheesecake filling. Set aside.

Make the cheesecake filling: In a large bowl, use the mixer to blend the cream cheese, eggs, sweeteners, and vanilla extract until smooth.

Carefully pour the filling over the cake batter in the springform pan, adding a little at a time. Spoon the filling into the center and outward and at least ½ inch up the side of the pan.

Bake for 1 hour 15 minutes to 1 hour 25 minutes, until the edges are browned and the center is set. Turn off the oven, leave the oven door ajar, and let the cake cool in the oven for

CALORIES: 301 | FAT: 28.6g | PROTEIN: 9.3g | CARBS: 4.1g | FIBER: 1.8g | ERYTHRITOL: 26.3g

ICING:

1 (8-ounce) package cream cheese, room temperature

¼ cup (½ stick) unsalted butter, softened

¼ cup powdered sweetener

½ teaspoon vanilla extract

at least an hour. Remove from the oven and let cool completely. Refrigerate for at least 6 hours or overnight before icing and serving.

Make the icing: In a large bowl, use a hand mixer or stand mixer to combine all the icing ingredients. Top the cake with the icing and spread it neatly to the edges. Garnish with a sprinkle of chopped walnuts and/or a few carrot shavings, if desired.

Healthy Peanut Butter Cups

makes
36 candies
(2 per serving)

I used to adore those egg-shaped peanut butter candies at Easter. As soon as they appeared in stores, I began consuming them, and as soon as Easter was over, I trolled the stores to buy them on clearance. They were my Easter addiction. When 2014 rolled around—my first low-carb Easter—I was sorely tempted to eat "just one." Fortunately, I turned my back (literally!) on that temptation and decided to go home and create my own version that I could enjoy while staying healthy. As I worked to develop the filling, my peanut butter–loving husband was more than happy to help with the testing. When I found the right ratios and texture, I had to ban him from the kitchen before he ate the entire batch! Even now, when I make these treats, I tend to make a double batch of the filling so that even with David stealing bites, I have enough to make a full batch of peanut butter cups. The peanut flour is optional, but it gives the filling a great texture.

1 cup peanut butter

½ cup powdered sweetener

¼ cup peanut flour (optional)

1/16 teaspoon ground cinnamon

1 teaspoon vanilla extract

2 (3-ounce) bars low-carb milk chocolate

2 teaspoons coconut oil

SPECIAL EQUIPMENT:

Mini-muffin pan(s) with at least 36 wells

Line 36 wells of a mini-muffin pan(s) with paper or foil liners.

In a bowl, mix together the peanut butter, sweetener, peanut flour (if using), cinnamon, and vanilla extract. Set aside.

Melt the chocolate in a small saucepan over low heat. Add the coconut oil and stir constantly with a small whisk. Continue heating until just melted and smooth.

Use a small spoon to coat the mini-muffin liners with the chocolate mixture. Shape the peanut butter filling into 36 discs about 1 inch in diameter. Place a small disc of peanut butter on top of the chocolate in each liner, then cover the disc with more of the melted chocolate. Do not be tempted use a lot of chocolate in each; you want a thin coating.

Once assembled, chill the peanut butter cups in the refrigerator until set. Remove the candies, still in their paper liners, from the pan(s) and place in an airtight container. Store in the refrigerator or freezer.

CALORIES: 72 | FAT: 6.5g | PROTEIN: 2.3g | CARBS: 1.9g | FIBER: 1g | ERYTHRITOL: 2g

05

may

Not only is MAY a month of traditionally beautiful weather, but it also signals the end of the school year, graduations, Cinco de Mayo, Mother's Day, and everyone's favorite kickoff to summer, Memorial Day. There are many reasons to celebrate in the lovely month of May!

May is the birthday month of my father. When I think of the desserts he really enjoys, two come to mind: strawberry shortcake and banana pudding. Because I love my low-carb banana pudding, I decided to make **Classic Keto No-Nana Pudding** the May birthday treat in my dad's honor. The "wafers" in this pudding are interesting because the recipe uses pork dust (ground pork rinds). No one is likely to guess that ingredient, but it gives the wafers a great texture. It also makes the wafers much lower in carbs than nut flour or coconut flour would.

In honor of Mother's Day, I've included three breakfast recipes so that you can surprise Mom with a simple breakfast in bed. The **Cream-Filled Crêpes with Blueberry Sauce** recipe involves multiple steps that will get the whole family involved, because sometimes it's the time in the kitchen working together that leaves us with the most cherished memories. The **Cinnamon Soul Bread** is wonderful toasted and smeared with butter, but if you really want to make Mom feel special, you can use it to make French toast. One bite and you will be her favorite for life! The **Faux Yogurt Parfaits** are easy enough that younger children can help prepare them while Dad cooks bacon. Our Mother's Day traditions often include breakfast in bed followed by a visit with one or the other grandmother and celebrations with extended family. The kids always find or make the best cards for me, and I cherish them.

While you won't find recipes for graduation parties or Memorial Day cookouts in this chapter, you will find outdoor party menu ideas in the months of July and August. In this chapter, I provide a few somewhat authentic Mexican recipes for a Cinco de Mayo celebration, which reminds me of Grandpa Frank, my mom's husband, who enjoys Mexican dishes and also celebrates his birthday in May. I love that some of these dishes are dairy-free. It was especially fun for me to learn about various chilies and flavor combinations used in Mexican cuisine. The best part of this process might have been searching out *tiendas,* or Mexican groceries, to find some of the chilies I needed, because many of these grocers also have small restaurants or grills inside. Tasting their offerings was just part of the hard work I felt obligated to put into developing these recipes for you! (You're welcome.) You can even celebrate Cinco de Mayo with an on-plan **Margarita** that is far more authentic, and tasty, than the sugary slushies served in most restaurants.

With **Everyone's Favorite Blueberry Cream Cheese Muffins** as the muffin of the month and **Peanut Butter Cup Ice Cream** as the featured frozen confection, May offers a delicious way to celebrate the ordinary and the extraordinary—or maybe just one more way to make the mundane last days of the school year less so.

Everyone's Favorite Blueberry Cream Cheese Muffins

makes
12 muffins
(1 per serving)

I must have made at least five versions of this muffin before I developed this recipe, which is one of my most popular baked goods. The basic muffin batter, without the blueberries and blueberry extract, can be adapted to make nearly any flavor you want. In fact, the blueberry extract can be omitted and the flavor from the blueberries is still sufficient. In addition to making a great treat for Mom, these muffins freeze well and are a nice option to add to a lunch box or travel bag.

⅓ cup blanched almond flour

⅓ cup whey protein isolate

⅓ cup oat fiber, or 2 tablespoons coconut flour

1 teaspoon baking powder

¼ teaspoon salt

½ cup (1 stick) salted butter, cold

¾ cup granulated sweetener

4 ounces cream cheese (½ cup), cold

3 large eggs

1 teaspoon blueberry extract

1 teaspoon vanilla extract

⅓ cup fresh or frozen blueberries

Preheat the oven to 350°F. Line a standard-size 12-well muffin pan with parchment paper liners.

In a large bowl, whisk together the almond flour, protein isolate, oat fiber, baking powder, and salt; set aside.

In a separate bowl, using a hand mixer or stand mixer, cream the butter and sweetener. When the butter has lightened in color, mix in the cream cheese and continue blending until everything is smooth and well incorporated.

Add the eggs one at a time, mixing well after each addition. Stir in the extracts by hand.

Add the dry ingredients to the wet ingredients and stir lightly. Do not overmix. Gently fold in the blueberries.

Divide the batter evenly among the wells of the prepared muffin pan, filling each well about two-thirds full. Bake for 24 to 28 minutes, until browned and just firm to the touch. Let cool in the pan for 5 to 10 minutes before serving.

Store leftovers in the refrigerator for up to 5 days.

CALORIES: 164 | FAT: 14.3g | PROTEIN: 5.5g | CARBS: 1.9g | FIBER: 0.4g | ERYTHRITOL: 9g | OAT FIBER: 5g

Classic Keto No-Nana Pudding

makes
12 servings

Banana pudding is a Southern classic. Traditionally, it's made with vanilla wafers, instant pudding, and Cool Whip—a blood glucose nightmare! The more authentic versions are topped with meringue and baked until the meringue is lightly browned. This version is made without bananas but uses banana extract, real eggs, and heavy cream to create a truly delicious low-carb dessert. The wafers are not like cookies at all; they are not crisp at first, although they do get crispier after 6 or 7 hours in the oven with the heat off, the light on, and the door ajar. At that point they become more like dried madeleines. This recipe may make more wafers than you need for the pudding. You can either halve the wafer recipe, freeze the extras to make another batch of pudding in the future, or enjoy the extras as plain wafer cookies.

WAFERS:

1 cup heavy cream

2 tablespoons white vinegar

1 cup blanched almond flour

½ cup pork dust (ground pork rinds)

½ cup granulated sweetener

⅓ cup plus 2 tablespoons whey protein isolate

2 tablespoons oat fiber

1½ teaspoons baking powder

½ teaspoon baking soda

¼ teaspoon salt

½ cup sour cream

¼ cup (½ stick) unsalted butter, melted but not hot

2 large eggs, beaten well

1 tablespoon vanilla extract

4 drops liquid sweetener

Preheat the oven to 325°F. Line two 11 by 17-inch rimmed baking sheets with parchment paper.

Make the wafers: Place the heavy cream in a small bowl. Pour in the vinegar and set aside.

In a separate bowl, whisk together the almond flour, pork dust, granulated sweetener, protein isolate, oat fiber, baking powder, baking soda, and salt; set aside.

In another bowl, use a spatula to mix the sour cream, melted butter, eggs, vanilla extract, and liquid sweetener.

Add the heavy cream mixture to the butter mixture and stir to combine. Then stir in the dry ingredients until smooth.

Spread half of the batter on each of the prepared baking sheets. Bake for 15 to 20 minutes, until browned. The "cake" will be soft and pliable. Let cool completely, then flip onto a cooling rack.

Cut the "cakes" into 1½-inch squares using a pizza cutter. Place the cooling rack in the oven with the light on and the door ajar for at least 6 hours; the longer the better. The wafers will dry out and become crispier.

While the wafers are drying, make the pudding: Melt the butter in a heavy saucepan over low heat. Whisk in the powdered sweetener and extracts.

CALORIES: 335 | FAT: 30.3g | PROTEIN: 11.3g | CARBS: 3.8g | FIBER: 1g | ERYTHRITOL: 14g | OAT FIBER: 1.9g

PUDDING:

½ cup (1 stick) unsalted butter

½ cup powdered sweetener

1½ teaspoons banana extract

½ teaspoon vanilla extract

6 large egg yolks

1½ cups heavy cream

6 drops liquid sweetener

When smooth, reduce the heat to the lowest setting and add the egg yolks, whisking constantly. Whisk for 4 to 6 minutes, until the pudding thickens slightly. Remove from the heat and refrigerate.

In a separate bowl, using a hand mixer or stand mixer, whip the heavy cream. As the cream begins to thicken, add the liquid sweetener. Gently fold the chilled pudding into the whipped cream. Mix very lightly so that it stays fluffy.

To assemble, layer half of the wafers in a 1½-quart dish, followed by half of the pudding. Repeat with a second layer of wafers, then the rest of the pudding. Crush a couple of wafers and sprinkle the crushed wafers (a tablespoon or two) over the top. Refrigerate the assembled dessert for at least 4 hours before serving.

This pudding is best eaten within 36 to 48 hours of being made, but it will keep in the refrigerator for up to 4 days.

Peanut Butter Cup Ice Cream

makes
6 servings

This ice cream adds my low-carb peanut butter cup candies to a vanilla ice cream base to create a classic ice cream flavor. The chocolate hardens and becomes crunchy, with soft bits of peanut butter sprinkled in between. You're gonna love this one!

1¾ cups heavy cream

¾ cup unsweetened almond milk

6 large egg yolks

½ cup powdered sweetener (see Tip)

2 teaspoons vanilla extract

½ teaspoon salt

⅓ batch Healthy Peanut Butter Cups (page 124)

SPECIAL EQUIPMENT:

Ice cream maker

Heat the heavy cream and almond milk in a heavy saucepan over low heat, stirring with a whisk. Add the egg yolks and continue whisking until just warmed.

Add the sweetener and whisk until completely dissolved. Continue heating, whisking constantly, until the custard thickens, about 10 minutes. When the custard coats the back of a wooden spoon or reaches 140°F on a candy thermometer, remove the pan from the heat. Do not allow the mixture to warm to over 140°F or the eggs will begin to cook.

Stir in the vanilla extract and salt. Place the mixture in the refrigerator to chill.

Meanwhile, chop the peanut butter cups into pieces the size of small pebbles.

When the ice cream mixture is cool, churn in an ice cream maker following the manufacturer's directions. Add the peanut butter cups to the ice cream while it is churning and after it has begun to freeze, but while it is still soft. Continue churning until it reaches your desired consistency.

Store leftovers in the freezer. When frozen, this ice cream will harden to a solid state. Allow to thaw at room temperature for about 10 minutes before enjoying.

tip

The type of sweetener used makes a huge difference in the texture of the ice cream. For the best texture, use allulose or xylitol; remember that each sweetener has different characteristics (see pages 19 and 20 for details). Use the sweetener that you prefer and that does not impact your blood glucose.

CALORIES: 186| FAT: 16g | PROTEIN: 5.8g | CARBS: 2g | FIBER: 0.2g | ERYTHRITOL: 21.5g

Margarita

makes
1 serving

Learning how to make a low-carb margarita was an eye-opening experience for me. An authentic margarita doesn't have to be full of sugar, and it isn't necessarily frozen. Once you've enjoyed this simple and authentic margarita, you won't miss the popular, overly sweetened version.

1 jigger (1½ ounces) tequila

2 tablespoons lime juice

1 tablespoon orange juice, or ⅛ teaspoon orange extract

4 drops liquid sweetener, or 1 tablespoon granulated sweetener

Lime slice or curl of lime zest, for garnish

Combine all the ingredients except the garnish. Pour over ice in a lowball or Old-Fashioned glass. Garnish with a lime slice or a curl of lime zest.

tip

To make this drink look really special, before filling the glasses, rub the rim of each glass with orange juice, then dip it in coarse salt, creating a thin coating of salt around the entire rim.

CALORIES: 111 | FAT: 0g | PROTEIN: 0g | CARBS: 3g | FIBER: 0g

Mother's Day

Cream-Filled Crêpes with Blueberry Sauce · 136

Cinnamon Soul Bread · 138

Faux Yogurt Parfaits · 140

Cream-Filled Crêpes with Blueberry Sauce

makes
12 crêpes
(3 per serving)

Spoil Mom with crêpes while spoiling everyone else, too! My daughter is especially fond of crêpes, so I love that we can enjoy these together on Mother's Day. In fact, the first time she tried crêpes, we were just finishing a full day of shopping. As we went into our favorite Greek restaurant for dinner, she pointed to a sign at a nearby store and exclaimed, "Look, Mom! Coffee and Creeps!" After explaining that a crêpe is like a very thin pancake, we went inside and tried a variety of sweet and savory crêpes. We still giggle about that fun experience, and we still point to the sign each time we see it. For easy planning, these crêpes can be made ahead of time and refrigerated until you are ready to use them. Store the plain crêpes with parchment paper between them until you assemble the dish.

CALORIES: 341 | FAT: 23.7g | PROTEIN: 15.7g | CARBS: 6.6g | FIBER: 1.1g | ERYTHRITOL: 21g

CRÊPES:

4 large eggs

1½ ounces cream cheese (3 tablespoons), room temperature

2 tablespoons heavy cream

½ teaspoon vanilla extract

¼ cup blanched almond flour

2 tablespoons oat fiber

2 tablespoons granulated sweetener

⅛ teaspoon baking powder

Dash of ground cinnamon

Ghee, for frying

FILLING:

4 ounces cream cheese (½ cup), room temperature

3 tablespoons heavy cream

¼ cup powdered sweetener

Juice of ½ lemon

3 drops liquid sweetener

¼ teaspoon vanilla extract

BLUEBERRY SAUCE:

1 cup fresh blueberries

⅓ cup water

2 tablespoons unsalted butter, softened

2 teaspoons powdered sweetener

FOR GARNISH (OPTIONAL):

A few fresh blueberries

Powdered sweetener

Whipped cream

Make the crêpes: Place all the ingredients except the ghee in a blender and blend until smooth.

Melt the ghee in a 7-inch nonstick skillet over low heat. Pour a thin layer of the crêpe batter into the skillet. Tilt the pan so that the batter completely covers the bottom. When the bottom of the crêpe is lightly browned, 4 to 6 minutes, flip it and brown on the other side, 2 to 3 minutes. Remove from the pan and place on a piece of parchment paper. Repeat with the remaining batter, layering the cooked crêpes between pieces of parchment.

Make the filling: Use a hand mixer or stand mixer to mix all the filling ingredients until smooth and creamy.

Make the sauce: Place all the sauce ingredients in a small saucepan over medium-low heat. Simmer for 6 to 7 minutes, until the berries have softened and you have a thin sauce. The sauce will thicken as it cools.

To assemble, smear a heaping tablespoon of the filling over each crêpe. Loosely roll up the crêpes like fat cigars. Spoon some of the blueberry sauce over the filled crêpes and serve warm. Garnish with a few fresh berries, a sprinkle of powdered sweetener, and/or a dollop of freshly whipped cream, if desired.

Cinnamon Soul Bread

makes
18 servings

Cinnamon Soul Bread reminds me of the cinnamon toast my mom used to make for me. She slathered margarine (gasp!) on one side, sprinkled sugar and cinnamon on top, and broiled it until it was toasty. As I got older, I often did the same with cinnamon raisin bread, which I adored. This version has no raisins, but it's perfect slathered with real butter, sprinkled with a little more cinnamon and powdered sweetener, and toasted or broiled. This bread can also be used to make amazing French toast!

12 ounces cream cheese (1½ cups), softened in the microwave

4 large eggs

¼ cup heavy cream

¼ cup (½ stick) unsalted butter, melted but not hot

¼ cup coconut oil, melted but not hot

2 tablespoons apple cider vinegar

2 teaspoons vanilla extract

½ teaspoon maple extract

1¼ cups whey protein isolate

½ cup oat fiber

2½ teaspoons baking powder

1 (1¼-ounce) packet active dry yeast

1 teaspoon xanthan gum

¼ teaspoon salt

½ cup granulated sweetener

1½ teaspoons ground cinnamon

Preheat the oven to 325°F. Liberally grease a 9 by 5-inch loaf pan.

In a large bowl, using a hand mixer or stand mixer, combine the cream cheese, eggs, heavy cream, butter, coconut oil, vinegar, and extracts; set aside.

In a separate bowl, whisk together the protein isolate, oat fiber, baking powder, yeast, xanthan gum, and salt. Use a sieve or sifter to sift the dry ingredients into the wet ingredients. Gently stir to combine. Do not overmix.

Pour the batter into the prepared loaf pan.

In a small bowl, combine the sweetener and cinnamon; sprinkle over the top of the bread.

Bake for 55 to 65 minutes, until the bread is golden brown and a toothpick inserted in the middle comes out clean. Don't underbake or the bread will sink as it cools. Let cool in the pan for at least 15 minutes before slicing with a serrated knife. The texture improves overnight.

CALORIES: 383 | FAT: 6.9g | PROTEIN: 0.7g | CARBS: 0.2g | FIBER: 0g | ERYTHRITOL: 6g | OAT FIBER: 5.7g

Faux Yogurt Parfaits

makes
2 servings

Grace and I were not making granola when we made this "granola." As soon as I sampled it, the idea for a yogurt parfait popped into my head. When we layered it up in a dessert dish, it looked far prettier and fancier than we imagined. It tasted terrific, too! This pretty dish is good for breakfast or brunch or as a fun dessert. Either option is perfect to help Mom celebrate her special day. This recipe makes more granola than you will need for two parfaits. The leftovers can be frozen for later use or enjoyed as a traditional granola cereal.

GRANOLA:

¼ **cup (½ stick) unsalted butter, softened**

½ **teaspoon vanilla extract**

4 **drops liquid sweetener**

½ **cup hazelnut flour or blanched almond flour**

¼ **cup plus 1 tablespoon oat fiber**

¼ **cup powdered sweetener**

¼ **cup finely chopped raw pecans**

¼ **teaspoon ground cinnamon**

FOR SERVING:

1 **cup Yogurt (page 344)**

½ **cup fresh berries, such as raspberries, blueberries, or blackberries**

Fresh mint leaves, for garnish (optional)

Whipped cream, for garnish (optional)

In a bowl, use a spatula to mix together the butter, vanilla extract, liquid sweetener, flour, oat fiber, sweetener, pecans, and cinnamon. The mixture will resemble coarse sand. Set aside.

To assemble, layer one-quarter of the yogurt, one-quarter of the berries, and 1 tablespoon of the granola in each of two 8-ounce tumblers, wine glasses, champagne flutes, or small mason jars; repeat the layers. Garnish with fresh mint or a dollop of freshly whipped cream, if desired.

CALORIES: 657 | FAT: 64g | PROTEIN: 6.5g | CARBS: 9.6g | FIBER: 32.6g | ERYTHRITOL: 18g | OAT FIBER: 30g

Cinco de Mayo

Slow Cooker Barbacoa

makes
8 servings

Akin to Mexican barbecue, barbacoa is a hearty, flavorful beef dish that is hard not to love. This recipe uses canned chipotle chilies in adobe sauce; when shopping, look for brands that don't contain added sugar. This dish is slightly spicier than Al Pastor (page 144), but you can reduce the number of chipotle and guajillo chilies to one each for less heat. The sauce in which the meat is cooked is the key to making this dish so flavorful, but it is also important to sear the meat before placing it in the slow cooker. I've tried making it without taking this step and have found that searing the meat adds a depth of flavor that is well worth the extra effort.

SAUCE:

2 chipotle chilies in adobe sauce, plus 2 tablespoons sauce

2 dried ancho or pasilla chili peppers, destemmed and seeded

2 dried guajillo chili peppers, destemmed and seeded

1½ cups beef bone broth

2 tablespoons apple cider vinegar

2 tablespoons lime juice

2 tablespoons ground cumin

2 tablespoons dried oregano

1 tablespoon garlic powder

1 tablespoon onion powder

2 teaspoons salt

½ teaspoon chili powder

½ teaspoon smoked paprika

¼ teaspoon ground cinnamon

¼ teaspoon ground cloves

1 (3-pound) chuck roast, cut into 2- to 3-inch chunks

2 bay leaves

In a small saucepan over low heat, combine all the ingredients for the sauce. Simmer for 15 to 20 minutes, until the peppers have softened. Remove from the heat and let cool for 20 to 25 minutes.

When the sauce mixture has cooled, process in a blender until smooth. Set aside.

In a large skillet over high heat, sear the pieces of chuck roast on all sides. Place the seared meat in a 4-quart or larger slow cooker. Pour the sauce over the meat. Add the bay leaves and push them into the sauce. Cover and cook on low for 6 to 8 hours, until the meat is tender.

To serve, shred the meat in the sauce with two forks. Remove the bay leaves before serving.

note ——————————
For safety, be sure to wear disposable gloves when seeding the peppers; the oils can cause painful skin irritation.

tip ——————————
Serve with queso fresco, sour cream, fresh cilantro, diced onions, chopped jalapeño, and/or sliced avocado.

CALORIES: 263 | FAT: 11g | PROTEIN: 35.5g | CARBS: 5.7g | FIBER: 1.6g

Al Pastor (Mexican Pork)

makes
8 servings

Traditional Al Pastor contains pineapple or other sweet fruits that make it not especially keto-friendly. This version gets a slight sweetness from lime juice, but its flavor is warm and savory. The chilies used in this dish are easily found in the ethnic section of most grocery stores or in a local tienda (Mexican grocery) if you have one. This dish is only mildly spicy because the seeds are removed from the chilies. If you want a spicier dish, you can use the whole chili or add an extra of each chili. The instructions call for using a slow cooker. If you don't have one, you can bake this dish in the oven or simmer it over low heat on the stovetop. The most important step is finishing the meat by frying it in a skillet; don't skip this step, as it intensifies the flavor.

SAUCE:

2 dried ancho or pasilla chili peppers, destemmed and seeded

2 dried guajillo chili peppers, destemmed and seeded

2 cloves garlic

1 cup beef bone broth

⅓ cup white vinegar

2 tablespoons lime juice

2 teaspoons dried oregano

2 teaspoons ground cumin

2 teaspoons salt

1½ teaspoons achiote powder

2½ pounds boneless country-style pork, cut into 1- to 2-inch chunks

Ghee or bacon fat, for frying

Queso fresco, for garnish

In a small saucepan over low heat, combine all the ingredients for the sauce. Simmer until the chilies have softened, 15 to 18 minutes. Remove from the heat and let cool.

When the sauce mixture has cooled, process in a blender until smooth.

Place the pork in a gallon-sized resealable plastic bag, pour the sauce over the pork, seal the bag, and place in the refrigerator to marinate for at least 6 hours or overnight.

After marinating, place the pork and sauce in a slow cooker, cover, and cook on low for 6 to 8 hours, until the meat is fork-tender. Remove the pork from the sauce and chop or shred the meat with two forks.

Heat the ghee in a large skillet over medium-high heat. Fry the pork in the ghee, adding a bit of the sauce to keep the meat from becoming too dry or burning. When the meat is browned, remove from the heat and serve immediately. Garnish with queso fresco. If desired, strain the sauce and serve it on the side.

note ————————

For safety, be sure to wear disposable gloves when seeding the peppers; the oils can cause painful skin irritation.

tip ————————

Serve with sour cream, fresh cilantro, chopped jalapeño, and/or sliced avocado.

CALORIES: 290 | FAT: 17.9g | PROTEIN: 28.3g | CARBS: 3.3g | FIBER: 0.6g

Wheat-Free Tortillas

makes
6 tortillas
(1 per serving)

A low-carb tortilla? Kind of. These are not authentic tortillas, but they are a good low-carb option if you miss the convenience of tortillas as a vehicle for Slow Cooker Barbacoa (page 142), Al Pastor (page 144), fajitas, or other yummy Mexican fillings. You can also double the recipe and freeze the tortillas for future use.

¼ **cup pork dust (ground pork rinds)**

1 tablespoon oat fiber

1 tablespoon whey protein isolate

Sprinkle of garlic powder, onion powder, ground cumin, and salt

¼ **cup egg whites (about 2 large eggs)**

¼ **cup water**

1 tablespoon ghee or olive oil

¼ **teaspoon corn extract**

Ghee, for frying

Mix all the ingredients except the ghee for frying in a blender or mix vigorously with a whisk.

In a 7-inch nonstick skillet over medium-low heat, heat some ghee. Use a rubber spatula or wooden spoon to spread one-sixth of the tortilla batter as thinly as possible around the base of the pan. Cook the tortilla until it is lightly browned, 3 to 4 minutes. Watch carefully so that it does not burn. Use a spatula to flip the tortilla and brown on the other side.

Remove to a plate or cooling rack to cool. Repeat with the rest of the batter, making a total of 6 tortillas. Layer the cooked tortillas between pieces of parchment paper and serve warm.

Store leftovers in the refrigerator for up to 5 days.

CALORIES: 39 | FAT: 1.9g | PROTEIN: 4.7g | CARBS: 0.2g | FIBER: 0g | OAT FIBER: 1.9g

Cheese Taco Shells

**makes
6 shells
(1 per serving)**

While the ingredients couldn't be simpler, these Cheese Taco Shells couldn't be more delicious. They are a great low-carb stand-in for traditional corn- or flour-based crunchy taco shells. The hardest part of this recipe is shaping the shells into the traditional taco shape. After baking the cheese, make sure to shape it before it cools. You can also drape the baked cheese over an inverted muffin pan or small ramekins to make taco bowls instead of shells. For crispier shells, use a mixture of 1½ cups shredded cheddar cheese and ½ cup freshly grated Parmesan cheese.

8 ounces cheddar cheese, shredded (about 2 cups)

¼ teaspoon chili powder

¼ teaspoon ground cumin

Preheat the oven to 400°F. Line a baking sheet with parchment paper.

In a small bowl, toss the cheese and spices together.

Measure ⅓ cup of the cheese mixture and spread it into a circle about 6 inches in diameter on the prepared baking sheet. Repeat with the remaining cheese to make a total of 6 circles, leaving at least 2 inches of space between circles. Bake for 4 to 6 minutes, until the edges have browned slightly.

Remove from the oven. Form each circle of cheese into a taco shell shape by draping it over the handle of a wooden spoon suspended over two cups. Let cool for 5 to 7 minutes, until firm.

Store leftover shells in an airtight container in the refrigerator for up to 5 days.

CALORIES: 148 | FAT: 12g | PROTEIN: 9.3g | CARBS: 1.1g | FIBER: 0g

Authentic Salsa Verde

makes
8 servings

Salsa verde, or green salsa, is a fantastic alternative to tomato-based salsas. Made with tomatillos, this simple and authentic sauce is mild and can be served with nearly any Mexican-inspired meal. This recipe was given to me by my friend Sandy, who walked me through each step. I'm so grateful for her willingness to teach me how to make delicious low-carb Mexican foods.

8 tomatillos, husked

1 large jalapeño pepper

¼ small onion

1 clove garlic

⅓ cup water

2 tablespoons fresh cilantro

1 tablespoon lime juice

½ teaspoon salt

Place the tomatillos, jalapeño, onion, and garlic in a small saucepan and cover with water. Bring to a boil, then reduce the heat and simmer until the tomatillos and jalapeño soften, 10 to 15 minutes. The color of the jalapeño will change to an army green.

Strain the vegetables and puree in a blender or food processor. Add the water, cilantro, lime juice, and salt and blend until smooth.

Store leftovers in the refrigerator for up to 5 days.

tip

For a creamy option, add half an avocado when you puree the cooked vegetables.

CALORIES: 20 | FAT: 0.3g | PROTEIN: 0.3g | CARBS: 3g | FIBER: 0.9g

Jalapeño Cheddar Bread

makes
16 servings

While we enjoy this bread plain, the jalapeño and cheddar cheese in this recipe give it a fun kick of flavor. It's especially nice for Cinco de Mayo. This bread is great for grilled sandwiches, croutons, or casseroles. Like many low-carb baked goods, the texture and flavor improve after it cools.

12 ounces cream cheese (1½ cups), softened in the microwave

4 large eggs

¼ cup heavy cream

¼ cup (½ stick) unsalted butter, melted but not hot

¼ cup bacon fat or coconut oil, melted but not hot

2 tablespoons apple cider vinegar

1¼ cups whey protein isolate

½ cup oat fiber

2½ teaspoons baking powder

1 (1¼-ounce) packet active dry yeast

1 teaspoon xanthan gum

¼ teaspoon baking soda

¼ teaspoon cream of tartar

¼ teaspoon salt

3 ounces sharp cheddar cheese, shredded (about ¾ cup)

2 jalapeño peppers, seeded and chopped

Preheat the oven to 325°F. Liberally grease a 9 by 5-inch loaf pan.

In a large bowl, use a hand mixer or stand mixer to blend the cream cheese, eggs, heavy cream, butter, bacon fat, and vinegar. Set aside.

In a separate bowl, whisk together the protein isolate, oat fiber, baking powder, yeast, xanthan gum, baking soda, cream of tartar, and salt.

Use a sieve or sifter to sift the dry ingredients into the wet ingredients. Stir lightly, adding the cheddar cheese and jalapeños as you stir. Do not overmix.

Pour the dough into the prepared pan. Bake for 60 to 70 minutes, until the bread is golden brown and a toothpick inserted in the middle comes out clean. Be careful not to underbake or the bread will sink as it cools.

Let cool in the pan for at least 15 minutes before slicing. Store leftovers in the refrigerator for up to a week.

CALORIES: 169 | FAT: 13.7g | PROTEIN: 6.6g | CARBS: 1.1g | FIBER: 0.3g | OAT FIBER: 5.7g

06

june

JUNE brings cheers for the laid-back days of summer. We can all celebrate the break from frantic mornings of packing lunches and tracking down that one sneaker that keeps you from flying out the door, and from evenings of homework and early bedtimes. Instead, fireflies light up the evening sky, and the best hours of the day are spent by the pool. June heralds summer vacations, comfortable clothing, and flip-flops. Because the only commercial holiday in June is Father's Day, I've included recipes that David particularly likes; however, all of these dishes can be enjoyed nearly anytime, especially **Creamy Parmesan Lemon Chicken with Artichokes** and **Hot Fudge Cake.**

Our June traditions include celebrating the end of the school year. When Grace was finishing kindergarten, I picked her up from school with a fun surprise. Using glass-safe markers, I decorated the windows of our SUV. I drew colorful flowers and wrote, "Grace is a first-grader!" on the hatchback window. On the rear side windows, I drew more hearts and flowers. On one side, I wrote, "School's out for summer!" On the other side, I wrote, "Honk if you love summer!" She adored it! We carried on that tradition for both kids until they started finishing middle school grades; eventually, their enthusiasm for Mom's colorful "art" waned.

We also celebrate Father's Day with David and the grandfathers. The process of picking out cards for the different grandfathers is as much fun as giving them, and each selection always seems to match the personality of the recipient. Like many celebrations, we often celebrate Father's Day with a meal. I try to make David's favorite dishes, which trend toward spicier foods. He enjoys any dish that contains chorizo, so I made it into a **Southwestern Breakfast Casserole.** While he doesn't have a huge sweet tooth, he does tend to like sweet foods for breakfast, so I've also included a recipe for **Cinnamon Bagels** that he particularly enjoys. From **Coffee Ice Cream** to **Shrimp Fra Diavolo** and **Sausage and Cheese Stuffed Mushrooms,** this month is dedicated to the man I love and the father of my children.

Just Like the Real Thing Chocolate Chip Muffins

makes
12 muffins
(1 per serving)

Grace named these muffins when she enthusiastically tried one and exclaimed, "Mom, this tastes just like the real thing!" I loved the smile on her face that told me my daughter wasn't feeling the least bit deprived. While I don't bake often, it's great to know that I can make these as a treat for her. Because they travel well, they're a great on-the-go option. The chocolate chips do tend to sink to the bottoms of the muffins, so I sprinkle them on top of the batter after pouring it into the pan to prevent them from clustering on the bottom.

⅓ cup blanched almond flour

⅓ cup whey protein isolate

⅓ cup oat fiber, or 2 tablespoons coconut flour

1 teaspoon baking powder

¼ teaspoon salt

½ cup (1 stick) unsalted butter, cold

⅔ cup granulated sweetener

4 ounces cream cheese (½ cup), cold

3 large eggs

2 teaspoons vanilla extract

½ cup low-carb milk chocolate chips or chopped low-carb milk chocolate

Preheat the oven to 350°F. Line a standard-size 12-well muffin pan with parchment paper liners.

In a large bowl, whisk together the almond flour, protein isolate, oat fiber, baking powder, and salt; set aside.

In a separate bowl, using a stand or hand mixer, cream the butter and sweetener. When the butter has lightened in color, mix in the cream cheese and continue blending until everything is smooth and well incorporated.

Add the eggs one at a time, mixing well after each addition. Add the vanilla extract and mix once more to combine.

Stir the dry ingredients into the wet ingredients by hand.

Divide the batter evenly among the wells of the prepared muffin pan, filling each well about two-thirds full. Sprinkle the chocolate chips over the muffins, pushing a few down into the batter.

Bake for 24 to 28 minutes, until browned on top and firm to the touch. Let cool in the pan for 5 to 10 minutes before serving.

Store leftovers in the refrigerator for up to 5 days.

CALORIES: 183 | FAT: 10g | PROTEIN: 6.1g | CARBS: 1.8g | FIBER: 0.5g | ERYTHRITOL: 10.7g | OAT FIBER: 5g

Summer's Here Strawberry Layer Cake

makes
16 servings

Like many other of my favorite recipes, I made this cake at my daughter's request. She spied what was supposed to be a low-carb version on a Pinterest board and then asked me to make it even lower in carbs for her. As you know by now, I enjoy a challenge—and I especially love strawberry cake. This cake is moist and gorgeous. It's perfect for any holiday, but especially nice for a relaxing summer get-together.

CALORIES: 366 | FAT: 34.1g | PROTEIN: 8.1g | CARBS: 5.5g | FIBER: 1.3g | ERYTHRITOL: 16.5g | OAT FIBER: 5.7g

CAKE:

1 cup heavy cream

2 tablespoons white vinegar

1 cup (2 sticks) unsalted butter, softened

1 cup granulated sweetener

4 ounces cream cheese (½ cup), room temperature

6 large eggs

1.2 ounces (34 g) unsweetened freeze-dried strawberries, powdered in a blender or clean coffee grinder (about ⅔ cup)

1 tablespoon unflavored gelatin

½ teaspoon citric acid (optional; see Note)

2 cups blanched almond flour

½ cup oat fiber

⅓ cup plus 1 tablespoon whey protein isolate

1 teaspoon baking powder

½ teaspoon baking soda

1½ teaspoons strawberry extract

1 teaspoon vanilla extract

6 drops liquid sweetener

ICING:

3 cups heavy cream

½ cup powdered sweetener

5 ounces cream cheese (½ cup plus 2 tablespoons), room temperature

4 drops liquid sweetener (optional)

Fresh berries, for garnish (optional)

Preheat the oven to 325°F. Generously grease two 9-inch cake pans and line with parchment paper.

Make the cake: Place the heavy cream in a small bowl. Pour in the vinegar and set aside.

In a separate bowl, use a hand mixer or stand mixer to cream the butter and granulated sweetener. When the butter has lightened in color, add the cream cheese and beat until creamy and well blended. Add the eggs one at a time, beating well after each addition.

In a separate bowl, whisk together the powdered strawberries, gelatin, citric acid (if using), almond flour, oat fiber, protein isolate, baking powder, and baking soda.

Add the dry ingredients to the butter mixture and mix by hand. Stir in the extracts and liquid sweetener. Taste the batter for sweetness and add more sweetener, if desired.

Divide the batter evenly between the prepared cake pans. Bake for 45 to 50 minutes, until slightly brown and springy to the touch; a toothpick inserted in the center should come out clean. Let cool in the pans for about 10 minutes before turning the cakes onto a cooling rack to cool completely.

While the cakes are cooling, make the icing: In a large bowl, use the mixer to whip the heavy cream. As it begins to thicken, slowly add the powdered sweetener. When thickened, add the cream cheese and whip until smooth. Taste for sweetness and add up to 4 drops of liquid sweetener, if desired.

After the cakes are completely cool, transfer one layer to a cake plate. Top with the icing. Add the second layer of cake and frost the sides and top of the entire cake with the remaining icing. Refrigerate the iced cake for at least 4 hours before serving.

Garnish with a few fresh berries just before serving, if desired.

note ————

The citric acid deepens the flavor of strawberries. It is commonly used in fruit-flavored foods to give them a bit of the characteristic tart fruit taste.

Coffee Ice Cream

makes
6 servings

Coffee-flavored ice cream just seems fitting for the month in which we celebrate fathers. While my dad never drank coffee, the father of my children definitely does, and he really likes this ice cream. Add 2 tablespoons of cocoa powder when you add the coffee to make a delicious mocha ice cream.

2¼ cups heavy cream

5 large egg yolks

¾ cup powdered sweetener (see Tip)

2½ teaspoons vanilla extract

1 tablespoon instant coffee granules or espresso powder

½ teaspoon salt

SPECIAL EQUIPMENT:

Ice cream maker

Heat the heavy cream in a heavy saucepan over low heat, stirring with a whisk. Add the egg yolks and continue whisking over low heat until just warmed.

Add the sweetener and whisk until completely dissolved. Continue heating, whisking constantly, until the custard thickens, about 10 minutes. When the custard coats the back of a wooden spoon or reaches 140°F on a candy thermometer, remove the pan from the heat. Do not allow the mixture to warm to over 140°F or the eggs will begin to cook.

Stir in the vanilla extract, coffee, and salt until dissolved. Transfer the mixture to a bowl and place in the refrigerator to cool.

When cool, churn the ice cream mixture in an ice cream maker following the manufacturer's directions until it reaches your desired consistency.

Store leftovers in the freezer. When frozen, this ice cream will harden to a solid state. Allow to thaw at room temperature for about 10 minutes before enjoying.

tip

The type of sweetener used makes a huge difference in the texture of the ice cream. For the best texture, use allulose or xylitol; remember that each sweetener has different characteristics (see pages 19 and 20 for details). Use the sweetener that you prefer and that does not impact your blood glucose.

CALORIES: 204 | FAT: 18.4g | PROTEIN: 4.9g | CARBS: 2g | FIBER: 0g | ERYTHRITOL: 18g

cocktail
of the month

Spiked Arnold Palmer

makes
4 servings

Admittedly, a true Arnold Palmer doesn't contain vodka, but I promised you a cocktail each month, so here it is! The vodka can be omitted if you prefer. This refreshing summer drink is easily enjoyed on the porch, by the lake, or in the cool of air-conditioning. We like to float slices of lemon in the serving pitcher or garnish the pitcher with fresh mint.

3 cups Iced Tea (page 352)

⅓ cup granulated sweetener

½ cup lemon juice (about 3 large lemons)

2 tablespoons finely grated lemon zest

1 tablespoon sugar-free lemon crystals (such as True Lemon)

4 ounces vodka (optional)

Fresh mint, for garnish (optional)

Lemon slices or curls of lemon zest, for garnish (optional)

Pour the tea and granulated sweetener into a large glass pitcher, then stir with a wooden spoon or rubber spatula to dissolve the sweetener. Add the lemon juice, lemon zest, and lemon crystals; stir well.

Refrigerate for at least 2 hours before serving. Pour the chilled mixture over ice. If using vodka, add 1 ounce to each glass just before serving.

Garnish with fresh mint and/or slices of lemon or curls of lemon zest, if desired.

CALORIES: 72 | FAT: 0.1g | PROTEIN: 0.1g | CARBS: 2.6g | FIBER: 0.3g | ERYTHRITOL: 16g

Father's Day

David's Favorite Southwestern Breakfast Casserole

makes
8 servings

David adores chorizo; if I combined chorizo with shoe leather and called it Southwestern Jerky, my husband would love it! This dish is similar to a frittata, but I've made the casserole more like a carnivore recipe by adding crumbled low-carb bread. The texture is familiar and the carbs are minimal, so I especially like to put this on a buffet table for others to enjoy. Somehow the Southwestern flavors make a brunch casserole more masculine, and I can assure you that this one is a hit with the fellas. I appreciate that it offers a chance to enjoy fresh cilantro, avocado, and sour cream for breakfast, as those items are perfect accompaniments to this dish!

8 large eggs

½ cup heavy cream

½ cup (1 stick) unsalted butter, melted but not hot

1 teaspoon mustard powder

½ teaspoon salt

Dash of ground black pepper

1 pound Mexican chorizo, casings removed

⅓ cup chopped green bell peppers

¼ cup finely chopped onions

2 jalapeño peppers, seeded and chopped

4 ounces cream cheese (½ cup), cut into small cubes

1½ cups crumbled Modified Soul Bread (page 342)

6 ounces cheddar cheese, shredded (about 1½ cups)

Preheat the oven to 350°F. Grease a 9 by 13-inch baking dish.

Use a blender to mix the eggs, heavy cream, melted butter, mustard powder, salt, and black pepper; set aside.

In a large skillet over medium heat, cook the chorizo, bell peppers, onions, and jalapeños, crumbling the meat as it cooks, until the chorizo is browned and the vegetables are tender. Spread the chorizo mixture evenly in the prepared baking dish.

Sprinkle the small cubes of cream cheese over the chorizo mixture. Top with the crumbled bread and shredded cheese. Pour the egg mixture over the entire dish. Use a fork to make sure that the egg mixture is distributed throughout the dish.

Bake for 45 to 55 minutes, until browned and set. Let cool for at least 10 minutes before slicing and serving.

note

For safety, be sure to wear disposable gloves when chopping and seeding the jalapeños; the oil can cause painful skin irritation.

CALORIES: 630 | FAT: 54.8g | PROTEIN: 27.7g | CARBS: 3.1g | FIBER: 0.3g | OAT FIBER: 5.2g

Cinnamon Bagels

makes
12 bagels
(1 per serving)

My husband is a picky man, and even though he likes to eat, he doesn't immediately embrace all the recipes I create, especially the low-carb baked goods. If he likes an item, it is a pretty safe bet that others will, too. The good news is that he really liked these bagels. When he tried one sliced and toasted, he looked at me sideways and said, "This is slightly chewy. How did you do that?" I just smiled and tried not to gloat because he called it "slightly chewy." While it's not your bagel shop–quality baked good, this bagel would give a supermarket bagel a bit of competition, especially when you factor in the very low carb count. David enjoys these toasted with butter. I enjoy them with a schmear of cream cheese.

8 ounces part-skim mozzarella cheese, shredded (about 2 cups)

2 ounces cream cheese (¼ cup), room temperature

2 ounces Parmesan cheese, grated (about ⅔ cup)

½ cup egg whites (about 4 large eggs)

3 tablespoons ghee, room temperature

1 tablespoon vanilla extract

¼ teaspoon maple extract

4 drops liquid sweetener

¾ cup whey protein isolate

½ cup granulated sweetener

¼ cup psyllium husk powder

1½ tablespoons ground cinnamon

1 teaspoon baking powder

½ cup very hot water

SPECIAL EQUIPMENT:

2 (6-well) donut pans

Preheat the oven to 350°F. Grease two 6-well donut pans.

In a large bowl, stir together the mozzarella, cream cheese, Parmesan, egg whites, ghee, extracts, and liquid sweetener; set aside.

In a separate bowl, whisk together the protein isolate, granulated sweetener, psyllium husk powder, cinnamon, and baking powder. Slowly add the hot water to the dry ingredients, stirring with the whisk so that the psyllium powder doesn't clump as you add the water.

When the hot water is fully incorporated, add the cheese mixture. Use a hand mixer or stand mixer to thoroughly incorporate all the ingredients, making sure that the cheese is fully blended into the batter. The batter will be runny.

Distribute the batter evenly among the wells of the prepared pans. Bake for 17 to 20 minutes, until the bagels are browned and firm to the touch. Let cool in the pans for 15 to 20 minutes before serving. Store leftovers in the refrigerator for up to 5 days.

note —————————————————————————————
These bagels are best served toasted a day after they are baked.

CALORIES: 116 | FAT: 6.3g | PROTEIN: 1g | CARBS: 2g | FIBER: 1g | ERYTHRITOL: 5.3g

Shrimp Fra Diavolo

makes
4 servings

When David and I were dating, one of his favorite restaurants in downtown Raleigh served a dish called Fra Diavolo. Because I never sought out spicy dishes, I had never heard of it. Twenty years later, I finally figured out how to make it for him. He enjoys it with a little more red pepper flakes than I do, so he generally gets this dish all to himself unless company's coming. While you could serve this meal over a pasta substitute like glucomannan noodles, zucchini noodles, sautéed spinach, or cabbage, David prefers to eat it more like a stew.

¼ cup olive oil

1 small onion, chopped

3 cloves garlic, crushed

1 (28-ounce) can crushed tomatoes

2 cups chicken bone broth or seafood stock

1 tablespoon lemon juice

1 tablespoon dried basil

2 teaspoons dried oregano

1½ teaspoons red pepper flakes, or more to taste

1 teaspoon salt

1½ pounds medium shrimp, peeled, deveined, and patted dry

2 tablespoons unsalted butter, softened

Warm the olive oil in a large skillet over medium heat. Add the onion and garlic and cook, stirring often, until the onion is browned.

Stir in the tomatoes, broth, lemon juice, basil, oregano, red pepper flakes, and salt. Simmer for about 20 minutes, until the sauce is reduced and slightly thickened.

Add the shrimp and simmer for another 3 to 5 minutes, until the shrimp are just pink. Remove from the heat.

Stir in the butter and serve immediately.

CALORIES: 314 | FAT: 20.3g | PROTEIN: 23.7g | CARBS: 10.3g | FIBER: 2g

Creamy Parmesan Lemon Chicken with Artichokes

makes
6 servings

Here's another option for a Dad's Day dinner if you're looking for something with a little less heat. This recipe was adapted from a family recipe of one of my favorite low-carb physicians, Dr. Sarah Hallberg. Actually, it was adapted from her husband's recipe that uses only artichokes. I decided to add chicken to make it an entree. This is as easy as a main dish can be, especially if you use canned artichokes and precooked chicken for a quick weeknight meal. If you want to get extra fancy, use fresh artichokes and roasted chicken.

2 (14-ounce) cans artichoke hearts

3 cups chopped cooked chicken

1½ cups heavy cream

Grated zest and juice of 1 large lemon

3 ounces Parmesan cheese, grated (about 1 cup)

1 tablespoon fresh thyme leaves

Dash of ground black pepper

Preheat the oven to 350°F.

Drain the artichokes. Use a clean towel to squeeze the excess moisture from the artichokes and chop them into bite-sized pieces.

Place the artichokes and chicken in a 9 by 13-inch baking dish; set aside.

In a small bowl, mix the heavy cream, lemon zest, and lemon juice. Pour the cream mixture evenly over the artichokes and chicken in the baking dish.

Sprinkle the Parmesan, thyme, and pepper evenly over the dish. Bake for 30 to 40 minutes, until lightly browned and bubbly. Let cool for at least 10 minutes before serving.

CALORIES: 280 | FAT: 15.7g | PROTEIN: 24.7g | CARBS: 5.8g | FIBER: 4g

Sausage and Cheese Stuffed Mushrooms

makes
8 servings

If you're serving this dish to a crowd, go ahead and make a double batch. Just trust me on this one. The ingredients are simple, but the taste is big. These stuffed mushrooms work well as a side dish or as an hors d'oeuvre.

1 pound button mushrooms

12 ounces Italian sausage, cooked and crumbled

6 ounces cream cheese (¾ cup), room temperature

5 ounces sharp cheddar cheese, shredded (about 1¼ cups)

1 green onion, finely chopped

¼ teaspoon garlic powder

Preheat the oven to 350°F. Line a baking sheet with aluminum foil or parchment paper.

Use a paper towel to clean the mushrooms. Remove and discard the stems. Set the caps aside.

In a mixing bowl, mix together the remaining ingredients with a large spoon. When well combined, use the spoon to stuff the sausage mixture into the mushroom caps. The back of the spoon is perfect for pressing the filling into the mushrooms. Do not overfill the mushroom caps.

Place the stuffed mushrooms in a single layer on the prepared baking sheet. Bake for 10 to 12 minutes, until the mushrooms are tender and the filling is bubbly and brown.

Serve warm.

CALORIES: 425 | FAT: 22.9g | PROTEIN: 12.9g | CARBS: 2g | FIBER: 0.5g

Hot Fudge Cake

makes
12 servings

Because we're celebrating dads, here's another recipe developed with my husband in mind. Before keto, David would hit the drive-thru for a version of this treat. He once confessed that he had a particular fondness for the hot fudge sauce. With the bar set high, I served my version to him with a little worry about whether he would like it. The verdict? "How'd you do that?" That reaction put a smile on my face. I also like to make this cake in a 9 by 13-inch baking dish (see Note, opposite) and cut it into 24 pieces. You can put a small scoop of Creamy Vanilla Ice Cream between two pieces of cake or one larger scoop on top of just one piece. Just don't forget the drizzle of hot fudge sauce and the freshly whipped cream!

1½ cups blanched almond flour

½ cup oat fiber

⅓ cup unsweetened cocoa powder

1½ teaspoons baking powder

1 teaspoon instant coffee granules

½ teaspoon salt

½ cup (1 stick) unsalted butter, softened

2 ounces cream cheese (¼ cup), room temperature

1 cup granulated sweetener

5 large eggs

8 drops liquid sweetener

2 teaspoons vanilla extract

3 ounces unsweetened baking chocolate, chopped

¼ cup heavy cream

1 batch Creamy Vanilla Ice Cream (page 348)

½ batch Hot Fudge Sauce (page 347)

Whipped cream (optional)

Preheat the oven to 350°F. Grease a standard-size 12-well muffin pan or line the wells with parchment paper.

In a large bowl, whisk together the almond flour, oat fiber, cocoa powder, baking powder, coffee, and salt, making sure the flour is well distributed. Set aside.

In a separate mixing bowl, use a hand mixer or stand mixer to cream the butter, cream cheese, and granulated sweetener. When the mixture is creamy, add the eggs one at a time, mixing well after each addition. Mix in the liquid sweetener and vanilla extract.

Microwave the chocolate in 15-second increments, stirring after each increment, until smooth and melted. (You can also melt the chocolate on the stovetop over low heat. Stir constantly until smooth and just melted, being careful not to let it burn.) Pour the melted chocolate into the butter mixture.

Add the dry ingredients to the chocolate mixture and mix well by hand, then stir in the heavy cream.

Divide the batter evenly among the wells of the prepared muffin pan and bake for 15 to 18 minutes, until a toothpick inserted in the center of a "muffin" comes out clean; they should be firm to a light touch. Let cool in the pan for at least 1 hour, then slice the "muffins" in half horizontally to make cakes.

To serve, place a cake on a serving plate and top with a ¼-cup scoop of vanilla ice cream. Place another cake on top. Drizzle with hot fudge sauce and top with a dollop of freshly whipped cream, if desired.

CALORIES: 495 | FAT: 36.9g | PROTEIN: 20.4g | CARBS: 7.5g | FIBER: 4g | ERYTHRITOL: 34g | OAT FIBER: 7.6g

note

You can also pour the batter into a 9 by 13-inch baking dish and bake at 350°F for 18 to 20 minutes, until a toothpick inserted in the center comes out clean. Let cool in the pan for at least 1 hour before cutting into 2-inch squares.

07
july

JULY is a busy month for our family. We have four birthdays to celebrate, including Grace's and David's. We also celebrate the Fourth of July, which is the birthday of my best friend's dad, who passed away in 2018. Mr. Jerry was indeed a Yankee Doodle Dandy, and he loved Independence Day as much as his birthday.

I grew up in a small town that has always celebrated the Fourth in a big way. In fact, my great-grandfather, who was the town barber, is believed to have welcomed the first crowds to what would become a longstanding tradition of July Fourth festivities that seem to grow larger each year in spite of the town staying small. The local fire department hosts the celebration, which includes carnival rides, entertainment, competitions, and even a fire queen pageant following a parade that lasts nearly an hour! Folks come from neighboring counties to join in the fun. The finale, of course, is a fireworks display that is pretty impressive for such a small town.

Even after going off to college and moving away, I rarely miss the Fourth of July parade. I meet my two best high school friends there each year to watch the parade with our families. Each year we take photos in front of an old oak tree. We line up our kids, who protest but eventually smile because we out-stubborn them. Then we line up as couples, and finally as just the three of us girls. It is always hot out, and each year we complain that we should have taken our photos *before* we all began to "glow." I cherish those photos and am glad to have them as a reminder of the healthier changes in me since I began a very-low-carb diet in June 2013.

Sometimes family and friends from outside the area even join us for the parade, curious as to why we enjoy it so much. David usually regales them with stories of the antique hearse that the local funeral home brings to the parade. When he started joining me at the parade in July 1999, he thought it was the oddest thing he had ever seen! Nearly two decades later, he still finds it odd, but he appreciates the event and always snaps a photo.

Afterward, we generally spend time with my extended family. We may or may not grill with them, so I've included several grill-friendly ideas in this chapter, including a refrigerated marinated cheese that Grace and I particularly love. Even if we make no other food for the Fourth, we traditionally make ice cream. While there are many ice cream recipes in this book, the July flavor, **Cookies and Cream,** is one of my very favorites.

After the fireworks come the birthdays. Grace celebrates the entire month, as one should. She loves our tradition of decorating her room with streamers and such while she sleeps. Even when she's away at camp, we decorate her room for her return. Her face always lights up, even if she sees the decorations a week after her birthday. On David's birthday, just five days after Grace's, the children decorate our bedroom. The birthday boy or girl gets to choose the meals for the day along with a birthday treat. For July, **Grace's Epic Banana Split Ice Cream Cake** is featured. This was Grace's thirteenth birthday request, and, while it is quite a bit of work, it is the best celebratory ice cream cake I've ever had. She was proud of that cake, and I was even more proud to have created it for her. In contrast, David's birthday treat is a simple **Private Island Key Lime Pie.** While it's equally delicious, the recipe is far less labor-intensive, befitting his more subdued personality. David also likes spicier dishes, so I included a recipe for **Jerk Chicken Thighs** with him in mind.

Lime in the Coconut Muffins

makes
12 muffins
(1 per serving)

You put the lime in the coconut… Even if we're landlocked, we all deserve dreams of islands teeming with fresh limes and coconuts. This muffin brings the taste of the islands to breakfast, brunch, or dessert. If you have coconut haters in your family, as we do, you can omit the coconut—or you can tell them to make their own muffins!

⅓ cup blanched almond flour

⅓ cup whey protein isolate

⅓ cup oat fiber, or 2 tablespoons coconut flour

1 teaspoon baking powder

¼ teaspoon salt

½ cup (1 stick) unsalted butter, cold

¾ cup granulated sweetener

4 ounces cream cheese (½ cup), cold

3 large eggs

⅓ cup lime-flavored sparkling water (such as Zevia or LaCroix)

2 teaspoons vanilla extract

1½ teaspoons lime extract

⅓ cup finely shredded unsweetened coconut

1 tablespoon finely grated lime zest

Preheat the oven to 350°F. Line a standard-size 12-well muffin pan with parchment paper liners.

In a large bowl, whisk together the almond flour, protein isolate, oat fiber, baking powder, and salt; set aside.

In a separate bowl, using a hand mixer or stand mixer, cream the butter and sweetener. When the butter has lightened in color, mix in the cream cheese and continue blending until everything is smooth and well incorporated.

Add the eggs one at a time, mixing well after each addition. Mix in the sparkling water and extracts.

3 in the dry ingredients by hand. Add the coconut and lime zest and stir to incorporate into the batter.

Divide the batter evenly among the wells of the prepared muffin pan, filling each well about two-thirds full. Bake for 24 to 28 minutes, until lightly browned and just firm to the touch. Let cool in the pan for 5 to 10 minutes before serving.

Store leftovers in the refrigerator for up to 5 days.

CALORIES: 158 | FAT: 14.4g | PROTEIN: 5.7g | CARBS: 1.5g | FIBER: 5.6g | ERYTHRITOL: 12g | OAT FIBER: 5g

Grace's Epic Banana Split Ice Cream Cake

makes
24 servings

In all honesty, this recipe is a lot of work! No one in her right mind would attempt it, but my Sweet G requested it for her thirteenth birthday. Actually, it was more of a challenge than a request, so of course this mama couldn't resist. If this amazing ice cream cake weren't such a special memory for us, I would not have included it in this book. When I made it, Grace was all smiles, and everyone who tried it loved it. The effort brings great reward and serves a large crowd. Thankfully, it also keeps well in the freezer.

To pull off this feat, you make the cake layers and three flavors of ice cream. You freeze the ice cream in the same size pans you use to make the cake, and then you layer the cake and ice cream in a similar manner to a banana split: banana cake, strawberry ice cream, banana cake, chocolate ice cream, banana cake, vanilla ice cream. The entire cake is topped with hot fudge sauce and chopped peanuts. Each slice can also be garnished with whipped cream. I like to drizzle the hot fudge sauce over individual pieces of cake rather than over the entire thing, especially if I expect to have leftovers.

You can make this cake in a traditional circular layer cake shape or in loaf pans. The loaf shape seems to be easier to slice and serve, but the round layers work well, too. Be sure to let the assembled cake sit out at room temperature for at least 20 minutes before attempting to slice it.

  CALORIES: 400 | FAT: 36.3g | PROTEIN: 12.3g | CARBS: 7.6g | FIBER: 3.4g | ERYTHRITOL: 25.5g | OAT FIBER: 3.8g

1½ cups blanched almond flour

½ cup banana-flavored whey protein isolate

½ cup oat fiber

¼ cup coconut flour

2 teaspoons baking powder

½ teaspoon salt

½ cup (1 stick) unsalted butter, softened

¾ cup granulated sweetener

5 large eggs

⅓ cup sour cream

⅓ cup heavy cream

2 teaspoons banana extract

2 teaspoons vanilla extract

5 drops liquid sweetener

1 batch Old-Fashioned Strawberry Ice Cream (page 110)

1 batch Chocolate Ice Cream (page 350)

1 batch Creamy Vanilla Ice Cream (page 348)

1 batch Hot Fudge Sauce (page 347)

Chopped peanuts

Whipped cream (optional)

Preheat the oven to 350°F. Grease three 8-inch round cake pans or two 9 by 5-inch loaf pans and line the pans with parchment paper.

In a large bowl, whisk together the almond flour, protein isolate, oat fiber, coconut flour, baking powder, and salt until well combined; set aside.

In a separate bowl, using a hand mixer or stand mixer, cream the butter and granulated sweetener. When the butter has lightened in color, add the eggs one at a time, mixing well after each addition.

Add the dry ingredients to the wet ingredients and mix well. Beat in the sour cream, heavy cream, extracts, and liquid sweetener.

Divide the batter among the prepared pans. If using round cake pans, bake for 14 to 18 minutes; if using loaf pans, bake for 20 to 24 minutes. The cakes are ready when the tops are lightly browned and a toothpick inserted in the middle comes out clean. Allow the cakes to cool completely.

If you used loaf pans, after the cakes have cooled, cut each loaf in half horizontally, creating four layers.

To assemble, begin with a layer of cake followed by a layer of strawberry ice cream. Add another layer of cake, then a layer of chocolate ice cream and another layer of cake. For a round cake, the vanilla ice cream should be the top layer. For a loaf pan cake (as pictured), you will end with a fourth layer of cake on top.

Cover the assembled cake with hot fudge sauce and chopped peanuts. If you are serving a smaller crowd and are confident that much of the cake will be frozen and eaten later, you may want to add more hot fudge sauce, chopped peanuts, and whipped cream to each slice as it is served.

notes

You can use unflavored whey protein isolate rather than banana-flavored isolate. If you use unflavored, increase the granulated sweetener to 1 full cup and the banana extract to 3 teaspoons.

If you make the cake in loaf pans, you will need only a half batch each of the ice creams and hot fudge sauce.

Cookies and Cream Ice Cream

makes
6 servings

July is hot, and ice cream can help cool things down. In fact, July is when we make all the ice cream flavors. This recipe was born of a July ice cream flavor frenzy that included many of the flavors in this book. Cookie bits in ice cream make for a doubly decadent treat. Although this recipe calls for a half batch of K-E-T-O cookies, you just might want to make a full batch and freeze the other half of the cookies so that you can easily make a second batch of ice cream later.

2½ cups heavy cream

1 cup unsweetened almond milk

6 large egg yolks

¾ cup powdered sweetener (see Tip)

2 teaspoons vanilla extract

½ teaspoon salt

½ batch K-E-T-O Chocolate Sandwich Cookies (page 222), unfilled, crumbled

Heat the heavy cream and almond milk in a heavy saucepan over low heat, stirring with a whisk. Add the egg yolks and continue whisking on low heat until just warmed.

Add the powdered sweetener and whisk until completely dissolved. Continue heating, whisking constantly, until the custard thickens, about 10 minutes. When the custard coats the back of a wooden spoon or reaches 140°F on a candy thermometer, remove the pan from the heat. Do not allow the mixture to warm to over 140°F or the eggs will begin to cook.

Stir in the vanilla extract and salt. Transfer the mixture to a bowl and place in the refrigerator to cool.

When cool, churn the ice cream mixture in an ice cream maker following the manufacturer's directions. Add the cookie bits to the ice cream while it is churning and after it has begun to freeze, but while the ice cream is still soft. Continue churning until it reaches your desired consistency.

Store leftovers in the freezer. When frozen, this ice cream will harden to a solid state. Allow to thaw at room temperature for about 10 minutes before enjoying.

tip

The type of sweetener used makes a huge difference in the texture of the ice cream. For the best texture, use allulose or xylitol; remember that each sweetener has different characteristics (see pages 19 and 20 for details). Use the sweetener that you prefer and that does not impact your blood glucose.

CALORIES: 328 | FAT: 22.1g | PROTEIN: 15.8g | CARBS: 3.9g | FIBER: 6.1g | ERYTHRITOL: 28g | OAT FIBER: 5g

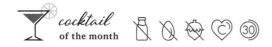
Kristie's Mojito Muy Bueno

makes
1 serving

This is a for-Kristie-by-Kristie kind of recipe! Yes, I developed this one just for me. I love the fresh flavors! I let mint grow wild in the backyard because fresh mint equals fresh mojitos. If you leave out the rum, this makes a great mocktail that kids can enjoy. If you haven't grown mint before, you might want to plant it in containers, as it really does want to take over the world. As long as the world has rum, that really isn't such a horrible thing...

Juice of 1 lime (about 2 tablespoons)

3 tablespoons chopped fresh mint

4 drops liquid sweetener, or 1 tablespoon granulated sweetener

6 ounces seltzer

2 ounces white rum

Lime wedges or slices, for garnish (optional)

Fresh mint, for garnish (optional)

In a large glass, combine the lime juice, mint, and sweetener. Use a muddler or the end of a wooden spoon to bruise the mint, being careful not to shred it. When the mint is crushed and fragrant, add the seltzer and rum.

Fill the glass with ice, garnish as desired, and serve.

CALORIES: 139 | FAT: 0g | PROTEIN: 0g | CARBS: 3.7g | FIBER: 0g

Fourth of July

Summertime Citrusy Shrimp

makes
4 servings

Summer should be no more complicated than flip-flops and t-shirts. If I ever run for president, that will be my platform. Grilling, cold salads, and simple seafood pair well with that philosophy, especially if you buy shrimp that is already peeled and deveined. Serve this dish with a cold salad and a Pinot Grigio and be thankful for 100 percent cotton.

MARINADE:

½ cup avocado oil

Finely grated zest of 2 large lemons (about 2 tablespoons)

Juice of 2 large lemons (about ⅓ cup)

4 cloves garlic, chopped

1 tablespoon plus 1 teaspoon dried parsley

2 teaspoons smoked paprika

¼ teaspoon salt

¼ teaspoon red pepper flakes (optional)

2 pounds large shrimp, peeled, deveined, and patted dry

Avocado oil or bacon fat, for grilling

SPECIAL EQUIPMENT:

Wooden skewers

Soak the skewers in water for at least 30 minutes. Set aside.

Make the marinade: Mix together all the marinade ingredients in a large bowl. Reserve and refrigerate ¼ cup of the marinade to serve as a dipping sauce.

Add the shrimp to the remaining marinade and toss to coat. Refrigerate for 20 to 25 minutes.

Preheat the grill.

Remove the shrimp from the marinade and discard the marinade. Thread the shrimp onto the prepared skewers by piercing the head and then the tail to secure the shrimp, leaving ¼ inch of space between them.

Use a brush to rub avocado oil over the hot grill grates. Grill the shrimp skewers for 2 to 3 minutes on each side, until the shrimp are just firm and turn pink. Do not overcook. Remove from the skewers and serve immediately with the reserved marinade.

tip

Alternatively, you can sauté the marinated shrimp in a large skillet instead of grilling them.

CALORIES: 362 | FAT: 28.1g | PROTEIN: 20.2g | CARBS: 7.2g | FIBER: 0.4g

Kristie's Southern Summer Tomato Pie

makes
12 servings

Even though I grew up Southern, I didn't discover tomato pie until the summer of 2012. You know a dish is good when you remember the first time you had it, right? When I went strictly low-carb in 2013, I thought I'd said goodbye to that deliciousness for the rest of my life. The summer of 2012 and my time with tomato pie stayed on my mind, though, and when I used this crust recipe for a different dish, the sweet memories came flooding back, and they triggered an idea to try making a low-carb tomato pie. I minimized the tomatoes to keep the carbs low, and I added bacon because life is just better with bacon. The flavors of this version are nothing short of amazing. The most difficult thing is getting 12 servings from it. We love it hot or cold, and I bet you will, too.

CRUST:

¾ cup blanched almond flour

⅓ cup oat fiber, or 2 tablespoons coconut flour

¼ teaspoon salt

3 ounces Parmesan cheese, grated (about 1 cup)

1 large egg

2 tablespoons bacon fat, coconut oil, ghee, or unsalted butter, softened

FILLING:

5 large tomatoes, peeled and sliced

⅓ cup chopped cooked bacon

⅓ cup finely slivered onions

4 ounces cheddar cheese, shredded (about 1 cup)

½ cup mayonnaise

½ teaspoon dried basil

¼ teaspoon dried oregano

Preheat the oven to 350°F.

Make the crust: Mix together all the crust ingredients until they have a doughlike consistency. Press into the bottom and up the sides of a 9-inch pie plate. Par-bake the crust for 15 minutes; allow to cool.

Fill the pie: Arrange the sliced tomatoes over the cooled crust. The slices should cover the crust and be about two slices deep. Sprinkle the bacon over the tomato slices, then top with onion slivers.

In a separate bowl, mix together the cheddar cheese and mayonnaise. Spread the cheese mixture over the tomatoes, bacon, and onions, pushing it to the edges of the crust to "seal" the toppings. Sprinkle the basil and oregano over the top.

Bake the pie for 30 to 40 minutes, until the topping is brown and bubbly. Let rest for at least 10 minutes before slicing and serving.

Store leftovers in the refrigerator for up to 4 days.

CALORIES: 198 | FAT: 15.8g | PROTEIN: 8.4g | CARBS: 4.8g | FIBER: 1.8g | OAT FIBER: 5g

Mediterranean Marinated Cheese

makes
24 servings

No more complicated than chopping the cheese, this simple dish brings great flavor to a buffet. Grace and I really love the Mediterranean flavors, and because David doesn't, we pile on the black olives, too! This is a perfect "make and take" dish because it can be assembled ahead of time. The ingredients are simple, but the dish always gets rave reviews. Leftovers pack well for lunches, and although I think of this as a summer dish, it also sits nicely on a holiday table.

1 (8-ounce) block white cheddar cheese or Monterey Jack cheese

1 (8-ounce) block sharp cheddar cheese

1 (8-ounce) package cream cheese, cold

⅓ cup olive oil

⅓ cup red wine vinegar

1 ounce sun-dried tomatoes, finely diced (about 2 tablespoons)

1 ounce pitted black olives, chopped (about 2 tablespoons) (optional)

2 cloves garlic, chopped

1 tablespoon chopped fresh rosemary

1½ teaspoons fresh thyme leaves

½ teaspoon salt

½ teaspoon ground black pepper

Cut the cheeses into 1½-inch squares or 1½ by 2-inch rectangles.

Layer the cheese pieces on their sides in a shallow rectangular dish, alternating white cheddar, sharp cheddar, and cream cheese and repeating in rows. Set aside.

Place the remaining ingredients in a jar with a screw-on lid. Cover and shake vigorously to mix. Pour the marinade over the cheeses. Cover the dish and refrigerate for at least 3 hours or overnight before serving.

Store leftovers in the refrigerator for up to 5 days.

CALORIES: 151 | FAT: 14.1g | PROTEIN: 5.3g | CARBS: 1.2g | FIBER: 0g

Seven-Layer Salad

makes
8 servings

Casseroles and layered salads are ubiquitous on buffet tables across the South, which is where my soul belongs. I call many of them Baptist dishes because you will not attend a covered-dish potluck at any self-respecting Baptist church that does not include a layered salad. Most of these salads have carb-heavy layers of shredded carrots, peas, or other non-keto foods. To keep myself off the "special" prayer list, I brainstormed all the potential layers that would work together in flavor and still be low-carb and high-fat. This works! You can slide this salad onto any buffet table and still get a "Halleluiah!" for good health and great taste.

SALAD:

3 cups shredded romaine lettuce

1 pound sliced deli turkey, chopped

½ cup cauliflower florets, chopped into small pieces

⅓ cup finely chopped green onions, plus more for garnish if desired

6 large eggs, hard-boiled, peeled, and chopped, plus more for garnish if desired

1 pound bacon, cooked and chopped, plus more for garnish if desired

12 ounces cheddar cheese, shredded (about 3 cups)

DRESSING:

1 cup mayonnaise

¾ cup sour cream

1 tablespoon apple cider vinegar

4 drops liquid sweetener (optional)

1 ounce Parmesan cheese, finely grated (about ⅓ cup)

Layer the salad: In a large glass bowl, layer the salad ingredients in the order listed, starting with the lettuce and ending with the cheddar cheese. Be sure to spread each layer all the way to the edges of the bowl so that the layers can be seen from the outside. Set aside.

Make the dressing: In a small bowl, mix together the mayonnaise, sour cream, vinegar, and sweetener, if using. Spread the dressing over the top of the layered salad, smoothing it into a solid layer and making sure it reaches the edges of the bowl so that it seals the edges of the salad.

Sprinkle the Parmesan over the dressing. If desired, garnish the salad with additional bacon, chopped or sliced hard-boiled eggs, and/or green onions.

CALORIES: 579 | FAT: 47g | PROTEIN: 36.5g | CARBS: 3g | FIBER: 0.9g

Jerk Chicken Thighs

makes
6 servings

"Honey, why didn't you make these before?" My husband loves food with a little spice, so I added this recipe to July in celebration of his birthday. Truthfully, I don't make these chicken thighs often because the children and I don't like a lot of heat in our food, even though this recipe is relatively mild. You will notice that I've not included the Scotch bonnet peppers that are traditionally found in jerk seasoning recipes. First, they aren't always easy to find in grocery stores, and second, I find them unreasonably spicy! If you want to add them to this dish, please do, but we've found this combination to be a perfect blend without the pain of Scotch bonnets. Also, I bake the chicken thighs, but you can grill or smoke them with equally delicious results.

This recipe makes more jerk seasoning than you will need for 2 pounds of chicken thighs. I like to store the extra in a labeled airtight container so that it's available whenever we want it.

2 pounds bone-in, skin-on chicken thighs

2 tablespoons bacon fat, melted

2 tablespoons Jerk Seasoning (recipe below)

Preheat the oven to 400°F.

Pat the chicken thighs dry and place skin side up in a single layer in a 9 by 13-inch baking dish. Drizzle the melted bacon fat over the thighs. Sprinkle the jerk seasoning liberally over the chicken, coating both sides well.

Bake for 25 to 35 minutes, depending on the thickness of the thighs, until the skin is dark brown and crispy and the juices run clear when the chicken is cut. The chicken should reach an internal temperature of 165°F for safety.

Jerk Seasoning

1 tablespoon garlic powder

1 tablespoon onion powder

1 tablespoon smoked paprika

1 tablespoon dried parsley

2 teaspoons ground dried thyme

2 teaspoons salt

2 teaspoons ground black pepper

1 teaspoon cayenne pepper

1 teaspoon allspice

¼ teaspoon ground cinnamon

¼ teaspoon ground nutmeg

Combine all the ingredients in a small bowl. Store leftovers in an airtight container for up to a month.

with seasoning
CALORIES: 376 | FAT: 29.2g | PROTEIN: 25.2g | CARBS: 1.2g | FIBER: 0.3g

Private Island Key Lime Pie

makes
12 servings

While Grace got ice cream cake for her birthday, David's favorite birthday treat is this Key lime pie. Lest you think my family will eat anything I make, let me assure you that my first attempt at Key lime pie was rejected. This was my second try. Fortunately, I nailed it! What's special about this pie, besides the fact that it was made to celebrate David's birthday, is the crust. The macadamia nuts push the flavor over the top. This crust is also excellent for other types of pie. Let your imagination be your guide.

CRUST:

½ cup (1 stick) unsalted butter, softened

½ cup granulated sweetener

½ cup crushed macadamia nuts

½ cup blanched almond flour

⅓ cup oat fiber

1 teaspoon vanilla extract

FILLING:

½ cup (1 stick) unsalted butter

½ cup powdered sweetener

½ cup Key lime juice

¼ cup grated lime zest

6 large egg yolks

1½ cups heavy cream

1 teaspoon vanilla extract

4 drops liquid sweetener

FOR GARNISH (optional):

Lime slices

Grated lime zest

Whipped cream

Preheat the oven to 350°F.

Make the crust: By hand in a bowl or in a food processor, mix together all the crust ingredients until a dough forms. Press the crust into the bottom and up the sides of a 10-inch glass pie pan. Bake for 12 to 14 minutes, until lightly browned. Set aside to cool.

Make the filling: Melt the butter in a heavy saucepan over low heat. Whisk in the powdered sweetener, Key lime juice, and lime zest. When the sweetener is dissolved, whisk in the egg yolks.

Keep the heat low and whisk constantly until the mixture has thickened. Remove from the heat and strain through a fine-mesh sieve to remove the zest. Refrigerate until cool, at least 1 hour.

In a large bowl, use a hand mixer or stand mixer to whip the heavy cream. As it begins to thicken, add the vanilla extract and liquid sweetener and continue whipping until the mixture is thick and creamy.

Gently fold the whipped cream mixture into the chilled lime juice mixture so that the filling remains fluffy.

Use a spatula to fill the crust with the filling and smooth the filling edge to edge. Place the pie in the refrigerator to chill for at least 4 hours or overnight before serving.

Garnish with lime slices, lime zest, and/or freshly whipped cream, if desired.

CALORIES: 397 | FAT: 41.8g | PROTEIN: 3.8g | CARBS: 4.4g | FIBER: 1.6g | ERYTHRITOL: 14g | OAT FIBER: 5g

08

august

AUGUST brings with it the end of summer and the start of the school year for most families. Even those who don't have school-aged children are often affected by the ringing of school bells and the waning summer days. By the end of August, most of us have enjoyed summer vacations and are tightening up our work schedules so that we can enjoy more time off for the holidays. While there are no federal holidays in the U.S. in August, there is plenty to celebrate.

In our family, we celebrate birthdays in August. My best friend's birthday is first, followed by my brother Tony; his wife, Sam; my sweet Aunt Jo; and her two grandsons! My other sister-in-law, Stephanie, also has an August birthday, and my son Jonathan's birthday is at the end of the month just as school is starting. With so many special birthdays in August, it was hard to choose a birthday treat to feature. I selected something that both Jonathan and Tony really like and that is versatile enough to please nearly anyone—**Perfect Pound Cake!** This pound cake can be used as a basic layer cake and paired with nearly any flavor of frosting you enjoy, or as a base for strawberry shortcake. You could make a low-carb chocolate buttercream and have a classic chocolate layer cake for a birthday celebration. In addition to birthday cakes, I've included a few other recipes that honor these special August birthdays. **Mint Chocolate Chip Ice Cream** is for Aunt Stephanie, who always enjoys helping me try new flavors of ice cream. The **Piña Colada** is for Aunt Sam, who was willing to help me experiment with cocktails. Aunt Jo and Jonathan both enjoy **Jonathan's Favorite Vegetable Beef Stew,** so there's a big pot for them. The **Best of Summer Seafood Casserole** is for Gwen, who rarely misses a chance to celebrate her birthday at the beach. Tony and Sam are fond of my **Cold Veggie Pizza,** so I made a low-carb version for family celebrations. Lastly, there's **Orange Danish Pull-Apart Bread** to provide a healthier version for David, Grace, and Jonathan, who used to adore the high-carb canned ones. It's pretty obvious that I love my family and friends with food, so making something just for them is a fun tradition.

As we bid farewell to summer and welcome the structure of another school year, the recipes I make for my family do change. School days call for quick meals of soups and sandwiches that pack easily in lunch boxes. I look for foods that travel well and can be grabbed easily for quick breakfasts. The **Simple Flatbread** is perfect for lunches that seem a bit more traditional and that don't require cutlery.

Like many families, our back-to-school traditions involve shopping trips. Some years the children need new backpacks, and some years we simply wash and recycle the old ones. After a summer of sandals on growing feet, the children nearly always need new tennis shoes, which turns into a family excursion. Finally, we clean out closets and drawers, discarding the clothes that somehow shrank over the summer and taking inventory of what the kids can actually wear to school and what needs to be replaced.

August, for us, is about savoring those last weeks of freedom from homework, school car lines, and a new daily routine. We squeeze in birthday parties and family reunions knowing that we won't have a chance for all those hugs again until the holiday season begins.

Peanut Butter No-Nana Muffins

makes
12 muffins
(1 per serving)

I'm old enough to equate August with Elvis, as it was the month of his death, and everyone in my generation knows that he loved peanut butter and banana sandwiches. As in the other banana-flavored recipes in this book, I've used banana extract here for just a hint of banana flavor. If you don't like banana, you can omit the banana extract and enjoy the full peanut flavor. These muffins are dense and moist. Try them for breakfast with a little softened butter. They're also a great option to toss a treat into kids' (or your own) lunches.

⅓ cup blanched almond flour

⅓ cup whey protein isolate

⅓ cup oat fiber, or 2 tablespoons coconut flour

1 teaspoon baking powder

¼ teaspoon ground cinnamon

¼ teaspoon salt

½ cup (1 stick) unsalted butter, cold

¾ cup granulated sweetener

2 ounces cream cheese (¼ cup), cold

3 large eggs

2 teaspoons vanilla extract

1½ teaspoons banana extract

½ teaspoon maple extract

⅓ cup peanut butter

Preheat the oven to 350°F. Line a standard-size 12-well muffin pan with parchment paper liners.

In a large bowl, whisk together the almond flour, protein isolate, oat fiber, baking powder, cinnamon, and salt; set aside.

In a separate bowl, using a hand mixer or stand mixer, cream the butter and sweetener. When the butter has lightened in color, add the cream cheese and continue blending until everything is smooth and well incorporated.

Add the eggs one at a time, mixing well after each addition. Add the extracts and mix well.

Add the dry ingredients to the wet ingredients and mix lightly by hand. Stir in the peanut butter.

Divide the batter evenly among the wells of the prepared muffin pan, filling each well about two-thirds full. Bake for 24 to 28 minutes, until browned and just firm to the touch. Let cool in the pan for 5 to 10 minutes before serving.

Store leftovers in the refrigerator for up to a week.

CALORIES: 170 | FAT: 15.5g | PROTEIN: 7g | CARBS: 2.6g | FIBER: 1g | ERYTHRITOL: 9g | OAT FIBER: 5g

Perfect Pound Cake

makes
12 servings

This is another recipe that celebrates my brother Tony and my son, Jonathan. Both have August birthdays, and both love my high-carb pound cakes. They nearly always request pound cake when I offer to make something special for them. Even though neither of them eats low-carb, I love that I can make a low-carb version of their favorite treat. The first time I made this pound cake, my brother said, "I wouldn't have known this wasn't real pound cake!" With as many cakes as I've made for him, I knew I'd nailed it.

⅓ cup coconut flour

¼ cup oat fiber

2 tablespoons whey protein isolate

1 teaspoon baking powder

½ teaspoon salt

½ cup (1 stick) unsalted butter, softened

½ cup granulated sweetener

4 large eggs

2 large egg whites

½ cup heavy cream

2 teaspoons vanilla extract

4 or 5 drops liquid sweetener, to taste

Preheat the oven to 350°F. Grease an 8½ by 4-inch loaf pan and line with parchment paper.

In a large bowl, whisk together the coconut flour, oat fiber, protein isolate, baking powder, and salt; set aside.

In a separate bowl, use a hand mixer or stand mixer to cream the butter and granulated sweetener.

In another bowl, using the mixer, beat the whole eggs and egg whites until frothy.

Add the beaten eggs to the butter mixture and beat until smooth. Stir in the heavy cream and vanilla extract by hand.

Add the dry ingredients to the wet ingredients and mix by hand, being careful not to overmix. Stir in the liquid sweetener.

Pour the batter into the prepared loaf pan and bake for 35 to 45 minutes, until the center is springy to the touch and a toothpick inserted in the middle comes out clean.

tip

You can also bake this cake in a greased and parchment paper–lined 9-inch round cake pan for 18 to 22 minutes.

CALORIES: 143 | FAT: 12.8g | PROTEIN: 5.1g | CARBS: 4.1g | FIBER: 1.8g | ERYTHRITOL: 6g | OAT FIBER: 3.8g

Mint Chocolate Chip Ice Cream

makes
6 servings

Jonathan's birthday is in August, and this recipe was inspired by his favorite flavor, mint chocolate chip. He didn't seem to think that we could make it at home, but we did. I love it when that happens! I use food-grade peppermint oil in this recipe, but you can also use peppermint extract.

1½ cups heavy cream

1 cup unsweetened almond milk

6 large egg yolks

½ cup powdered sweetener (see Tip)

6 drops liquid sweetener

2 teaspoons vanilla extract

2 drops food-grade peppermint oil

½ teaspoon salt

2 ounces dark chocolate (85% cacao or higher), finely chopped

In a heavy saucepan over low heat, heat the heavy cream and almond milk, stirring with a whisk. Add the egg yolks and continue whisking until just warmed.

Add the sweeteners and whisk until completely dissolved. Continue heating, whisking constantly, until the custard thickens, about 10 minutes. When the custard coats the back of a wooden spoon or reaches 140°F on a candy thermometer, remove the pan from the heat. Do not allow the mixture to warm to over 140°F or the eggs will begin to cook.

Stir in the vanilla extract, peppermint oil, and salt. Transfer the mixture to a bowl and place in the refrigerator to cool.

When cool, churn the ice cream mixture in an ice cream maker following the manufacturer's directions. Add the chocolate to the ice cream while it is churning and after it has begun to freeze, but while the ice cream is still soft. Continue churning until it reaches your desired consistency.

Store leftovers in the freezer. When frozen, this ice cream will harden to a solid state. Allow to thaw at room temperature for about 10 minutes before enjoying.

tip

The type of sweetener used makes a huge difference in the texture of the ice cream. For the best texture, use allulose or xylitol; remember that each sweetener has different characteristics (see pages 19 and 20 for details). Use the sweetener that you prefer and that does not impact your blood glucose.

CALORIES: 206 | FAT: 9.4g | PROTEIN: 14.4g | CARBS: 3.8g | FIBER: 1g | ERYTHRITOL: 12g

Piña Colada

makes
1 serving

I always think of my sister-in-law, Sam, married to my brother Tony, when I make this cocktail. Before Sam and Tony married, Sam helped me make a low-carb cocktail video. We had a blast! In hindsight, we shouldn't have attempted to make six cocktails in one video. Even with just a few sips of each, we were getting a little silly by the time we finished filming. This Piña Colada recipe was one of the six that we made, and Sam was surprised that it could be made without all the fruit and sugar.

4 ounces coconut cream

2 ounces white rum

1 teaspoon lime juice

½ teaspoon coconut extract

¼ teaspoon orange extract

¼ teaspoon strawberry extract

⅛ teaspoon vanilla extract

6 drops liquid sweetener, or 1 tablespoon granulated sweetener

1 cup crushed ice

Lime wedge, for garnish (optional)

Unsweetened shredded coconut, for garnish (optional)

In a blender, blend all the ingredients except the garnishes until smooth. Pour into a chilled highball glass. Garnish with a lime wedge and a sprinkle of shredded coconut, if desired.

CALORIES: 368 | FAT: 24g | PROTEIN: 2g | CARBS: 6g | FIBER: 0g

Farewell to Summer

Tony's Favorite Cold Veggie Pizza

makes
12 servings

My younger brother, Tony, was always a picky eater, but one holiday I made the traditional crescent roll pizza with raw veggies, and he liked it! From then on, it was a recipe I always made for him. When we went low-carb, I continued to make that pizza for him, but my low-carb family couldn't enjoy it. Finally, it dawned on me to ditch the tube of crescent rolls and use a low-carb crust, my homemade ranch seasoning mix, and very-low-carb veggies. Problem solved! Now I can make just one version and keep peace in the family. The only problem is that I still need to make two pizzas since my spoiled baby brother never did learn how to share!

CALORIES: 203 | FAT: 18.9g | PROTEIN: 5.9g | CARBS: 3.2g | FIBER: 6g | OAT FIBER: 5g

CRUST:

1½ cups shredded mozzarella cheese

1 ounce cream cheese (2 tablespoons), softened

⅓ cup blanched almond flour

⅓ cup oat fiber

1 large egg

1 teaspoon garlic salt

1 teaspoon Italian seasoning

SAUCE:

1 (8-ounce) package cream cheese, softened

½ cup mayonnaise

2 tablespoons Dry Ranch Mix (page 339)

TOPPINGS:

½ cup broccoli florets, finely chopped

½ cup cauliflower florets, finely chopped

⅓ cup finely chopped peeled cucumbers

¼ cup radishes, finely chopped

¼ cup finely chopped red bell peppers

¼ cup finely chopped yellow bell peppers

¼ cup finely chopped carrots

1 tablespoon finely chopped red onions

Preheat the oven to 350°F. Line a 9 by 13-inch baking dish with parchment paper.

Make the crust: Melt the mozzarella and cream cheese in a saucepan over medium heat or in the microwave. Mix well. Add the almond flour and oat fiber and incorporate into the melted cheeses. It's easiest to do this with well-oiled hands. If the dough becomes stringy, warm it again. Add the egg, garlic salt, and Italian seasoning and mix well.

Use your hands to flatten the dough and spread it evenly over the prepared baking dish. Bake for 12 to 16 minutes, until lightly browned. Remove from the oven and let cool on a cooling rack.

Make the sauce: In a small bowl, mix the cream cheese, mayonnaise, and ranch seasoning mix until creamy. Spread the sauce over the cooled crust, making sure that the crust is completely covered.

Sprinkle the vegetable toppings over the sauce, distributing them evenly.

Refrigerate the pizza for at least 30 minutes before serving. Store leftovers in the refrigerator for up to 4 days.

tip

To reduce the carbs further and make this recipe nut-free, you can substitute ½ cup pork dust (ground pork rinds) for the almond flour and oat fiber in the crust.

Best of Summer Seafood Casserole

makes
8 servings

This farewell-to-summer recipe is rich and hearty and extremely versatile. You can use whatever seafood you like, including pieces of cod, catfish, or snapper, instead of the shrimp and scallops featured here. I nearly always include crab meat because I love the texture. This dish is easy to assemble ahead of time and to bake after guests arrive.

¼ **cup (½ stick) unsalted butter**

3 **cloves garlic, minced**

6 **ounces mushrooms, sliced**

2 **stalks celery, chopped**

2 **tablespoons minced onions**

1 **cup heavy cream**

⅓ **cup dry white wine or chicken bone broth**

1 **tablespoon lemon juice**

1 **teaspoon paprika**

¼ **teaspoon salt**

1 **pound small shrimp, peeled, deveined, and patted dry**

8 **ounces crab meat, cartilage removed**

4 **ounces bay scallops, drained and patted dry**

CRUMB TOPPING:

½ **cup pork dust (ground pork rinds)**

1 **ounce Parmesan cheese, grated (about ⅓ cup)**

1 **tablespoon dried parsley**

¼ **teaspoon ground black pepper**

Preheat the oven to 375°F.

Melt the butter in a 2½-quart oven-safe pot (preferably not cast iron) over medium heat. Add the garlic and cook until fragrant, about 30 seconds. Add the mushrooms, celery, and onions and sauté for 2 to 3 minutes, until the vegetables are just tender.

Reduce the heat to low and pour in the heavy cream and wine. Simmer until the sauce thickens, 5 to 7 minutes.

Remove the pot from the heat. Add the lemon juice, paprika, salt, and seafood and stir until thoroughly combined.

In a small bowl, combine all the crumb topping ingredients. Sprinkle the topping mixture over the seafood mixture in the pot.

Bake the casserole for 20 to 24 minutes, until browned and bubbly. You may want to broil the dish for 1 minute to brown the top just before serving. Do not overbake or the shrimp will become tough.

CALORIES: 307 | FAT: 18.3g | PROTEIN: 30.4g | CARBS: 3.9g | FIBER: 0g

Classic Caesar Salad

makes
4 servings

I know, I don't like anchovies, either, but I love Caesar salad dressing, and if you don't add the anchovy fillet paste, it won't taste like the real thing. You're going to have to trust me. This delicious fatty dressing can be made in a small mason jar and stored in the refrigerator for up to a week. I love having it on hand to use as a dipping sauce for meats, both roasted or from the deli, or for a quick salad like this one during the work week. Guests are often impressed that I make my own Caesar dressing. I just don't tell them about the anchovy paste.

DRESSING:

¾ **cup mayonnaise**

3 **cloves garlic, minced**

2 **tablespoons lemon juice**

2 **teaspoons anchovy fillet paste**

2 **teaspoons Dijon mustard**

1 **teaspoon Worcestershire sauce**

¼ **teaspoon salt**

Dash of ground black pepper

Dash of hot sauce

1 **ounce Parmesan cheese, grated (¼ cup)**

2 **heads romaine lettuce, chopped**

2 **ounces Parmesan cheese, grated (about ½ cup)**

Make the dressing: In a mixing bowl, whisk together all the ingredients except the Parmesan cheese. Refrigerate the dressing for at least 1 hour before serving. Just before dressing the salad, mix in the Parmesan.

To assemble the salad, place the lettuce in a large bowl and toss with the dressing to coat. Sprinkle the Parmesan cheese over the tossed salad and serve immediately.

Store leftover dressing in the refrigerator for up to 5 days.

CALORIES: 202 | FAT: 18.9g | PROTEIN: 4.1g | CARBS: 2.2g | FIBER: 0.9g

Back to School

Orange Danish Pull-Apart Bread

makes
12 servings

Although it took more than four years, I was excited to finally perfect this recipe. My husband's family always made this bread from the refrigerated biscuit aisle. David and the children adored those high-carb rolls. Once I saw him look longingly at a fresh batch, so I was determined to give him a keto option. This version is even better than the original because it is low-carb. I do use ¼ teaspoon of real sugar (gasp!). The sugar is eaten by the yeast, so it should not impact blood glucose. If you are uncomfortable using the yeast and sugar, then omit them. The yeast improves the texture and gives the bread a great flavor, but you can still enjoy it without the yeast. Rolling the dough into balls gives you a loaf that resembles pull-apart bread. This sweet bread would make a great back-to-school breakfast as a special treat to get the kids up and moving.

CALORIES: 183 | FAT: 12.4g | PROTEIN: 9.4g | CARBS: 2.5g | FIBER: 0.5g | ERYTHRITOL: 16.7g | OAT FIBER: 7.6g

1 (1¼-ounce) packet active dry yeast

¼ teaspoon sugar

2 tablespoons hot water

½ cup blanched almond flour

½ cup oat fiber

⅔ cup granulated sweetener, divided

1 tablespoon baking powder

½ teaspoon salt

3 ounces cream cheese (¼ cup plus 2 tablespoons), softened

2 ounces full-fat mozzarella cheese, shredded (about ½ cup)

2 large eggs

1 teaspoon orange extract

1 teaspoon vanilla extract

3 tablespoons unsalted butter, softened

1 teaspoon finely grated orange zest

½ teaspoon ground cinnamon

ICING:

2 ounces cream cheese (¼ cup), softened

½ cup powdered sweetener

6 tablespoons (¾ stick) unsalted butter, softened

½ cup heavy cream

½ teaspoon orange extract, or 1 tablespoon fresh orange juice

½ teaspoon vanilla extract

Dash of salt

1 tablespoon finely grated orange zest

Make the bread: Preheat the oven to 350°F.

In a small bowl, dissolve the yeast and sugar in the hot water. Set aside.

In a separate bowl, use a hand mixer or stand mixer to mix the almond flour, oat fiber, ⅓ cup of the granulated sweetener, baking powder, salt, cream cheese, mozzarella, eggs, and extracts. Stir in the yeast mixture by hand; let the dough sit while you prepare the pan.

Place the butter in a 9-inch round cake pan and put the pan in the oven to melt the butter. When melted, remove the pan from the oven.

In a small bowl, combine the remaining ⅓ cup of granulated sweetener with the orange zest and cinnamon. Set aside.

Form the dough into 20 balls, 1½ to 2 inches in diameter. Roll each ball in the cinnamon mixture. Place the coated balls in the prepared pan so that the sides are touching.

Bake for 20 to 25 minutes, until the bread has risen and is just firm to the touch. Let cool for 15 to 20 minutes.

While the bread is cooling, make the icing: In a bowl, using the mixer, whip the cream cheese and sweetener until fully incorporated. Add the butter, heavy cream, extracts, and salt and continue whipping until smooth and creamy. Stir in the orange zest by hand. Refrigerate until ready to use.

After the bread has rested, cover with the icing. Serve warm.

Simple Flatbread

makes
4 to 8 servings

Flatbread sandwiches make packing school lunches easier. My daughter uses these flatbreads as a dipper for hummus, as a base for pizza, for a quick grilled sandwich, or as an on-the-go option with deli meat, cheese, and mayo. I enjoy them with chicken or tuna salad. You can change the seasonings easily to make any flavor you like; we like to make a rosemary and cracked black pepper version for sandwiches. This flatbread reminds me more of pita bread than any other low-carb substitute I've attempted.

½ cup coconut flour

1 tablespoon psyllium husk powder

¾ teaspoon Italian seasoning

¼ teaspoon granulated garlic

¼ teaspoon sea salt

¼ cup olive oil

1½ ounces mozzarella cheese, shredded (about ⅓ cup)

1 cup boiling water

Preheat the oven to 350°F. Line a 9 by 13-inch rimmed baking sheet with parchment paper.

In a large bowl, whisk together the coconut flour, psyllium husk powder, Italian seasoning, garlic, and salt. Add the oil and mozzarella and mix together. Pour in the hot water last, stirring as you add it so that the psyllium absorbs the water but does not clump.

Transfer the dough to the prepared baking sheet and flatten until it is thin and even. I lay a second piece of parchment paper on top of the dough and use my hands to flatten and smooth it. Be sure that the dough is a uniform thickness and less than ⅛ inch thick. When flattened, it should cover the baking sheet.

Bake for 25 to 28 minutes, until browned. The baking time will depend on how thin you've made the bread. Transfer to a cooling rack, peel away the parchment paper, and let cool completely.

Use a pizza cutter to cut the bread into squares for sandwiches. Store leftovers in the refrigerator for up to a week.

CALORIES: 50 | FAT: 2.4g | PROTEIN: 2.8g | CARBS: 4.5g | FIBER: 2.5g

Jonathan's Favorite Vegetable Beef Stew

makes
6 servings

Leftover beef roast can easily become a low-carb vegetable beef soup. I'll admit that this hearty soup isn't as good as my grandmother's, which was loaded with starchy veggies, but it hits the spot. Truthfully, I'm not sure that any other high-carb version would be as good as my grandmother's, but I'm betting she would approve of this keto version. The flavor of this soup improves when you warm it as leftovers, and my kids love it in their packed lunches when the days turn cooler.

2 tablespoons unsalted butter

¼ cup finely diced onions

2 cloves garlic, minced

1 stalk celery, chopped

1 small zucchini, chopped

¾ cup bite-sized cabbage strips

½ cup diced radishes

½ cup chopped green beans

⅓ cup chopped cauliflower florets

2 cups beef bone broth

2 (8-ounce) cans tomato sauce

2 bay leaves

½ teaspoon salt

¼ teaspoon ground black pepper

3 cups cubed cooked beef roast

Melt the butter in a 2½-quart saucepan over medium heat. Add the onions, garlic, and celery and sauté until the onions are translucent and the celery is just tender.

Stir in the remaining ingredients except the beef. Reduce the heat and simmer, uncovered, until the vegetables are tender and the broth has thickened, 20 to 25 minutes.

Mix in the beef and simmer for another 5 to 7 minutes, until the beef is warm. Remove the bay leaves before serving.

Store leftovers in the refrigerator for up to 5 days.

CALORIES: 262 | FAT: 12.6g | PROTEIN: 26.6g | CARBS: 6.7g | FIBER: 2.2g

Grilled Ham and Cheese with Red Pepper Strips

makes
1 sandwich

Treat the kids to a grilled ham and cheese with or without the red pepper strips! I love that this sandwich has melty cheese that oozes out when the grilled goodness is sliced diagonally. I love the buttery toasted outside and the smell of the skillet when it's done. I also love that I can serve this sandwich with a warm bowl of soup and it feels about as "normal" as what the kids next door are eating.

1½ tablespoons salted butter, softened, divided

1 tablespoon mayonnaise

2 slices Modified Soul Bread (page 342)

2 slices mild cheddar cheese

1 ounce shaved deli turkey breast

3 strips red bell pepper

In a 9-inch skillet over medium heat, melt 1 tablespoon of the butter.

Spread a generous dollop of mayonnaise on one side of each slice of bread. Top the mayonnaise on one slice of bread with a slice of cheese, the turkey, the red pepper strips, the second slice of cheese, and the other slice of bread, mayonnaise side down.

Place the sandwich in the skillet with the melted butter. Use a knife to spread the remaining butter on the top slice of bread. Cook the sandwich for 2 to 3 minutes, until the bottom slice of bread is browned.

Flip the sandwich over and cook the other side for 2 to 3 minutes, until toasted and golden.

CALORIES: 699 | FAT: 64g | PROTEIN: 29.9g | CARBS: 3.5g | FIBER: 1g | OAT FIBER: 22.8g

K-E-T-O Chocolate Sandwich Cookies

makes
12 cookies
(1 per serving)

It took thirteen months and eight attempts to perfect this recipe, a low-carb version of those little chocolate sandwich cookies that we all grew up dunking in milk. While I mostly use them in other recipes, these little rascals are pretty good center stage, too. You can pack them in back-to-school lunches. While the other kids are eating the impersonal factory-made versions, your well-loved kiddos get to show off their homemade healthier cookies packed with love. Don't get me wrong, I loved my kids when I used to toss the packaged kind into their lunch boxes, but homemade is often coveted. If I can make these treats and keep the kids healthy and happy, it's worth the extra effort to provide a sense of "normalcy."

Please try these as cookie sandwiches. Individually, the cookies and crème filling do not taste the same. Together, like many things in life, is where the magic happens. The cookies, without the filling, are also used for Cookies and Cream Ice Cream (page 182).

Adding the glucomannan and coconut oil to the crème filling is optional. These ingredients change the texture of the filling, but not the flavor. My family enjoys the cookies without these ingredients, but I prefer the texture when I include them. Either way, these cookies are delicious.

COOKIES:

1 cup blanched almond flour

½ cup granulated sweetener

¼ cup oat fiber

¼ cup Hershey's Special Dark unsweetened cocoa powder

¼ teaspoon salt

3 tablespoons refined coconut oil

2 large egg whites

1 teaspoon vanilla extract

4 drops liquid sweetener

Make the cookies: Combine the almond flour, granulated sweetener, oat fiber, cocoa powder, and salt in a food processor; add the coconut oil and egg whites and process into a thick dough. Add the vanilla extract and liquid sweetener and combine.

Roll the dough into a 2-inch-diameter log and refrigerate for at least 1 hour.

Preheat the oven to 350°F. Line a cookie sheet with parchment paper.

Cut the chilled dough into ⅛-inch slices, making a total of 24 slices, and place on the prepared cookie sheet. Bake for 6 to 8 minutes, until just firm. Do not overbake, as these cookies burn easily. Remove from the oven and let cool on a cooling rack. The cookies will crisp up as they cool.

CALORIES: 162 | FAT: 16.3g | PROTEIN: 2.1g | CARBS: 2.2g | FIBER: 5.9g | ERYTHRITOL: 10g | OAT FIBER: 5g

CRÈME FILLING:

¼ cup (½ stick) unsalted butter, softened

½ cup heavy cream

½ cup powdered sweetener

1½ teaspoons vanilla extract

¼ teaspoon salt

4 teaspoons glucomannan (optional)

1 teaspoon refined coconut oil (optional)

While the cookies are cooling, make the crème filling: In a large bowl, use a hand mixer or stand mixer to combine the butter, heavy cream, and sweetener. Add the vanilla extract and salt and mix well. Sprinkle the glucomannan, if using, into the filling, mixing as you add it to avoid clumps. When the glucomannan is fully incorporated, mix in the coconut oil, if using.

When the cookies have cooled, assemble the sandwiches by topping a cookie with 1½ teaspoons of filling; top with another cookie. Repeat with the remaining cookies and filling to make a total of 12 sandwich cookies. Store in an airtight container in the refrigerator.

09

september

SEPTEMBER heralds the fifth season: pumpkin spice everything! While others are standing in long lines at coffee shops, Grace and I kick off the season with our own low-carb version of **Pumpkin Spice Coffee.** And when the kids are away and friends drop in, a **Pumpkin Spice Margarita** is a fun and easy way to celebrate the arrival of autumn. With cooler weather and football season, September also calls for tailgating and warm breakfasts that are just a bit heartier than the lighter fare of summer.

In September, my family is back to the grind of school and adapting to new routines. We try to sneak in a trip to the mountains when we can, although extracurricular activities can make getting there difficult. Because we're often on the go, I've included recipes that travel well, like decadent **Glazed Maple Cinnamon Donuts, Mason Jar Chili and Cornbread,** and **Mexican Meatballs** for tailgating. If you're tailgating, it's great to have foods that everyone can enjoy and not think of as "diet food."

September is also the birthday month of my brother-in-law, Greg. Although he is the baby of the family, and the youngest is usually the pickiest eater, I appreciate that Greg will try anything I make! He might look at it closely or give it a sniff first, but he graciously samples any creation I take to a family gathering. Even better is the fact that he usually *likes* my creations. The birthday treat for this month is a low-carb version of the ubiquitous Baptist **Chocolate Éclair Cake.** Although the version Greg is familiar with uses all packaged products, my version uses real chocolate, homemade pudding, and handcrafted graham crackers. The first time I made it for the family, Greg didn't know it was low-carb until he realized I had made it. Then he simply said, "That's good. That's rich. I don't know how you make stuff like that," as he took a second serving.

What I love most about September are the cooler weather, the gorgeous fall colors, and the delicious flavors of the season—apple, pumpkin, maple, and cinnamon. Even though fall signals the beginning of the end of the calendar year, September, to me, is about a renewed focus. Perhaps it's because of the new academic year, but I believe September is a month to get things done, like cleaning out closets, trimming shrubs, and starting Christmas lists. September is about moving forward while enjoying the journey.

Perfect Pumpkin Spice Muffins

makes
12 muffins
(1 per serving)

There is so much to love about these moist and hearty muffins, but I especially love that they are nut-free for those with allergies. The texture resembles that of a pumpkin spice bread, which means they are perfect for a smear of cream cheese and butter. These muffins are naturally moist, but note that some brands of canned pumpkin puree are thicker than others. I tend to use Libby's brand, which has less moisture than other products.

½ cup (1 stick) unsalted butter, cold

4 ounces cream cheese (½ cup), cold

¾ cup brown sugar substitute, plus more for garnish if desired

5 large eggs

½ cup pumpkin puree (not pumpkin pie filling)

⅓ cup coconut flour

¼ cup oat fiber

1 teaspoon baking powder

¼ teaspoon salt

1½ teaspoons vanilla extract

½ teaspoon maple extract (optional)

1 teaspoon pumpkin pie spice

½ teaspoon ground cinnamon, plus more for garnish if desired

¼ teaspoon ground cloves (optional)

¼ cup heavy cream

5 drops liquid sweetener (optional)

Preheat the oven to 350°F. Line a standard-size 12-well muffin pan with parchment paper liners.

In a large bowl, using a hand mixer or stand mixer, blend the butter and cream cheese until creamy and well blended. Add the brown sugar substitute and blend until smooth.

Add the eggs one at a time, beating well after each addition. Beat in the pumpkin puree. Set aside.

In a separate bowl, whisk together the coconut flour, oat fiber, baking powder, and salt. Stir the dry ingredients into the wet ingredients by hand.

Add the extracts, pie spice, cinnamon, and cloves, if using, and mix well. Mix in the heavy cream and liquid sweetener, if desired.

Divide the batter evenly among the wells of the prepared muffin pan, filling each well about three-quarters full. Sprinkle the tops with brown sugar substitute and cinnamon, if desired.

Bake for 24 to 28 minutes, until browned and just firm to the touch. Let cool in the pan before serving. The taste and texture are best after 30 minutes out of the oven.

Store leftovers in the refrigerator for up to a week.

Chocolate Éclair Cake

makes
24 servings

This recipe uses two parts of the Classic Keto No-Nana Pudding (page 130) to make a traditional Baptist potluck dish. My mother-in-law always makes this cake for a church crowd. Her version uses graham crackers layered in the bottom of a 9 by 13-inch baking dish, covered by a layer of vanilla pudding. She places graham crackers on top and then spreads a layer of chocolate icing over the graham crackers. The dish is refrigerated overnight. The graham crackers soften between the chocolate icing and the pudding, and they form a cakelike dessert. My keto version begins with a base of homemade low-carb graham crackers and is topped with real vanilla pudding and covered in hot fudge sauce. Over several hours, or overnight, the cracker layer becomes moist. I'd be proud to put this on the dessert table at any potluck dinner!

GRAHAM CRACKERS:

½ cup heavy cream

1 tablespoon white vinegar

½ cup blanched almond flour

¼ cup pork dust (ground pork rinds)

¼ cup whey protein isolate

1 tablespoon oat fiber

¾ teaspoon baking powder

¼ teaspoon baking soda

⅛ teaspoon salt

¼ cup sour cream

2 tablespoons unsalted butter, melted but not hot

¼ cup granulated sweetener

3 drops liquid sweetener

1 large egg

1½ teaspoons vanilla extract

PUDDING:

¾ cup (1½ sticks) unsalted butter

⅔ cup powdered sweetener

8 large egg yolks

1½ cups heavy cream

2 teaspoons vanilla extract

6 drops liquid sweetener

1 batch Hot Fudge Sauce (page 347)

Make the graham crackers: Preheat the oven to 325°F. Line an 11 by 17-inch rimmed baking sheet with parchment paper.

In a small bowl, combine the heavy cream and vinegar; set aside.

In a separate bowl, whisk together the almond flour, pork dust, protein isolate, oat fiber, baking powder, baking soda, and salt; set aside.

In a third bowl, use a spatula to mix the sour cream, melted butter, sweeteners, egg, and vanilla extract until well combined. Add the cream and vinegar mixture to the sour cream mixture, then stir in the dry mixture by hand until smooth.

Spread the batter on the prepared baking sheet. Bake for 18 to 22 minutes, until browned. The cake will be soft and pliable. Let cool, then flip over onto a cooling rack.

When cool, use a pizza cutter to cut the cake into 2-inch squares. Place the cooling rack in the oven with the light on and the door ajar for at least 2 hours; the longer the better. The graham crackers will dry out and become crisp.

While the crackers are drying out, make the pudding: Melt the butter in a heavy saucepan over low heat. Whisk in the powdered sweetener. When smooth, reduce the heat to the lowest setting and add the egg yolks, whisking constantly. Continue whisking for 4 to 6 minutes, until the pudding thickens slightly. Remove from the heat, transfer the pudding to a bowl or other container, and refrigerate.

In a separate bowl, using a hand mixer or stand mixer, whip the heavy cream to soft peaks. As the cream begins to thicken, add the vanilla extract and liquid sweetener. Gently fold the chilled pudding into the whipped cream by hand so that it stays fluffy.

To assemble, layer half of the graham crackers in a 9 by 13-inch baking dish. Smooth the pudding mixture on top of the graham crackers. Top the pudding with the rest of the graham crackers. Pour the hot fudge sauce over the graham crackers, being sure to cover the crackers and pudding completely.

Refrigerate for at least 6 hours or overnight. This cake is best eaten within 12 to 48 hours of being made but will keep in the refrigerator for up to 4 days.

tip

For a beautiful finish, garnish each serving with a dollop of whipped cream or a sprinkle of powdered sweetener.

Pumpkin Spice Ice Cream

makes
6 servings

When pumpkin spice season descends, commercial ice cream makers start bragging about their pumpkin spice flavors. Instead of letting those products torture us, I get to work in the kitchen making my own version. Truly, if food manufacturers are adding sugar and thickeners, then their versions can never be as good as the ones we can make with cream, eggs, and spices. This version is thick and rich. If paired with a low-carb crust, such as the one I use for Private Island Key Lime Pie (page 196), this would make a fantastic ice cream pie.

1½ cups heavy cream

1 cup unsweetened almond milk

6 large egg yolks

⅓ cup powdered sweetener (see Tip)

⅓ cup pumpkin puree (not pumpkin pie filling)

1 teaspoon vanilla extract

½ teaspoon maple extract

1 teaspoon pumpkin pie spice

½ teaspoon ground cinnamon

⅛ teaspoon ground cloves (optional)

⅛ teaspoon salt

In a heavy saucepan over low heat, heat the heavy cream and almond milk, stirring with a whisk. Add the egg yolks and continue whisking until just warmed.

Add the powdered sweetener and whisk until completely dissolved. Continue heating, whisking constantly, until the custard thickens, about 10 minutes. When the custard coats the back of a wooden spoon or reaches 140°F on a candy thermometer, remove the pan from the heat. Do not allow the mixture to warm to over 140°F or the eggs will begin to cook.

Add the remaining ingredients and mix well. Transfer the mixture to a bowl and place in the refrigerator to cool.

When cool, churn the ice cream mixture in an ice cream maker following the manufacturer's directions until it reaches your desired consistency.

Store leftovers in the freezer. When frozen, this ice cream will harden to a solid state. Allow to thaw at room temperature for about 10 minutes before enjoying.

tip ———————————————————————

The type of sweetener used makes a huge difference in the texture of the ice cream. For the best texture, use allulose or xylitol; remember that each sweetener has different characteristics (see pages 19 and 20 for details). Use the sweetener that you prefer and that does not impact your blood glucose.

CALORIES: 169 | FAT: 13.9g | PROTEIN: 5.2g | CARBS: 3.9g | FIBER: 0.7g | ERYTHRITOL: 8g

Pumpkin Spice Margarita

makes
1 serving

You just have to taste this drink once to love it. The earthiness of the tequila is a perfect match for the flavors of fall. This cocktail is especially fun to serve to guests who aren't low-carb because it's so darned delicious.

¼ **cup heavy cream**

1 **ounce tequila**

1 **tablespoon powdered sweetener**

½ **teaspoon pumpkin pie spice**

½ **teaspoon vanilla extract**

¼ **teaspoon maple extract**

¼ **teaspoon ground cinnamon, plus extra for garnish if desired**

½ **cup ice**

Whipped cream, for garnish (optional)

Combine all the ingredients except the garnishes in a cocktail shaker. Shake well and strain the drink into a stemmed margarita or martini glass.

Garnish with freshly whipped cream and a sprinkle of cinnamon, if desired.

tip

For a beautiful presentation, before filling the glasses, rub the rim of each glass with water or heavy cream, then dip it in a mix of 1 teaspoon granulated sweetener and ⅛ teaspoon ground cinnamon.

CALORIES: 172 | FAT: 10.8g | PROTEIN: 0.8g | CARBS: 1.1g | FIBER: 0g | ERYTHRITOL: 9g

The Fifth Season: Pumpkin Spice

tip

Additional recipes for celebrating pumpkin spice season include Perfect Pumpkin Spice Muffins (page 226), Pumpkin Spice Ice Cream (page 230), and the Pumpkin Spice Margarita (opposite). Thanksgiving's Pumpkin Pie Cheesecake (page 292) extends the season even further.

Pumpkin Spice Fudge

makes
12 servings

In addition to back to school and apple picking, September ushers in the season of pumpkin spice everything. While it isn't my favorite flavor, I, too, fall victim to the need to celebrate the season that is Pumpkin Spice. This fudge is high-fat and flavorful. It makes a nice sweet treat to enjoy at the end of a meal or with a cup of coffee on a cool evening.

4 ounces refined coconut oil

½ cup (1 stick) salted butter or ghee

¾ cup pumpkin puree (not pumpkin pie filling)

⅓ cup powdered sweetener

1 teaspoon vanilla extract

½ teaspoon maple extract

1 teaspoon pumpkin pie spice

½ teaspoon ground cinnamon

¼ teaspoon ground cloves (optional)

SPECIAL EQUIPMENT (optional):

24 (½-ounce) paper or silicone candy molds

Place the coconut oil and butter in a 1½-quart saucepan over low heat until just melted.

Remove from the heat, add the pumpkin and sweetener, and stir until the sweetener is dissolved. Mix in the extracts and spices. Use an immersion blender to thoroughly mix the ingredients. The fudge should be barely warm (see Tip). Pour into 24 individual candy molds or an 8-inch square baking dish.

Refrigerate for at least 2 hours, until set. If you used a baking dish, cut the fudge into 24 squares. I like to store this fudge in the freezer.

tip

The fudge should be barely warm after being mixed with the immersion blender. If it is too warm when it is placed in the fridge to cool, it will separate as it cools. Should this happen, you can correct the fudge by barely melting it, blending again, and refrigerating.

CALORIES: 127 | FAT: 21.7g | PROTEIN: 0.7g | CARBS: 0.9g | FIBER: 0.3g | ERYTHRITOL: 4g

Creamy Pumpkin Spice Coffee

makes
1 serving

Once you make your own pumpkin spice coffee, you will never stand in line for it again. The real butter blended in along with the pumpkin and spices makes this drink far richer and better for you than the "natural flavors" added to commercial versions. Grace and I enjoy this drink with breakfast or as a dessert when fall evenings turn cooler.

12 ounces freshly brewed coffee, hot

2 tablespoons heavy cream

1 tablespoon unsalted butter, softened

1 tablespoon pumpkin puree (not pumpkin pie filling)

¼ teaspoon vanilla extract

¼ teaspoon pumpkin pie spice

¼ teaspoon ground cinnamon, plus extra for sprinkling

⅛ teaspoon ginger powder

Liquid sweetener, to taste

Whipped cream, for garnish

Place all the ingredients except the whipped cream in a blender and whip until frothy.

Serve hot with a dollop of freshly whipped cream and a sprinkle of cinnamon.

CALORIES: 173 | FAT: 17.4g | PROTEIN: 0.5g | CARBS: 3.8g | FIBER: 0g

Tailgating

Faux Apple Danish

makes
12 servings

The first time I made this Danish, David and I were going out of town, and I left it for Grace to enjoy with her grandparents. I distinctly remember not wanting to leave it behind! While I don't make it often, this treat satisfies my fall apple cravings. We like this recipe well enough to share it with friends and family at Christmas, and this Danish has been part of our Christmas morning meal more than once. I've provided directions for making individual Danishes or one large pastry. When I'm serving this to a crowd, I usually make the large version.

tip

You can omit the oat fiber from the pastry dough. If you do, increase the amount of almond flour and coconut flour by 1 tablespoon each.

CALORIES: 199 | FAT: 13.8g | PROTEIN: 10.9g | CARBS: 3.6g | FIBER: 1.1g | ERYTHRITOL: 12.3g | OAT FIBER: 2.8g

"APPLES":

1 cup peeled and chopped zucchini

2 tablespoons unsalted butter

1 teaspoon vanilla extract

½ teaspoon apple extract (optional)

¼ cup granulated sweetener

½ teaspoon apple pie spice

½ teaspoon ground cinnamon

CREAM CHEESE FILLING:

6 ounces cream cheese (¾ cup), softened

1 large egg yolk

2 teaspoons lemon juice

1 teaspoon vanilla extract

¼ cup powdered sweetener

PASTRY:

5 tablespoons blanched almond flour

¼ cup granulated sweetener

3 tablespoons oat fiber (see Tip)

2 tablespoons coconut flour

1 teaspoon ground cinnamon

1 teaspoon allspice

½ teaspoon baking powder

3 tablespoons unsalted butter, softened

2 large eggs

½ teaspoon vanilla extract

6 ounces mozzarella cheese, shredded (about 1½ cups)

ICING:

2 ounces cream cheese (¼ cup), softened

¼ cup heavy cream

3 tablespoons powdered sweetener

1 teaspoon apple pie spice

1 teaspoon ground cinnamon

½ teaspoon vanilla extract

Make the "apples": Combine all the ingredients for the "apples" in a saucepan over medium-low heat until the butter is melted and the sweetener is dissolved. The zucchini should be just tender. Set aside to cool.

Make the filling: Use a hand mixer or stand mixer to beat the filling ingredients together until smooth and creamy.

Make the pastry dough: Combine all the ingredients except the mozzarella cheese in a large mixing bowl. Melt the cheese in the microwave or on the stovetop over low heat. When the cheese is thoroughly melted, combine it with the other ingredients. Mix with your hands until a dough forms.

To make individual Danishes, preheat the oven to 400°F and grease a muffin top pan. Divide the dough evenly among the wells, pushing it in as if making a crust. Top each Danish with a generous tablespoon of the cream cheese filling. Place the "apples" on top of the cream cheese filling, dividing the mixture evenly among the Danishes.

Bake for 15 to 20 minutes, until browned and set. Let the Danishes cool in the pan slightly, then remove to a cooling rack and let cool for at least 12 minutes, until cool enough to handle.

To make one large braided Danish, preheat the oven to 375°F and line a 9 by 13-inch jelly roll pan with parchment paper. Use your hands to smooth the dough into one large rectangle. Visually, divide the dough into thirds along the longer side. Leaving the middle third alone, use a sharp knife to cut horizontal slits along the outer thirds. Once assembled, you will use these slits to fold the dough over the filling and "apples" to resemble a braid.

Smooth the cream cheese filling down the middle third of the crust. Top the cream cheese filling with the "apples." Fold the cut pieces of dough over the center, alternating folding from left to right until all the strips of dough have been folded over the center.

Bake for 20 to 25 minutes, until browned and set. Let cool until cool enough to handle.

While the Danish(es) are cooling, make the icing: Use a spatula to mix the cream cheese, heavy cream, and sweetener in a small bowl. Stir in the pie spice, cinnamon, and vanilla extract. The icing should be thin enough to pipe over the Danish. If it's too thick, thin it with a little more cream.

Transfer the icing to a small resealable plastic bag. Use scissors to cut a small hole in one corner of the bag and drizzle the icing over the Danish(es). Serve warm.

Glazed Maple Cinnamon Donuts

makes
12 donuts
(1 per serving)

Donuts on a diet? That's why we call it a lifestyle! These donuts will not disappoint you as long as you start with blocks of full-fat mozzarella cheese, which are usually sold at Walmart. The texture isn't nearly as good if you use preshredded part-skim cheese. Beyond that, these donuts can be mixed up in one bowl and made really quickly. If I don't have time to glaze them, I sprinkle them with powdered sweetener, which my family loves as much as the glaze.

7 ounces full-fat mozzarella cheese, shredded (about 1¾ cups)

4 ounces cream cheese (½ cup), softened

½ cup (1 stick) unsalted butter, softened

½ cup whey protein isolate

⅓ cup oat fiber

⅓ cup granulated sweetener

⅓ cup brown sugar substitute, or ⅓ cup granulated sweetener mixed with ¼ teaspoon maple extract

2 large eggs

1 teaspoon baking powder

1 teaspoon ground cinnamon

¼ teaspoon salt

1 tablespoon vanilla extract

½ teaspoon maple extract

GLAZE:

½ cup (1 stick) unsalted butter

⅓ cup powdered sweetener

2 tablespoons refined coconut oil

2 tablespoons heavy cream

¼ teaspoon maple extract

¼ teaspoon vanilla extract

SPECIAL EQUIPMENT:
2 (6-well) donut pans

Preheat the oven to 350°F. Grease two 6-well donut pans.

Make the donuts: In a large bowl, combine all the donut ingredients. Using a hand mixer or stand mixer, mix until well blended.

Divide the batter evenly among the wells of the prepared pans. Bake for 16 to 18 minutes, until golden brown and firm to the touch. Let cool in the pans for 5 to 10 minutes, until cool enough to handle.

While the donuts are cooling, make the glaze: Place all the ingredients in a small saucepan over low heat. Stir until the sweetener is dissolved and all the ingredients are mixed well.

Drizzle the glaze over the warm donuts or dip the donuts in the glaze. Let dry on a cooling rack. Serve warm.

CALORIES: 231 | FAT: 26.9g | PROTEIN: 9.9g | CARBS: 1.1g | FIBER: 5.0g | ERYTHRITOL: 4g | OAT FIBER: 10.3g

Mason Jar Chili and Cornbread

makes
8 servings

This fall favorite uses one of the cornbread recipes in this book to make a great tailgating chili dish. You can assemble it in 8- or 12-ounce mason jars. My family swears that the 12-ounce jars I use to serve it aren't large enough, but they are! Layer the jars with chili, a generous sprinkle of shredded cheese, a serving of crumbled cornbread, a dollop of sour cream, and some chopped green onions. Who needs football when you can tailgate?

CHILI:

1 pound ground beef

1 pound cubed pork loin or bulk sausage

1 pound beef round steak, cut into bite-sized pieces

2 tablespoons dried minced onions, or ½ cup chopped onions

2 teaspoons minced garlic

2 teaspoons salt

3 tablespoons chili powder

2 teaspoons ground cumin

2 teaspoons paprika

1 teaspoon onion powder

¼ teaspoon ground cinnamon

2 cups beef bone broth

1½ cups strained tomatoes (lowest carb count possible)

1 cup water

½ cup (1 stick) unsalted butter, softened

FOR ASSEMBLY:

8 ounces cheddar cheese, shredded (about 2 cups)

½ batch Kristie's Keto Cornbread (page 42) or Jalapeño Cheddar Cornbread (page 268), crumbled

½ cup sour cream

2 green onions, chopped

Make the chili: In a 6-quart or larger saucepan over medium heat, brown the meats one at a time. Drain the fat, if desired. Return the meats to the pan and add the onions, garlic, salt, and spices. When heated through, stir in the broth, tomatoes, water, and butter. Reduce the heat and simmer, uncovered, for 35 to 45 minutes, until the chili has thickened and the meats are tender.

To assemble, fill each jar about two-thirds full of chili. Sprinkle ¼ cup of shredded cheddar on top of the chili and 2 to 3 tablespoons of crumbled cornbread on top of the cheese. Finish each jar with a 1-tablespoon dollop of sour cream and about 1 teaspoon of chopped green onions. Serve immediately.

CALORIES: 681 | FAT: 56.2g | PROTEIN: 37g | CARBS: 7.6g | FIBER: 3.1g | OAT FIBER: 3.75g

Mexican Meatballs

makes
24 meatballs
(6 per serving)

If a recipe can be masculine, this one is, which is just one reason it makes a great tailgating option. Also, the meatballs are bite-sized and don't have to be super-hot to be tasty. They are delicious served with Authentic Salsa Verde (page 150), sour cream, sliced jalapeños, and/or crumbled queso fresco.

1 pound ground beef

1 pound Mexican-style fresh (raw) chorizo, casings removed

2 ounces pepper Jack cheese, shredded (about ½ cup)

1 large egg

⅓ cup pork dust (ground pork rinds)

2 jalapeño peppers, seeded and finely chopped

1 tablespoon finely chopped onions

1 clove garlic, minced

1 teaspoon smoked paprika, plus extra for garnish

Preheat the oven to 375°F.

Place all the ingredients in a large bowl and use your hands or a large rubber spatula to mix thoroughly. Shape the mixture into twenty-four 1½-inch balls.

Place the meatballs on a rimmed baking sheet, spacing them at least ½ inch apart. Bake for 12 to 14 minutes, until browned and cooked through. Let cool for 10 to 15 minutes before serving. Serve with your desired accompaniments, garnished with a little smoked paprika.

note ————————————————
For safety, be sure to wear disposable gloves when chopping and seeding the jalapeño peppers; the oil can cause painful skin irritation.

CALORIES: 513 | FAT: 40.4g | PROTEIN: 32.7g | CARBS: 2.5g | FIBER: 0g

10

october

OCTOBER is one of my favorite months. Nights become crisp, and being outside in the daytime is pleasant again. The sky seems brighter and the air cleaner. If you've never had a chance to enjoy fall, with the brightly colored leaves, the smell of smoke from bonfires, and perhaps a **Hot Buttered Rum** warming your hands, then you haven't lived.

October is a time for fueling up with a good breakfast like **Baked Cinnamon Faux Apple Oatmeal** and then hitting a pumpkin patch to find the perfect future jack-o'-lantern. It is also a good time to share a hearty meal of **Zuppa Toscana (Sausage and Kale Soup)** with a side of **Jalapeño Cheddar Cornbread** before tagging along after the trick-or-treaters as they zigzag through the neighborhood.

My family traditionally reserves the teenth weekend (the weekend that ends in "–teenth," as in sixteenth or nineteenth) in October to travel to the mountains. Mother Nature puts on a spectacular show in those hills, and the teenth weekend is usually when the colors peak. It is also when the small town of Banner Elk, North Carolina, hosts the Woolly Worm Festival. Yes, there is a woolly worm, and he and his tribe have their own festival. The humble woolly worm is credited with the ability to predict the winter, so he is celebrated with three days of festivities. One of the highlights of the festival is the woolly worm races. If you can't find your own woolly worm (hunting them is not for the faint of heart), then you can buy one for a dollar or two. You can then name your worm and register it for a race. When your worm's heat begins, you place it at the end of a string and then cheer like mad as the worm, along with thirteen others, races to the top of the string. Each worm that wins a heat goes on to compete again. The final, winning worm gets the distinction of forecasting the upcoming winter's weather. The guide to the forecast is woven into the woolly worm's bands of fur. Darker brown stripes are said to represent harsher weather, while lighter bands indicate milder weather.

We often enjoy smoked meats from our favorite mountain BBQ place, The Pedalin' Pig, after we leave the festival. Our eyes bigger than our bellies, we simply box up the leftovers, and I use them later to make a big pot of **Brunswick Stew.** Those leftover smoked meats make the best stew you will ever eat. We also like to travel with **No-Apple Spice Muffins** or **Cinnamon Roll Pull-Apart Bread** for a treat on the long drive.

I don't know how accurate the woolly worms' bands are, but I do know that my grandmother always suggested we watch nature to see what the future held. She swore that a bumper crop of pecans meant a harsh winter was on the way. I loved it when the pecan trees were loaded down because winter was my favorite season. In a climate that rarely saw snow, hearing the elders say "harsh winter" gave me hope for snow days, which meant cancelled schools and snow cream. October still represents a month of hope, whether it comes from woolly worms or pecan trees, but the promise of winter sprouts just as everything else is going dormant.

Perhaps that is why I am so fond of pansies and sasanqua camellia. Both bloom in my region throughout the fall and winter. It seems that anything can bloom in spring, but to have the stamina and the sheer determination to blossom when everything else is dying is unique. The pansies smile and the deep pink camellias brighten the edge of the yard while the rest of nature is cloaked in uniforms of gold, orange, or brown. While I love those brilliant fall colors, the flowering plants that remind us that life goes on even as the cycle of dying surrounds us are my favorite.

No-Apple Spice Muffins

**makes
12 muffins
(1 per serving)**

This is another recipe that makes me think of my brother Tony and his wife, Sam. Once I made this as a sweet bread for Christmas Eve. When Sam told me how much she liked it, Tony quipped, "There's no apple in it." She poked her finger at a piece of zucchini and asked him, "Then what's that?" They both looked at me. I smiled as I explained that the pieces of "apple" were really peeled cubes of zucchini. Sam laughed and said, "If anyone can make zucchini taste like apple, it would be you!" The leftovers went home with them that night. I use hazelnut flour in these muffins, which is not only lower in carbs than almond flour but also has a richer flavor.

CALORIES: 210 | FAT: 21g | PROTEIN: 7.3g | CARBS: 3.6g | FIBER: 6.5g | ERYTHRITOL: 9g | OAT FIBER: 5g

"APPLES":

1 cup peeled and chopped zucchini

1 teaspoon apple pie spice

½ teaspoon ground cinnamon

1 teaspoon vanilla extract

1 teaspoon apple extract

5 drops liquid sweetener

MUFFIN BATTER:

⅔ cup hazelnut flour or blanched almond flour

⅓ cup oat fiber

⅓ cup whey protein isolate

2 teaspoons ground cinnamon

2 teaspoons apple pie spice

1 teaspoon baking powder

1 teaspoon salt

½ cup (1 stick) unsalted butter, softened

3 ounces cream cheese (¼ cup plus 2 tablespoons), softened

1 cup brown sugar substitute, or ¾ cup granulated sweetener

4 large eggs

2 tablespoons sour cream

1½ teaspoons apple extract

1 teaspoon vanilla extract

4 drops liquid sweetener

½ cup chopped raw pecans or walnuts

Preheat the oven to 350°F. Line a standard-size 12-well muffin pan with parchment paper liners.

Make the "apples": Mix the zucchini with the remaining "apples" ingredients. Set aside.

Make the muffin batter: In a large bowl, whisk together the hazelnut flour, oat fiber, protein isolate, cinnamon, pie spice, baking powder, and salt; set aside.

In a separate bowl, use a hand mixer or stand mixer to blend the butter and cream cheese. Add the brown sugar substitute and mix until well blended and creamy.

Add the eggs one at a time, mixing well after each addition. Stir in the sour cream, extracts, and liquid sweetener by hand. Taste for sweetness and adjust if necessary.

Stir the prepared "apples" and the nuts into the batter. Divide the batter evenly among the wells of the prepared muffin pan, filling each well about two-thirds full. Bake for 24 to 28 minutes, until browned and just firm to the touch. Let cool in the pan for 5 to 10 minutes before serving.

Store leftovers in the refrigerator for up to 5 days.

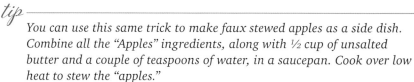

tip

You can use this same trick to make faux stewed apples as a side dish. Combine all the "Apples" ingredients, along with ½ cup of unsalted butter and a couple of teaspoons of water, in a saucepan. Cook over low heat to stew the "apples."

Peanut Butter Pie

**makes
8 servings**

I might have been in high school when my friend Gwen and her mother taught me how to make peanut butter pie. That high-carb version used all convenience foods and could be made in 20 minutes or less. This low-carb version can be made in just 15 minutes, even though it doesn't rely on any convenience foods. After I made this pie the first time, I shared the recipe with my Facebook group. Kristin Parker, an admin in the group and one of my favorite people, was among the first to make it. Her entire family adored it, and she even made it for her birthday. She has also made it to celebrate Sundays, rainy days, snowstorms, and her new kitten—in short, for any reason! I'm sharing this recipe in October in honor of Kristin's birthday and her sweet friendship.

CRUST:

⅓ cup blanched almond flour

⅓ cup granulated sweetener

¼ cup unsweetened cocoa powder

¼ cup oat fiber

¼ cup (½ stick) unsalted butter, melted

¼ teaspoon vanilla extract

¼ teaspoon salt (optional)

⅛ teaspoon instant coffee granules

FILLING:

1 (8-ounce) package cream cheese, softened

½ cup peanut butter, room temperature

¾ cup powdered sweetener

¼ cup heavy cream

1 teaspoon vanilla extract

4 drops liquid sweetener

¼ teaspoon salt

Make the crust: Mix together all the crust ingredients until the mixture resembles coarse crumbs. Use your fingers to press the crust mixture into the bottom and up the side of a 9-inch pie plate.

Make the filling: In a large bowl, use a hand mixer or stand mixer to blend the cream cheese and peanut butter until creamy and thoroughly blended.

Add the powdered sweetener and blend until dissolved. Beat in the heavy cream, vanilla extract, liquid sweetener, and salt. Continue mixing until the filling is fluffy and smooth, 2 to 3 minutes.

Pour the filling into the prepared crust and smooth the top. Refrigerate the pie for at least 2 hours or overnight before serving. Store leftovers in the refrigerator for up to a week.

Brownie Ice Cream

makes
6 servings

This is another of those desserts that remind me I can keto for life. People say it's hard or not sustainable. Bless their hearts! They don't know what they don't know. I can eat Brownie Ice Cream, still feel good, and not fear my skinny jeans. That, my friends, is living! This brownie is meant to be a little crumbly so that it works well with the ice cream. It also makes a nice treat on its own with a little freshly whipped cream.

2½ cups heavy cream

¼ cup (½ stick) salted butter

6 large egg yolks

½ cup powdered sweetener (see Tip)

2 teaspoons vanilla extract

¼ teaspoon salt

½ batch Brownie Bits (opposite)

SPECIAL EQUIPMENT:

Ice cream maker

tip

The type of sweetener used makes a huge difference in the texture of the ice cream. For the best texture, use allulose or xylitol; remember that each sweetener has different characteristics (see pages 19 and 20 for details). Use the sweetener that you prefer and that does not impact your blood glucose.

In a heavy saucepan over low heat, heat the heavy cream and butter, stirring with a whisk until the butter is melted. Stir in the egg yolks and continue whisking over low heat until just warmed.

Add the sweetener and whisk until completely dissolved. Continue heating, whisking constantly, until the mixture thickens, about 10 minutes. When the mixture coats the back of a wooden spoon or reaches 140°F on a candy thermometer, remove the pan from the heat. Do not allow it to warm to over 140°F or the eggs will begin to cook.

Add the vanilla extract and salt and stir to combine. Transfer the mixture to a bowl and place in the refrigerator to cool.

When cool, churn the ice cream mixture in an ice cream maker following the manufacturer's directions. Add the brownie bits to the ice cream while it is churning and after it has begun to freeze, but while the ice cream is still soft. Continue churning until it reaches your desired consistency.

Store leftovers in the freezer. When frozen, this ice cream will harden to a solid state. Allow to thaw at room temperature for about 10 minutes before enjoying.

CALORIES: 630 | FAT: 58g | PROTEIN: 17.3g | CARBS: 7.6g | FIBER: 3.5g | ERYTHRITOL: 36g

Brownie Bits

2 ounces unsweetened baking chocolate

½ cup (1 stick) unsalted butter, softened

2 ounces cream cheese (¼ cup), softened

¾ cup granulated sweetener

3 large eggs

¼ cup unsweetened almond milk

1 teaspoon vanilla extract

⅓ cup blanched almond flour

¼ cup whey protein isolate

¼ cup unsweetened cocoa powder

¼ teaspoon salt

Preheat the oven to 350°F. Grease an 8-inch round cake pan and line with parchment paper.

In a small microwave-safe bowl, melt the chocolate in the microwave, stirring frequently so that it doesn't burn; set aside.

In a separate bowl, use a hand mixer or stand mixer to blend the butter and cream cheese. Add the sweetener and mix until smooth. Add the eggs one at a time, mixing well after each addition. Pour in the melted chocolate, beating as you add it. Add the almond milk and vanilla extract and mix well. Stir in the almond flour, protein isolate, cocoa powder, and salt by hand.

Pour the batter into the prepared cake pan and smooth the top. Bake for 15 to 20 minutes, until just set. Do not overbake. Let the brownie cool for 15 to 20 minutes before removing from the pan. Crumble into small pieces just larger than pebbles. Freeze the unused portion to make a second batch of ice cream later.

Hot Buttered Rum

makes
1 serving

No, there isn't a half cup of butter in this one cocktail! You start by making a flavored butter that you will add to the rum and hot water. After you make the butter, you can enjoy this hot cocktail anytime you want. The flavored butter is also fantastic slathered on Modified Soul Bread (page 342) or Cinnamon Soul Bread (page 138), with or without the cocktail!

FLAVORED BUTTER:

(makes ¾ cup)

½ cup (1 stick) unsalted butter, softened

2 teaspoons orange zest

1 teaspoon maple extract

¼ cup powdered sweetener

¼ teaspoon ground cinnamon

⅛ teaspoon ground cloves

HOT BUTTERED RUM:

2 tablespoons flavored butter (from above)

½ cup hot water

2 ounces dark rum

Make the flavored butter at least 1 day in advance. In a bowl, mix the butter, orange zest, maple extract, sweetener, cinnamon, and cloves until thoroughly combined. Store in an airtight container in the refrigerator until ready to use. You might prefer to roll the softened butter into a log and wrap tightly in parchment paper before refrigerating. Store in the refrigerator for up to 2 weeks or freeze for up to 2 months.

To prepare the cocktail, place 2 tablespoons of the flavored butter in an 8-ounce mug. Pour the hot water over the butter. Add the rum and mix well to combine. Serve immediately.

CALORIES: 329 | FAT: 23g | PROTEIN: 0g | CARBS: 0g | FIBER: 0g | ERYTHRITOL: 36g

Cozy Fall Foods

Baked Cinnamon Faux Apple Oatmeal · 256

Cinnamon Roll Pull-Apart Bread · 258

Korean Short Ribs · 260

Smoked Gouda Cauli Mash · 262

Baked Cinnamon Faux Apple Oatmeal

makes
2 servings

For a woman who doesn't love fake anything, I sure love some faux! This recipe resembles a high-carb baked oatmeal with apples and apple pie spice, but there are no apples and no oatmeal. Those things will kill you! Still, there's something about the texture of oatmeal, the warm spice of cinnamon, and the tingle of maple that fall simply demands. If you're one of those people who craves a warm breakfast option for the cooler mornings of October, you're gonna love this recipe. While you can simply microwave all of the ingredients (about 1½ minutes at full power), I prefer to bake this faux oatmeal. The flavor seems richer and the texture more authentic. On a Sunday morning, it warms the whole house and the tummies of those you love.

"OATMEAL":

2 tablespoons salted butter

½ cup chopped peeled zucchini

1 tablespoon water

½ cup hemp hearts

¼ cup plus 1 tablespoon brown sugar substitute

2 tablespoons oat fiber

½ teaspoon ground cinnamon

½ teaspoon apple pie spice

¼ teaspoon salt

3 ounces heavy cream

1½ teaspoons vanilla extract

½ teaspoon apple extract

½ teaspoon maple extract

3 drops liquid sweetener

TOPPING:

½ cup chopped raw pecans

2 tablespoons oat fiber

2 tablespoons brown sugar substitute

2 tablespoons unsalted butter, melted

Preheat the oven to 350°F.

Make the "oatmeal": Melt the butter in a medium saucepan over medium heat. Add the zucchini and water and cook for about 5 minutes, until the zucchini is just barely tender; do not let it get soft or mushy. Add the remaining ingredients for the "oatmeal" and stir until well mixed. Reduce the heat to low and heat until warmed through. Pour the "oatmeal" into two 7-ounce ramekins.

Make the topping: In a small bowl, mix together the topping ingredients. Sprinkle the topping over the "oatmeal," dividing it evenly between the ramekins.

Bake for 20 to 25 minutes, until browned and thickened. Let stand for 5 to 10 minutes before serving.

CALORIES: 567 | FAT: 53.7g | PROTEIN: 14.9g | CARBS: 8.7g | FIBER: 5.5g | ERYTHRITOL: 38g | OAT FIBER: 16.9g

Cinnamon Roll Pull-Apart Bread

makes
12 servings

This sweet bread really does sound and taste too good to be true. When I tell you that it is as close to a cinnamon roll as I've ever made low-carb, I mean it. You need to understand that I have tried no fewer than a dozen times to make an acceptable—not even delicious, but just acceptable—low-carb cinnamon roll. Not one was worth sharing or repeating until I developed this recipe. I had nearly given up; I can't tell you why I even tried once more. This version resembles a pull-apart bread, like the Orange Danish Pull-Apart Bread (page 214). If you've ever bought Sister Schubert's brand cinnamon rolls in the disposable aluminum tray, this recipe will seem familiar to you. I won't say my version tastes exactly like Sister Schubert's, but I'd argue it's better because it's healthier. I do use a small amount of real sugar, but only to feed the yeast, which adds flavor and texture and makes this bread seem more authentic. If you prefer not to use it, simply omit the sugar, yeast, and water. I think you will be pleased with the end result either way.

1 (1¼-ounce) packet active dry yeast

¼ teaspoon sugar

2 tablespoons hot water

½ cup blanched almond flour

½ cup oat fiber

⅓ cup granulated sweetener

1 tablespoon baking powder

½ teaspoon salt

3 ounces cream cheese (¼ cup plus 2 tablespoons), softened

2 ounces full-fat mozzarella cheese, shredded (about ½ cup)

2 large eggs

3 tablespoons unsalted butter, softened

CINNAMON COATING:

⅓ cup brown sugar substitute

2 teaspoons ground cinnamon

Preheat the oven to 350°F.

In a small bowl, dissolve the yeast and sugar in the hot water. Set aside.

In a separate bowl, use a hand mixer or stand mixer to blend the almond flour, oat fiber, granulated sweetener, baking powder, salt, cream cheese, mozzarella, and eggs. Stir in the yeast mixture by hand and let the dough sit while you prepare the pan.

Place the butter in a 9-inch round cake pan and put the pan in the oven to melt the butter. When the butter is melted, remove the pan from the oven.

Meanwhile, make the cinnamon coating: In a small bowl, mix together the brown sugar substitute and cinnamon.

Form the dough into 20 balls, 1½ to 2 inches in diameter. Roll each ball in the cinnamon mixture, completely coating each ball. Place the coated balls in the prepared pan so that the sides are touching.

Bake for 20 to 24 minutes, until the bread has risen and is just firm to the touch. Let cool in the pan for about 15 minutes.

ICING:

4 ounces cream cheese (½ cup), softened

¼ cup (½ stick) unsalted butter, softened

½ cup heavy cream, room temperature

⅓ cup powdered sweetener

½ teaspoon vanilla extract

Dash of salt

While the bread is baking, make the icing: Use a hand mixer or stand mixer to blend the cream cheese and butter. When smooth and creamy, mix in the heavy cream, sweetener, vanilla extract, and salt. Continue beating until thoroughly mixed.

After the bread has cooled for 15 minutes, spread the icing over the top and serve warm. Refrigerate leftovers for up to 5 days.

Korean Short Ribs

makes
6 servings

My friend Kristin Parker gave me her recipe for Korean Short Ribs. I've modified it only slightly for this book because her version was pretty tasty! She likes to make these in an Instant Pot. While I appreciate the convenience of the Instant Pot, I have also made these in the oven, which makes them a little more flavorful and tender. If you have time, try them both ways. You may want to reserve some of the marinade to serve at the table; simply set aside ¼ cup or so before adding the meat to the marinade. This marinade is also fantastic with roasted, broiled, or grilled chicken wings.

½ cup coconut aminos (see Tip)

⅓ cup olive oil

⅓ cup rice vinegar

2 tablespoons brown sugar substitute

1 tablespoon five-spice powder

¼ teaspoon salt

2½ pounds boneless country-style pork ribs, cut into strips

Marinate the ribs: Mix the coconut aminos, olive oil, vinegar, brown sugar substitute, five-spice powder, and salt in a gallon-sized freezer bag. Add the ribs to the marinade and refrigerate for at least 1 hour or preferably overnight.

To cook the ribs in an electric pressure cooker such as an Instant Pot, place the ribs and marinade in the cooker and cook on high pressure for 15 minutes; allow the pressure to release naturally.

To cook the ribs in the oven, preheat the oven to 325°F. Remove the ribs from the marinade; discard the marinade. Place the ribs on a rimmed baking sheet and bake for 1 hour 20 minutes, or until the meat is tender.

tip
You can substitute soy sauce or tamari for the coconut aminos. If you use either of those substitutes, omit the salt.

CALORIES: 448 | FAT: 22.3g | PROTEIN: 46.7g | CARBS: 3.2g | FIBER: 0g | ERYTHRITOL: 5.3g

Smoked Gouda Cauli Mash

makes
6 servings

My family is a little obsessed with smoked Gouda cheese. In fact, we happily say, "Gouda makes it gooder!" which seems to ring true regardless of what "it" is. The smoked Gouda in this recipe thickens the cauli mash and adds a subtle smoky flavor. You can serve it with Korean Short Ribs (page 260) or any grilled or roasted meat. When I make cauli mash, I prefer to steam the cauliflower in the microwave before mashing it. You can steam it on the stovetop, but if you do, be sure to squeeze the excess moisture from the cauliflower before making the mash.

3 cups chopped cauliflower

4 ounces smoked Gouda cheese, shredded or chopped (about 1 cup), plus extra for garnish if desired

½ cup (1 stick) unsalted butter, softened

⅓ cup heavy cream

1 ounce cream cheese (2 tablespoons), softened

½ teaspoon salt

⅛ teaspoon smoked paprika, for sprinkling

Dried chives, for garnish (optional)

Steam the cauliflower by placing it in a microwave-safe dish and microwaving, uncovered, for 4 to 5 minutes, until soft. Do not add water to the dish before microwaving. Use a clean kitchen towel or paper towel to squeeze the moisture from the steamed cauliflower.

Transfer the steamed cauliflower to a blender. Add the Gouda, butter, heavy cream, cream cheese, and salt. Blend until creamy. Sprinkle the smoked paprika and dried chives, if using, over the cauli mash just before serving.

Store leftovers in the refrigerator for up to 4 days.

CALORIES: 253 | FAT: 20.1g | PROTEIN: 11g | CARBS: 3.2g | FIBER: 1.1g

Pre–Trick-or-Treating

Brunswick Stew

makes
6 servings

If you're not from the South, you might not have heard of Brunswick Stew, bless your heart. If you are from the South, you probably have your own preferred version. Truly authentic Brunswick Stew features various meats and often includes wild game such as squirrel or rabbit. My version is more "tame" and uses leftover smoked or grilled meats, which add an unbelievable flavor. The inspiration for this recipe came from a follower who asked me to create it. The fact that David and Grace both have a fondness for it made the challenge to create a low-carb version even more fun. This dish is great for a Halloween party, a fall potluck, or a simple dinner with loved ones on a chilly fall evening.

1½ pounds chopped smoked meat, such as pulled pork, brisket, or chicken, or a combination

2 cups beef bone broth

1 (14½-ounce) can green beans, drained, or 3 ounces fresh green beans, trimmed and snapped

1 cup chopped zucchini

½ cup strained tomatoes

½ cup cabbage strips

¼ cup chopped jicama or water chestnuts (optional)

½ cup (1 stick) unsalted butter

½ cup Classic BBQ Sauce (page 340)

½ cup Eastern NC BBQ Sauce (page 341)

2 tablespoons dried minced onions

½ teaspoon garlic powder

Combine all the ingredients in a large saucepan over medium heat. When the stew begins to simmer, reduce the heat to low. Simmer, uncovered, until the vegetables are tender and the stew thickens, 45 to 55 minutes.

Store leftovers in the refrigerator for up to 5 days.

CALORIES: 303 | FAT: 21.4g | PROTEIN: 24.2g | CARBS: 4.3g | FIBER: 1.3g

Zuppa Toscana (Sausage and Kale Soup)

makes
8 servings

Traditionally, this soup is made with potatoes, which makes it impossible to enjoy on a low-carb lifestyle. Many folks simply replace the potatoes with cauliflower, which isn't a bad solution; however, chopped zucchini is a lower-carb option, which is especially helpful because kale, also used in this soup, has more carbs than you might expect. Whenever I serve this soup, I find that my children's friends enjoy it. In fact, Grace has even asked for it during the heat of summer. If you aren't serving it to a crowd, enjoy the leftovers heated up for weekday lunches.

2 pounds Italian sausage, casings removed

½ cup chopped onions

1 clove garlic, minced

¼ teaspoon salt

Dash of ground black pepper

4 cups beef bone broth

2 cups chopped zucchini

3 cups chopped kale

1 cup heavy cream

1 ounce Parmesan cheese, grated (about ⅓ cup)

2 tablespoons cooked bacon pieces (optional)

In a stockpot or Dutch oven over medium heat, brown the sausage. Add the onions, garlic, salt, and pepper and sauté in the sausage drippings until the onions are browned. Drain the fat, if desired.

Add the broth and zucchini to the pot. Simmer for 15 to 20 minutes, until the zucchini is tender. Stir in the kale and simmer for an additional 10 to 15 minutes, until the kale is just tender.

Pour in the heavy cream and simmer over low heat until the soup thickened, 15 to 20 minutes.

Remove from the heat. Just before serving, sprinkle the Parmesan and bacon, if using, over the top of the soup.

Store leftovers in the refrigerator for up to 5 days.

CALORIES: 347 | FAT: 30.3g | PROTEIN: 15.6g | CARBS: 4.7g | FIBER: 0.6g

Jalapeño Cheddar Cornbread

makes
8 servings

My husband told me never to make this bread again. He enjoyed it too much! If you can stick to just one serving, this is a really tasty low-carb cornbread. Not only do I enjoy putting it on a buffet to fool the carbivores, but I love eating it warmed up with softly scrambled eggs and a pat of butter—not a traditional breakfast option, but trust me, it's a great way to start the day. You can also enjoy it with soups or as a side with grilled or roasted meats.

⅓ cup oat fiber

⅓ cup whey protein isolate

¼ cup coconut flour

1½ teaspoons baking powder

¼ teaspoon salt

4 large eggs

½ cup (1 stick) salted butter, melted but not hot

⅓ cup bacon fat or salted butter, melted but not hot

¼ cup heavy cream

¼ cup water

¼ teaspoon corn extract

2 ounces cheddar cheese, shredded (about ½ cup)

⅓ cup chopped cooked bacon

1 jalapeño, seeded and finely chopped

1 tablespoon dried minced onions

3 tablespoons salted butter

Preheat the oven to 350°F.

In a small bowl, whisk together the oat fiber, protein isolate, coconut flour, baking powder, and salt; set aside.

Place the eggs, melted butter, bacon fat, heavy cream, water, and corn extract in a large bowl. Use a hand mixer or stand mixer to mix until frothy.

Sift the dry ingredients into the wet ingredients and stir to combine. Stir in the cheese, bacon, jalapeño, and onions.

Place the butter in a 9-inch cast-iron skillet and put the skillet in the oven until the butter is melted and sizzling. Remove the skillet from the oven and tilt it to cover the bottom with the melted butter.

Pour the cornbread batter into the skillet and use a rubber spatula to distribute it evenly. Bake until lightly browned, 25 to 30 minutes. The bread should be firm to the touch. Let cool in the pan for 5 to 10 minutes before serving. Refrigerate leftovers for up to a week.

note ——————————————————

For safety, be sure to wear disposable gloves when chopping and seeding the pepper; the oil can cause painful skin irritation.

CALORIES: 314 | FAT: 35.4g | PROTEIN: 12.1g | CARBS: 5.3g | FIBER: 9.5g | OAT FIBER: 7.5g

11

november

"Remember, remember the Fifth of NOVEMBER, the gunpowder treason and plot!" In England, those words are used in the recognition of Guy Fawkes Day. I learned about that holiday as a college student studying in Leeds, England. I've never forgotten the phrase, in part, because November 5 was the day I met my husband. We've remembered that day by saying, "Remember, remember, the Fifth of November!"

When we met, David and I were participating in a retreat for a leadership conference. I was wearing a very tight pair of size 14 jeans. We were both dating others, but we stayed up talking well into the morning hours that night. On my way home the next day, I called my best friend, told her everything about him, and breathlessly said, "I met the man I'm gonna marry and the father of my children." By May, David and I had begun dating. I used to pray, "Lord, if he's not the one, then let it be someone just like him. He can be taller, shorter, fatter, or thinner, but please let him have the same heart." From time to time we still celebrate the Fifth of November. I will always remember it as the day my heart fell in love with his.

November is also my mother's birthday month. She is a red-headed Scorpio, and although she is a pushover most of the time, when she would say, "Don't tell me 'no'!" or when her faced reddened to the same hue as her hair, we all fell in line quickly. My mother's favorite flavor of ice cream has always been **Butter Pecan,** so this month's ice cream recipe is in her honor. Grace and I love it as much as she does, and I love giving my mother, Grace, and myself a low-carb version that we all can enjoy.

My mother is diabetic, so it is very important for her to avoid sugar. One year, just before Thanksgiving, she called me to discuss the menu we were going to enjoy with extended family. As she listed what each person was bringing, she said, "Hilda is bringing Cherry Yum-Yum, but we can't have that." Now, my hair is not naturally red, but I'm pretty sure it was supposed to be. I replied, "Well, we *can* have it, but I choose not to eat that high-carb stuff." I could almost see her roll her eyes as she replied, "I know, but you know what I mean. It's full of sugar, and I hate that it is, because I sure do love it." I knew before we finished that call that I was going to create a low-carb **Cherry Yum-Yum** even if I did nothing else that Thanksgiving!

I set about scheming how to make cherries without cherries. I made the first test batch, and Grace hovered as I finished assembling it. She was happy to do the taste-testing for me and exclaimed, "Mom! I think that's the best thing you have ever made!" Then she elbowed me out of the way, ignoring my protests that it needed to be chilled. David's reaction was similar, so I quickly scribbled down the recipe.

By the time we joined my extended family for Thanksgiving, I had made the Cherry Yum-Yum twice more. Even though David, Grace, and I enjoyed it, I cringed when my sister-in-law set it down right beside her grandmother's version. My little low-carb creation was pitted against one made by a grandmother who could make shoe leather taste like filet mignon! We went on with the meal, and before long everyone turned their attention to dessert. My mom was excited to try my Cherry Yum-Yum, but somehow the rest of the family had gotten excited, too. I watched with horror as my tall, thin brother scooped a generous helping of each version, side by side, onto his plate. I held my breath as folks began to take their first bites. I wanted to yell that it wasn't fair to put the family favorite next to my version, but I kept quiet and said a little prayer under my breath. My brother was first: "That's actually really good! I love it!" My mom had tasted mine by then as well and asked, "How did you do that?" The general consensus was that it was hard to believe my version was sugar-free! As everyone tried a bite, my mother began to get a little protective of "her" dessert. She whispered to me, "Why don't they leave mine alone? They can eat that other one." I giggled and assured her that I had an extra one in the car that she could have all to herself!

The Cherry Yum-Yum debuted at our fifth low-carb Thanksgiving, but I very much remember our first low-carb Thanksgiving. I never dreamed of including anything high-carb because I set to work determined to make delicious low-carb options, including a stuffing that the carbivores enjoyed! I made a low-carb cranberry sauce and a twice-baked cauliflower dish. We didn't feel deprived at all. Best of all—and I remember this vividly—as we drove home late in the day, it occurred to me that I wasn't hungry. We had eaten a large meal at around 1 p.m. It was nearly 8 p.m., and none of us had begun to think about dinner. We hadn't stopped for food on the two-hour drive home. No one was asking when we would eat dinner. I looked at David with tears in my eyes. Alarmed, he asked, "What's wrong?" I choked out, "I'm not hungry. Are you?" He paused for a second and then said, "No. I hadn't thought about it." I reminded him of how we used to eat a large meal, then get a snack for the road, buy a snack on the way home, and then eat dinner. We were always hungry and nearly always afraid of being hungry. I was in tears because I realized that I was finally free from the hunger. Not only did I feel good, but I could focus on other things besides eating. I remember being especially thankful for keto that first Thanksgiving.

Now that we no longer eat foods that put us in a carb coma, we enjoy the Thanksgiving holiday so much more. While others are wearing their stretchy pants or loosening their belts after dinner, we are ready to shop, play games, and kick off the holiday season. Nearly every year, we do our great Christmas tree trek the weekend after Thanksgiving. We bundle up, pack the car, and head out early to the mountains. Along the three-hour drive,

we talk about how we want to decorate our trees (yes, trees, plural) and what we want to do for the holidays. For several years we have selected a very tall tree for the two-story family room. Most often we find one that is 14 to 16 feet tall. One year, I got overly ambitious and insisted on a tree that took three strong men several hours to bring into the house. It barely squeezed through the open French doors. When they finally righted it, the commercial tree stand broke. That poor tree lay on the floor of our great room for a week. Unable to find a commercial tree stand that was large enough, David used a chainsaw to dismantle it so that we could more easily carry it to the curb!

In addition to our mall-sized tree, we have another special tree tradition. In late February 2003, when I was newly pregnant with Grace, David and I drove up to our family property in the mountains. He found a tree grower in Ashe County who let us buy two dozen seedlings. It was snowing that day when we set out those trees on our land. We dreamed of a time when we might be able to cut one of those Fraser firs for our family's Christmas. We wondered how old the baby we were expecting might be when the trees could be harvested. We daydreamed about the time when those seedlings, many less than a foot tall at the time, might hold cherished family ornaments.

Nearly a decade later, in December 2012, we were preparing to celebrate Christmas in our new home. We had built a room adjacent to the kitchen that we called the hearth room because it has a wood-burning fireplace. Unlike the two-story great room, that room is cozy and connected to the kitchen. On our annual Christmas tree trek, we visited our property and decided that those tiny saplings, most of which were taller than me by then, were ready. The kids, then ages nine and six, chose a tree from our very own "lot." They helped David saw it down and load it onto the roof of the car. Keep in mind that neither of us knew what to do with those trees other than fertilize them a few times over the decade. We had not trimmed or shaped them. When we got that scraggly, lopsided tree up in its stand, we all declared it perfect. We decorated it with a mix of white lights pushed in toward the center and strands of multicolored lights woven along each branch. The tree was so sparse that hiding the cords was impossible, but none of us minded. We had purchased brightly colored ornaments in nontraditional shapes reminiscent of Dr. Seuss.

Every year since, we have chosen our hearth room tree from those seedlings that David and I planted with love and hope as newlyweds. Since then, we have planted more trees, with the children's help. We wondered aloud what our tradition might be when those new seedlings were ready to be harvested. Would we be waiting for them to come home from college? Would our grandchildren get to choose from that lot? We intend to keep planting seedlings every three to five years so that future generations may enjoy similar traditions of their own.

November is indeed our month in which to give thanks. David and I are thankful for each other and for falling in love with one another's hearts; we are thankful for my mother and all that she means to us; and we are thankful for nonfood traditions that sustain and connect us.

Cinnamon Pecan Muffins

makes
12 muffins
(1 per serving)

It happens every year: the shopping and prepping and cooking consume three or four days leading up to the Thanksgiving meal. Each of those days, I find myself working in the kitchen early in the morning and late at night to prepare. Inevitably, family members wander into the kitchen, often at different times, and ask, "Hey Mom, what can I eat?" Sometimes my response is just a guttural growl. David has learned to grab the car keys and ask, "Do you want me to pick up something for you, too?" There I am dirtying every dish in the house, and my family is eating takeout because I'm too busy to make a meal for them. These muffins, made ahead of time, make a great meal that the family can grab and get out of your way so that you can finish the cooking marathon known as Thanksgiving. They are also delicious on school mornings as the weather turns cooler. I love to warm them up, slather them with butter or a bit of softened cream cheese, and enjoy with coffee.

⅓ cup blanched almond flour

⅓ cup whey protein isolate

⅓ cup oat fiber, or 2 tablespoons coconut flour

2 teaspoons ground cinnamon

1 teaspoon baking powder

¼ teaspoon salt

½ cup (1 stick) unsalted butter, cold

¾ cup granulated sweetener

4 ounces cream cheese (½ cup), cold

3 large eggs

1 tablespoon sour cream

2 teaspoons vanilla extract

1 teaspoon maple extract

½ cup chopped pecans, toasted

Preheat the oven to 350°F. Line a standard-size 12-well muffin pan with parchment paper liners.

In a large bowl, whisk together the almond flour, protein isolate, oat fiber, cinnamon, baking powder, and salt; set aside.

In a separate bowl, using a hand mixer or stand mixer, cream the butter and sweetener. When the butter has lightened in color, add the cream cheese and blend until everything is smooth and well incorporated. Add the eggs one at a time, mixing well after each addition. Add the sour cream and extracts.

When the wet ingredients are well blended, stir the dry ingredients into the wet ingredients by hand. Add the pecans and stir lightly to combine.

Divide the batter evenly among the wells of the prepared muffin pan, filling each well about two-thirds full. Bake for 24 to 28 minutes, until lightly browned and just firm to the touch. Let cool for 5 to 10 minutes before serving.

Store leftovers in the refrigerator for up to 5 days.

CALORIES: 200 | FAT: 20.8g | PROTEIN: 6.9g | CARBS: 2.8g | FIBER: 1.5g | ERYTHRITOL: 12g | OAT FIBER: 5g

Cherry Yum-Yum

makes
9 servings

This is the ketogenic version that took on the full-sugared, high-carb traditional Cherry Yum-Yum one Thanksgiving and won! I use hazelnut flour in the crust; it not only has a lower carb count than almond flour, but it also gives the crust a nice flavor and texture because it's slightly coarser. I also use just enough cherries and cherry extract to make the fruit sauce taste like cherries while stretching it with cranberries, which are lower in carbs. You could lower the carb count even more by using all blueberries or raspberries if you prefer. Both are equally yum-yum!

FRUIT FILLING:

2 ounces fresh cranberries

2 ounces pitted and chopped fresh Bing cherries

½ cup cold water, divided

1 teaspoon unflavored gelatin

2 teaspoons cherry extract

½ teaspoon vanilla extract

⅓ cup powdered sweetener

Liquid sweetener, to taste

CRUST:

½ cup hazelnut flour

¼ cup plus 1 tablespoon oat fiber

¼ cup granulated sweetener

¼ cup (½ stick) unsalted butter, softened

½ teaspoon vanilla extract

¼ teaspoon ground cinnamon (optional)

4 drops liquid sweetener

CREAM LAYER:

1 cup heavy cream

1 (8-ounce) package cream cheese (1 cup), softened

⅓ cup powdered sweetener

1½ teaspoons cherry extract

½ teaspoon vanilla extract

8 drops liquid sweetener (or to taste)

Make the filling: In a small saucepan over low heat, combine the cranberries, cherries, and 6 tablespoons of water.

Meanwhile, in a small bowl, mix the remaining 2 tablespoons of water with the gelatin. Stir to combine and set aside.

When the cranberries are soft and have popped, add the extracts and sweeteners to the fruit mixture. Remove from the heat and stir in the gelatin until thoroughly combined. Set aside to cool.

While the filling is cooling, make the crust: Combine all the crust ingredients in a food processor and pulse to combine. The mixture will resemble coarse sand. Sprinkle all but 2 tablespoons of the crust mixture into a 9-inch round glass baking dish, press to flatten, and set aside.

Make the cream layer: In a large bowl, using a hand mixer or stand mixer, whip the heavy cream until it begins to thicken. Add the cream cheese and whip until smooth and thick. Beat in the remaining ingredients and refrigerate the cream mixture until ready to assemble.

To assemble, pour half of the cream mixture over the prepared crust. Pour the cooled fruit mixture on top of the cream mixture. Top with the remainder of the cream mixture and sprinkle with the reserved crust mixture. Place in the refrigerator to chill for at least 4 hours before serving.

Butter Pecan Ice Cream

makes
6 servings

Butter pecan has always been one of my favorite ice cream flavors, mostly because it is also my mom's favorite flavor. I had to share this recipe in November, which is her birthday month. It was fun to make this version and even more fun to watch her enjoy it. This ice cream is buttery with crunchy bits of roasted pecans in every bite. The dark rum adds a deeper flavor but can be omitted if you prefer.

½ **cup finely chopped raw pecans**

2 **tablespoons unsalted butter**

¾ **teaspoon salt, divided**

2 **tablespoons brown sugar substitute**

1¾ **cups heavy cream**

¾ **cup unsweetened almond milk**

5 **large egg yolks**

¾ **cup powdered sweetener (see Tip)**

2 **teaspoons vanilla extract**

1 **teaspoon maple extract**

1 **teaspoon dark rum (optional)**

SPECIAL EQUIPMENT:

Ice cream maker

tip

The type of sweetener used makes a huge difference in the texture of the ice cream. For the best texture, use allulose or xylitol; remember that each sweetener has different characteristics (see pages 19 and 20). Use the sweetener that you prefer and that does not impact your blood glucose.

In a small skillet over low heat, combine the pecans, butter, and ¼ teaspoon of the salt. Stir constantly until the pecans are lightly browned and toasted; do not allow them to burn. Remove the pecans from the pan and toss them with the brown sugar substitute until they are lightly coated. Set aside to cool.

Pour the browned butter in the skillet into a small bowl, avoiding the solids that have fallen to the bottom of the pan; the browned butter should easily pour from the pan while the solids remain. Set aside.

In a heavy saucepan over low heat, combine the heavy cream and almond milk, stirring with a whisk. Add the egg yolks and continue whisking until just warmed. Add the powdered sweetener and whisk until completely dissolved. Continue heating, whisking constantly, until the custard thickens, about 10 minutes. When the custard coats the back of a wooden spoon or reaches 140°F on a candy thermometer, remove from the heat. Do not allow it to warm to over 140°F or the eggs will begin to cook.

Stir in the extracts, the remaining ½ teaspoon of salt, and the rum, if using. Transfer the mixture to a bowl and place in the refrigerator to cool.

When cool, freeze the ice cream mixture in an ice cream maker following the manufacturer's directions. Add the browned pecans and butter to the ice cream while it is churning and after it has begun to freeze, but while the ice cream is still slightly softer than soft serve. Continue churning until it reaches your desired consistency.

Store leftovers in the freezer. When frozen, this ice cream will harden to a solid state. Allow to thaw at room temperature for about 10 minutes before enjoying.

CALORIES: 277 | FAT: 26.6g | PROTEIN: 5.8g | CARBS: 3.1g | FIBER: 1.2g | ERYTHRITOL: 18g

Mint Julep

makes
1 serving

My family members were teetotalers on both sides, so our table wine at every meal, including Thanksgiving, was sweet tea. I do wonder sometimes if some of those gatherings might have been just a bit more enjoyable had the adults enjoyed a Mint Julep or two. While we don't serve cocktails at our Thanksgiving meals, if we did, I'd serve this drink after dinner.

2 ounces bourbon

1 teaspoon granulated sweetener

6 fresh mint leaves

2 tablespoons water

1 cup crushed ice

Fresh mint sprig, for garnish

Place the bourbon, sweetener, and mint in a chilled highball glass or silver julep cup. Use a muddler or the handle of a wooden spoon to bruise the mint. Add the water and crushed ice. Stir before serving. Garnish with a sprig of mint.

CALORIES: 128 | FAT: 0g | PROTEIN: 0g | CARBS: 0g | FIBER: 6g

Thanksgiving

Sausage Stuffing

makes
12 servings

Yes, the stuffing used to be my favorite, too. It covered half my plate, and I strategically placed slices of turkey over the top to hide just how much stuffing I'd taken. While I'm sure no one ever has made a stuffing as wonderful or flavorful as your dear grandmother's, I'm gonna hand you some tough love: If you want to be healthy, if you want to stay on plan, if you want to outrun the crowd at the Black Friday doorbuster events, back away from your grandmother's stuffing. Give her a kiss on the cheek and explain that you made this one with sausage and you cannot wait to hear what she thinks of it!

You make this recipe by baking the bread several days in advance, cubing or crumbling it, and letting it dry out. You can also substitute an equal amount of crumbled Kristie's Keto Cornbread (page 42).

1 pound mild breakfast sausage

1 cup chopped button mushrooms

½ cup finely chopped celery

⅓ cup finely chopped onions

1 clove garlic, minced

1 tablespoon unsalted butter, softened

1 teaspoon dried sage

¼ teaspoon salt

⅛ teaspoon ground black pepper

2 large eggs

½ cup chicken bone broth

¼ cup heavy cream

4 cups Soul Bread Crumbs (page 342)

Preheat the oven to 350°F. Butter a 9 by 13-inch baking dish.

Brown the sausage in a large skillet. When the sausage is browned, add the mushrooms, celery, onions, and garlic. As it all browns, stir in the butter, sage, salt, and pepper. Set aside to cool.

In a separate bowl, mix together the eggs, chicken broth, and heavy cream. Toss together the cooled sausage mixture, the egg mixture, and the bread crumbs. Spread in the prepared baking dish and bake for 25 to 30 minutes, until browned.

CALORIES: 177 | FAT: 10.3g | PROTEIN: 7.8g | CARBS: 1.8g | FIBER: 0.3g | OAT FIBER: 7.6g

Green Bean Casserole

makes
6 servings

Yes, you can still have your green bean casserole. Put away the canned fake onions, but don't tell granny. Just set this dish right down between the turkey and the low-carb stuffing and give thanks. If you're feeding a crowd, you'd better double the recipe if you want a scoop for your own plate.

10 slices bacon, chopped

4 ounces button mushrooms, chopped

⅓ cup minced onions

1 clove garlic, minced

1½ pounds green beans, trimmed if fresh or thawed and squeezed with paper towel if frozen

⅓ cup beef, chicken, or vegetable broth

½ cup heavy cream

3 ounces cream cheese (¼ cup plus 2 tablespoons), softened

¼ cup sour cream

¼ teaspoon salt

TOPPING:

½ cup pork dust (ground pork rinds)

1 ounce Parmesan cheese, grated (about ⅓ cup)

1 tablespoon onion powder

2 tablespoons unsalted butter, softened

Preheat the oven to 350°F.

In a medium skillet over medium-high heat, cook the bacon. When the bacon just begins to brown, add the mushrooms, onions, and garlic. Cook until the bacon is crisp and the onions are just browned, 12 to 15 minutes.

Toss the green beans into the pan with the bacon and vegetables. Stir to coat with the bacon fat and sauté until the beans are a bright, shiny green, 5 to 7 minutes.

Add the broth, reduce the heat, and simmer for 4 to 6 minutes, until the green beans are tender.

Use a slotted spoon to remove the green bean mixture from the pan and place in a 9-inch square baking dish. Set aside.

Add the heavy cream and cream cheese to the skillet and reduce the heat to low. As the cream cheese melts, use a wooden spoon to scrape up the pan drippings and stir the cream. Simmer over low heat for 3 to 5 minutes, until thickened. Remove from the heat and stir in the sour cream and salt to make a thick gravy. Pour the gravy over the green bean mixture in the baking dish.

Make the topping: In a separate bowl, use a fork or spatula to mix together the pork dust, Parmesan cheese, onion powder, and butter until it forms coarse crumbs. Sprinkle the topping mixture over the green beans.

Bake the casserole for 25 to 35 minutes, until the topping is lightly browned and the juices have thickened. Let cool for at least 10 minutes before serving.

CALORIES: 230 | FAT: 20.2g | PROTEIN: 12.4g | CARBS: 7.1g | FIBER: 3g

Harvest Squash Casserole

makes
8 servings

My grandmother made this recipe with square cheese slices, Duke's mayonnaise, cream of something soup, and crushed saltine crackers. It was one of my absolute favorites, especially when she let that cheese get browned on top. With apologies to my grandmother, my healthier version truly does taste better. I know what some of you are thinking: "I hate pork rinds, and I would never eat them." My picky husband used to say that, too. Just try it. This is the best squash casserole you will ever say the blessing over. Amen!

⅓ cup water

3 tablespoons unsalted butter

4 cups sliced yellow squash

⅓ cup chopped onions

½ cup mayonnaise

½ cup sour cream

¼ teaspoon ground black pepper

8 ounces cheddar cheese, shredded (about 1 cup), divided

¾ cup pork dust (ground pork rinds)

Sliced green onions, for garnish (optional)

Preheat the oven to 350°F.

In a 2½-quart saucepan over medium heat, heat the water and butter. Add the squash and onions and sauté until the squash is tender and the water has evaporated. Let cool.

Add the mayonnaise, sour cream, and pepper; mix to combine. Stir in 6 ounces of the shredded cheese and the pork dust. When thoroughly combined, pour the mixture into a 9 by 13-inch baking dish.

Sprinkle the remaining 2 ounces of shredded cheese over the top of the casserole. Bake until browned and bubbly, about 25 minutes. Let sit for 10 to 15 minutes before serving.

Garnish with sliced green onions, if desired.

CALORIES: 326 | FAT: 22.2g | PROTEIN: 7.3g | CARBS: 3.8g | FIBER: 0.8g

Keto-Friendly Cranberry Sauce

makes
6 servings

If you're missing traditional cranberry sauce, this version will definitely fill the void. I take it to every Thanksgiving meal, and someone usually asks for the recipe or compliments the orange flavor. You can turn this into an easy dessert by mixing the finished cranberry sauce with 4 ounces of cream cheese and 2 cups of freshly whipped cream.

¼ teaspoon unflavored gelatin

¼ cup cold water

⅔ cup water

1 cup fresh cranberries

1 tablespoon unsalted butter, softened

¼ cup granulated sweetener, or more to taste

¼ teaspoon vanilla extract

⅛ teaspoon orange extract, or 1 drop food-grade orange oil

⅛ teaspoon salt

In a small bowl, mix the gelatin with ¼ cup of cold water. Stir until well dissolved; set aside.

Place the ⅔ cup of water and the cranberries in a small saucepan over medium heat. After the berries soften and begin to pop, add the butter and sweetener and mix well.

When the sweetener is dissolved and the mixture has thickened, add the gelatin and stir until dissolved. Mix in the extracts and salt. Taste for sweetness, adding more sweetener if needed.

Place in the refrigerator to chill for an hour before serving. If the cranberry sauce becomes too thick after cooling, stir in 2 tablespoons of water and warm over low heat.

CALORIES: 24 | FAT: 1.4g | PROTEIN: 1.3g | CARBS: 1.8g | FIBER: 0.6g | ERYTHRITOL: 6g

Perfect Keto Pecan Pie

makes
8 servings

More goo or more pecans? Most folks have a firm preference as to which makes a pecan pie "best." Unfortunately, a smooth, silky goo is hard to get when you're using keto-friendly sweeteners. Fortunately, my family prefers a pie full of pecans. This pie reminds me of the ones I enjoyed growing up. It was the one kind of pie my mother always made for the holidays, and the pecans nearly always came from the hardy trees that grew around my grandmother's home. Part of our Thanksgiving tradition was to go outside after the meal and pick up fallen pecans. The adults urged the children to compete to see who could fill their paper bags the fastest. I would crawl around on my hands and knees instead of standing and stooping, and sometimes my knee would land right on top of a whole pecan. That hurt! Picking up pecans was fun, though, because we talked as we worked, and I got to eavesdrop on the adults' conversations. I also knew what my mama was going to make with those pecans, and that made the work even more rewarding.

CRUST:

1½ cups blanched almond flour

¼ cup oat fiber, or 2 tablespoons coconut flour

3 tablespoons powdered sweetener

½ teaspoon salt

5 tablespoons unsalted butter, cold

1 large egg white

1 teaspoon water

1 teaspoon vanilla extract

FILLING:

¾ cup (1½ sticks) unsalted butter

¼ cup water

¾ cup powdered sweetener

½ cup brown sugar substitute or granulated sweetener mixed with ½ teaspoon maple extract

Preheat the oven to 350°F. Grease a 9-inch pie plate.

Make the crust: Place the almond flour, oat fiber, sweetener, salt, and butter in a food processor and pulse until the mixture has the texture of coarse crumbs. Add the egg white, water, and vanilla extract and process until a thick dough forms.

Press the dough into the bottom and up the sides of the prepared pie plate. You may need to refrigerate the dough for 30 to 45 minutes to make it easier to shape the edges of the crust.

Par-bake the crust for 7 to 9 minutes, until just golden, then set aside to cool.

While the crust is cooling, make the filling: Melt the butter in a 2-quart saucepan over low heat. Whisk in the water, sweeteners, salt, cinnamon, and extracts until well blended. When the mixture has thickened, remove from the heat and let cool slightly.

Add the beaten eggs to the filling mixture and mix well. Stir in the pecans. Pour the filling into the cooled crust.

Bake the pie for 35 to 40 minutes, until softly set. After 15 minutes, cover the pie loosely with foil to keep the top from browning too much. Do not overbake. Let cool for at least 30 minutes before serving. The pie will set up further as it cools.

CALORIES: 613 | FAT: 62.1g | PROTEIN: 10.9g | CARBS: 9.5g | FIBER: 6g | ERYTHRITOL: 28.9g | OAT FIBER: 5.6g

1½ teaspoons salt

¼ teaspoon ground cinnamon

1 tablespoon vanilla extract

2 teaspoons maple extract

2 large eggs, beaten

2½ cups raw pecan halves

note —————————————

The filling may become grainy after the pie is refrigerated because of the erythritol. Warming the pie will reduce the graininess. Powdering the granulated sweetener before adding it to the filling also may help.

Pumpkin Pie Cheesecake

makes
16 servings

We have had great family debates about this recipe. Should the cheesecake be on the bottom with a layer of pumpkin on top, or should it be blended like a creamy pumpkin pie? I prefer it blended because the pumpkin flavor is more pronounced in each bite. I don't add a lot of spices to this pumpkin pie filling because we like the buttery taste of pumpkin with just a bit of cinnamon and pumpkin pie spice sprinkled in. If you like cloves and nutmeg, you can easily add more spices. Don't be tempted to skip the cheesecake filling and double the pumpkin pie filling, though. The cheesecake part is much lower in carbs than the pumpkin filling, so if you skip the cheesecake, you will end up with a much higher-carb dessert.

CRUST:

1 cup raw pecan halves

¼ cup blanched almond flour or hazelnut flour

2 tablespoons oat fiber, or 1 tablespoon coconut flour

¼ cup granulated sweetener

½ teaspoon ground cinnamon

½ teaspoon pumpkin pie spice (optional)

½ teaspoon vanilla extract

4 or 5 drops liquid sweetener, to taste

¼ cup (½ stick) unsalted butter, melted

CHEESECAKE FILLING:

2 (8-ounce) packages cream cheese, softened

¼ cup heavy cream

2 large eggs

⅓ cup granulated sweetener

5 to 7 drops liquid sweetener, to taste

1 teaspoon vanilla extract

½ teaspoon lemon juice

Preheat the oven to 350°F.

Make the crust: Place all the crust ingredients in a food processor and pulse until they have the texture of coarse crumbs. Press into a 9-inch springform pan. Set aside.

Make the cheesecake filling: In a large bowl, mix together the cream cheese, heavy cream, eggs, and sweeteners until creamy and well blended. Stir in the vanilla extract and lemon juice. Pour the cheesecake filling on top of the crust and refrigerate while you make the pumpkin pie filling.

Make the pumpkin pie filling: In a large bowl, mix together the pumpkin, heavy cream, melted butter, and eggs until smooth. Add the sweeteners, baking powder, cinnamon, and salt and mix well. Stir in the vanilla extract. Pour the pumpkin mixture on top of the cheesecake filling.

Bake the cheesecake for 1 hour 20 minutes to 1 hour 30 minutes; after 20 to 30 minutes, cover it loosely with foil to prevent it from browning too much. The cheesecake is fully baked when it is slightly browned and just set. Turn off the oven, leave the oven door ajar, and let the cheesecake cool in the oven for at least 1 hour.

Remove from the oven and let cool completely. Refrigerate for at least 6 hours, preferably overnight, before serving.

PUMPKIN PIE FILLING:

1 (15-ounce) can pumpkin puree (not pumpkin pie filling)

¾ cup heavy cream

½ cup (1 stick) unsalted butter, melted but not hot

2 large eggs, beaten

⅓ cup granulated sweetener

8 drops liquid sweetener

1 teaspoon baking powder

1 teaspoon ground cinnamon

½ teaspoon salt

2 teaspoons vanilla extract

variation ———————————————

Instead of layering the pumpkin pie filling on top of the cheesecake filling, you can blend them together, then pour the combined filling on top of the crust and bake as instructed.

Italian Cream Cake

makes
16 servings

This delicious cake is moist and tender, and the pecans and coconut flakes add a texture that makes you want another bite, and then another. It's also an eye-catcher on a buffet with the toasted pecans and toasted coconut arranged on top of the white icing. I appreciate that it tastes better when made at least a day ahead of time. If you cover the cake well and refrigerate it, the slices will be perfectly moist even a day or so after baking.

CAKE:

⅔ cup coconut flour

½ cup oat fiber

¼ cup whey protein isolate

2 teaspoons baking powder

½ teaspoon salt

1 cup (2 sticks) unsalted butter, softened

1 cup granulated sweetener

8 large eggs

1 cup heavy cream

2 teaspoons vanilla extract

½ teaspoon coconut extract

5 or 6 drops liquid sweetener, to taste

⅔ cup chopped raw pecans

⅔ cup unsweetened coconut flakes

4 large egg whites

ICING:

2 (8-ounce) packages cream cheese, softened

1 cup (2 sticks) unsalted butter, softened

⅔ cup powdered sweetener

3 drops liquid sweetener

½ teaspoon coconut extract

Preheat the oven to 350°F. Liberally grease two 8-inch round cake pans and line the pans with parchment paper.

Make the cake: In a large bowl, whisk together the coconut flour, oat fiber, protein isolate, baking powder, and salt; set aside.

In a separate large bowl, use a hand mixer or stand mixer to whip the butter and granulated sweetener. Add the whole eggs one at a time, beating well after each addition. Stir in the heavy cream and extracts by hand. Add the dry ingredients and mix by hand until just incorporated. Add the liquid sweetener, pecans, and coconut and stir until thoroughly combined.

In a third bowl, use the mixer to whip the egg whites until stiff peaks form. Fold the whipped whites into the batter, being careful to not overmix.

Divide the batter evenly between the prepared cake pans. Bake for 20 to 25 minutes, until a toothpick inserted in the middle of a cake comes out clean. Let the layers rest for about 10 minutes before removing from the pans to cooling racks to cool completely.

While the cakes are cooling, make the icing: Use the hand mixer or stand mixer to whip the cream cheese and butter until fluffy. Beat in the sweeteners and extracts. Stir in the pecans by hand.

To assemble, slice each cake round in half horizontally. Place one layer on a cake plate and spread about ⅓ cup of the icing on top. Add another layer of cake followed by a layer of icing until the four layers of cake are assembled. Cover the top and sides of the assembled cake with the remaining icing. Sprinkle toasted

CALORIES: 463 | FAT: 45.5g | PROTEIN: 10g | CARBS: 7.3g | FIBER: 4.6g | ERYTHRITOL: 18g | OAT FIBER: 5.7g

¼ teaspoon maple extract

¼ teaspoon vanilla extract

¼ cup finely chopped toasted pecans

FOR GARNISH:

Toasted unsweetened coconut flakes

Toasted pecans

coconut and toasted pecans over the top of the cake. Cover and refrigerate for at least 6 hours or overnight before serving. If wrapped well, the cake will keep in the refrigerator for up to 5 days.

Leftover Turkey Pot Pie

makes
12 servings

Anyone can cook a turkey, but figuring out what to do with the leftovers can be a real challenge. I find myself looking for creative ways to use leftover turkey that seem different enough from the Thanksgiving meal that my family doesn't know they are eating another round. Leftover Turkey Pot Pie is a perfect solution. If your family decorates for the holidays immediately after Thanksgiving, this is also a great one-pot dish to enjoy after decking the halls. Not only is it warm and filling, but it makes the house smell fantastic. Jonathan, my die-hard carbivore, actually prefers this pot pie to commercial or restaurant versions, which makes this mama super happy!

¼ cup (½ stick) unsalted butter

1 cup chopped zucchini

¾ cup chopped cauliflower

½ cup chopped broccoli stems

½ cup sliced button mushrooms

⅓ cup chopped carrots

⅓ cup chopped onions

1 (14½-ounce) can green beans, drained, or 3 ounces fresh green beans, trimmed and snapped

2 stalks celery, chopped

2 cups chicken bone broth

4 ounces cream cheese (½ cup), softened

½ cup heavy cream

½ teaspoon dried thyme

½ teaspoon salt

¼ teaspoon poultry seasoning

¼ teaspoon ground black pepper

4 cups chopped cooked turkey

½ batch Belle's Biscuits (recipe opposite), unbaked

Preheat the oven to 375°F.

Melt the butter in a 12-inch ovenproof skillet over medium heat. Add the vegetables and sauté until just tender, 10 to 12 minutes.

Add the chicken broth and simmer for about 10 minutes, until the broth is reduced by half.

Add the cream cheese and heavy cream and stir until the cream cheese is melted. Simmer until the sauce is thickened, 5 to 7 minutes.

Add the thyme, salt, poultry seasoning, and pepper and mix well. Add the turkey and mix into the vegetables and sauce.

Drop the biscuit dough in small scoops on top of the pot pie filling in the skillet, covering the entire pan. Bake for 30 to 35 minutes, until the biscuits are browned on top and not doughy underneath. Let cool for 15 to 20 minutes before serving.

CALORIES: 315 | FAT: 23g | PROTEIN: 18.3g | CARBS: 6.8g | FIBER: 1.6g | OAT FIBER: 2.8g

Belle's Biscuits

makes
6 biscuits, or enough dough
for 2 batches of pot pie

6 large egg whites

1½ cups fine blanched almond flour

3 tablespoons oat fiber, or 1½ tablespoons coconut flour

1½ teaspoons baking powder

1 teaspoon salt

1½ ounces mozzarella cheese, shredded (about ⅓ cup)

5 tablespoons unsalted butter, softened

If baking the biscuits separately instead of using them for pot pie, preheat the oven to 350°F and grease a standard-size 6-well muffin pan.

Use a hand mixer or stand mixer to beat the egg whites until frothy but not stiff. Add the almond flour, oat fiber, baking powder, salt, and mozzarella cheese; mix well. Add the butter and beat until well blended.

To bake the biscuits, divide the batter evenly among the wells of the prepared muffin pan, filling each well three-quarters full. Bake for 12 to 15 minutes, until golden brown and firm on top. Let cool for at least 10 minutes before serving. Refrigerate leftovers for up to a week.

12

december

Because we begin decorating for Christmas in late November, DECEMBER is spent in a flurry of shopping, wrapping, cooking, and celebrating. With multiple extended-family celebrations, I try to stay organized with lists. As much as I hate to admit it, my favorite way to organize for Christmas is by using spreadsheets. I have one file for gifts, another for foods I will make (with a tab for each meal), and a third one for groceries. Using a cloud service enables me to access those files wherever I go, which comes in handy when I'm out and have forgotten what I need. Admittedly, I've become glassy-eyed more than once over a fantastic sale (75 percent off!) on an item that neither I nor anyone on my list actually needs. We try to stay organized because our extended families live at least two hours away in opposite directions. We often celebrate three different times with three different sets of family, which has us traveling at least four hours per day over the course of a long weekend. We love that time with extended family, but scheduling the food, gifts, and travel takes some effort.

I do the bulk of my shopping online, although I often look for special gifts at locally owned stores, and I love shopping with family and friends. David and I often take a vacation day during the week to finish buying gifts. My mom and I also try to set aside a weekday to shop, even when my list is mostly checked off. We covet the chance to spend that time together as we enjoy the Christmas decorations and share the excitement of the season. It takes us at least two days to shop and wrap. My mother is an expert gift-wrapper. Not only does she take the job seriously, but she instructs me to leave the wrapping to her. My job is to have the gifts purchased and labeled so that she can wrap until her heart is content. I also have the job of coordinating wrapping paper for our three Christmas trees.

While I used to be ashamed to admit it, I will confess that I buy paper to wrap gifts so that the colors and style of the wrapping paper match the style of the tree. The whimsical tree in the hearth room gets brightly colored wrapping paper that appeals to children. All the children who get gifts from us find their presents under the hearth room tree. Because David has a large family, and because we always travel to his parents' house, the gifts for his family gatherings go under the tree in the dining room. We tend to have long drives on subsequent days, so separating the gifts saves us a little time; we can simply load the car without having to look at each tag. The huge tree in the great room is where we put the gifts for each other on the right and the gifts for my extended family on the left, again so that we can load up the car quickly in the bustle of the holidays. The center is reserved for people who will be celebrating Christmas at our house. That's not to say that chaos doesn't ensue, especially when a well-meaning husband, who can't seem to understand the color coordination, wraps a gift in the "wrong" paper. Since I can't have chartreuse and lavender snowmen with puppies under the formal dining room tree, we just have to make a mental note of the exception and move forward. By Christmas morning, we've given up trying to bring order to anything and have learned to savor the craziness.

When we gather with friends and family, I look forward to sharing food with them just as I did before we began eating keto, including my low-carb versions of traditional favorites such as **Cheese Straws** and **Grandmother's Christmas Coconut Cream Cake.** It's especially gratifying when they enjoy a recipe that I've created or an old favorite that I've tweaked to make it healthier, like my **Breakfast Strata.** Even though I still do a lot of cooking throughout the holidays, I've learned to focus more on the people and much less on the food. Instead of hovering around the buffet, I find myself lingering longer over conversations with friends and family.

David and I have made a point to focus on nonfood traditions related to the holidays. For example, we usually pick two different evenings to drive around and look at Christmas lights. We cruise through local neighborhoods awarding a thumbs-up to the houses whose decorations we admire most. As we go, we listen to Christmas music, often singing along off-key. We also like to attend Christmas Eve candlelight services when our travel schedule allows. When the children were little, I stomped my mama foot and announced that regardless of anyone's schedule, our family of four was going to spend Christmas morning at our house. Anyone was welcome to join us, but I refused to leave my house before noon. Even though it felt a bit selfish at the time, it was unpleasant to make the children leave their Santa gifts behind and stick them in the car for several hours. In addition, because I always cook for family celebrations, I didn't want to miss Christmas morning with the children because I was in the kitchen finishing up the **Baked Macaroni and Cheese with Crab Meat** or the **Sausage Balls.** Thankfully, David agreed, so Christmas morning has become a special time for us, with nowhere to hurry off to when we really just want more time in our PJs by the Christmas tree. For that reason, I try to make dishes for Christmas morning that can be prepped ahead of time, like **French Toast Casserole.** I want to provide food that my family enjoys, but more importantly I want to be present for them among the presents.

Another tradition that we enjoy is buying puzzles for the grandparents. When the extended family gathers, we eat, unwrap gifts, and then sit around visiting. We've found that when we give the grandparents puzzles, more of the family is likely to sit around the table. Throughout the day, people will come and go, talking and working toward finding that one missing piece. Over the years, they've learned to set up the puzzle in a space that is out of the way, just in case it isn't finished until well into the new year. In that case, folks continue to take turns working on the puzzle as they come and go.

David and I recognize that many of the memories we make each year have nothing to do with the perfectly plated delicacies on our holiday menus. Even though we love making classic Christmas cookies like **Gingerbread Cookies, Shortbread Cookies,** and **No-Bake Chocolate Cow Patty Cookies,** we cherish the doing—making our Christmas tree trek, decking the halls, coordinating the wrapping paper, and laughing over the insanity of our overscheduled celebrations. We often hold hands in the car during the harried hither and yon, reminding us both that it's the journey that matters most.

Sparkling Orange Cranberry Muffins

makes
12 muffins
(1 per serving)

Don't skip using the sparkling water in these muffins; it adds a fantastic texture and flavor. These muffins are perfect for Christmas morning or any holiday brunch. You can also bake them as mini-muffins for a buffet.

⅓ cup blanched almond flour

⅓ cup whey protein isolate

⅓ cup oat fiber, or 2 tablespoons coconut flour

1 teaspoon baking powder

¼ teaspoon salt

½ cup (1 stick) unsalted butter, cold

¾ cup granulated sweetener

4 ounces cream cheese (½ cup), cold

3 large eggs

⅓ cup orange-flavored sparkling water

2 teaspoons vanilla extract

1 teaspoon orange extract

⅓ cup fresh cranberries

Preheat the oven to 350°F. Line a standard-size 12-well muffin pan with parchment paper liners.

In a large bowl, whisk together the almond flour, protein isolate, oat fiber, baking powder, and salt until well combined; set aside.

In a separate bowl, using a hand mixer or stand mixer, cream the butter and sweetener. When the butter has lightened in color, mix in the cream cheese and blend until everything is smooth and well incorporated. Add the eggs one at a time, mixing well after each addition. Mix in the sparkling water and extracts.

When the wet ingredients are well blended, stir in the dry ingredients by hand. Gently stir in the cranberries.

Divide the batter evenly among the wells of the prepared muffin pan, filling each well about two-thirds full. Bake for 20 to 25 minutes, until lightly browned and just firm to the touch. Let cool for 5 to 10 minutes before serving.

Store leftovers in an airtight container in the refrigerator for up to a week.

tip

This batter can be baked in a 9 by 5-inch loaf pan and served as a sweet bread along with the butter from the Hot Buttered Rum recipe (page 254). YUM!

CALORIES: 152 | FAT: 13.8g | PROTEIN: 5.6g | CARBS: 1.7g | FIBER: 0.5g | ERYTHRITOL: 9g | OAT FIBER: 5g

Mocha Brownie Torte

makes
16 servings

This is a special birthday dessert for dear friends of mine, Gwen and Sean McCarthy. Gwen and I met in first grade. She knows things about me that even I don't know. Although Sean went to high school with us, they didn't start dating until after we all finished college. Around that same time, we got together with a few others for an impromptu dinner. Always in a hurry, I grabbed a packaged brownie mix, a tub of Cool Whip, instant coffee, and cocoa powder and made a tiered mocha brownie torte. It looked impressive for the little bit of time I spent on it. We all were excited to enjoy a piece after dinner. Suddenly, Sean turned to me with the most horrific look on his face. I could hear crunching as he chewed. We figured out that the instant coffee granules had not been smoothly incorporated into the whipped topping. Uh-oh! Laughter and good-natured ribbing ensued and never ebbed. One mention of mocha brownie torte and we all giggle as if it were yesterday. Gwen and Sean have been married for 25 years now! I'm proud to include this keto version in honor of Sean's birthday month. Be sure to stir in those coffee granules, y'all!

BROWNIE:

1½ cups blanched almond flour

½ cup oat fiber

⅓ cup unsweetened cocoa powder

1½ teaspoons baking powder

½ teaspoon salt

1 teaspoon instant coffee granules or espresso powder

½ cup (1 stick) unsalted butter, softened

2 ounces cream cheese (¼ cup), softened

1 cup granulated sweetener

5 large eggs

2 teaspoons vanilla extract

8 drops liquid sweetener

3 ounces unsweetened baking chocolate, chopped

¼ cup heavy cream

Preheat the oven to 350°F. Grease two 8-inch round cake pans and line the pans with parchment paper.

Make the brownie: In a large bowl, whisk together the almond flour, oat fiber, cocoa powder, baking powder, salt, and coffee until they are well mixed. Set aside.

In a separate bowl, use a hand mixer or stand mixer to cream the butter, cream cheese, and granulated sweetener. When the mixture is creamy, add the eggs one at a time, beating well after each addition. Mix in the vanilla extract and liquid sweetener and set aside.

In a small microwave-safe bowl, melt the chocolate in the microwave until smooth, stirring frequently so that it doesn't burn. (You can also melt the chocolate on the stovetop over low heat.) When melted, pour the chocolate into the butter mixture. Add the dry ingredients and mix well by hand, then stir in the heavy cream.

Divide the batter evenly between the prepared pans and smooth the tops. Bake for 18 to 22 minutes, until just set. Do not overbake. Let the brownie cool in the pans for 15 to 20 minutes before removing to a cooling rack to cool completely.

CALORIES: 235 | FAT: 22.8g | PROTEIN: 6g | CARBS: 5.2g | FIBER: 2.6g | ERYTHRITOL: 16.5g

FILLING:

1 teaspoon instant coffee granules or espresso powder

1 tablespoon unsweetened cocoa powder

1 tablespoon warm water

1½ cups heavy cream

½ cup powdered sweetener

1 teaspoon vanilla extract

3 or 4 drops liquid sweetener, to taste

Make the filling: In a small bowl, dissolve the coffee and cocoa powder in the water. Set aside.

In a separate bowl, use the hand mixer or stand mixer to whip the heavy cream. Add the powdered sweetener and vanilla extract and beat until creamy and stiff peaks just begin to form. Add the coffee mixture and whip until incorporated and thick. Taste for sweetness. Add the liquid sweetener.

To assemble the torte, slice each brownie round in half horizontally. Place one layer on a cake plate or serving platter. Top with one-quarter of the filling. Alternate layers of brownie and filling. Use the remaining filling to top the last brownie round, leaving the sides of the torte uncovered. Place in the refrigerator to chill for at least 1 hour before serving. Store leftovers in the refrigerator for up to 5 days.

Gingerbread Ice Cream

makes
6 servings

Another Grace recipe was created when she quipped, "Let's make gingerbread ice cream for Christmas!" I'm not sure either of us had ever eaten it, but it sure sounded good. We spent some time talking about how the ice cream should taste. We agreed that the custard base needed the flavors of gingerbread, but it also needed cookie bits. As we set to work making the gingerbread cookies, we debated using raw cookie dough or crumbled cookies. Our indecision led us to try both, and we agreed that the baked cookie pieces were our preference because of the texture they added to the creamy ice cream. We have since made this frozen treat for two different family gatherings in addition to making a couple of batches for ourselves. I eventually learned to freeze extra cookies so that the ice cream could be made quickly without spending time to make the cookies first.

1½ cups heavy cream

1 cup unsweetened almond milk

6 large egg yolks

⅓ cup powdered sweetener (see Tip)

1 teaspoon vanilla extract

½ teaspoon maple extract

½ teaspoon ground cinnamon

¼ teaspoon ginger powder

¼ teaspoon ground cloves

¼ teaspoon salt

3 un-iced Gingerbread Cookies (page 330), crumbled

SPECIAL EQUIPMENT:

Ice cream maker

In a heavy saucepan over low heat, heat the heavy cream and almond milk, stirring with a whisk. Add the egg yolks and continue whisking until just warmed.

Add the sweetener and whisk until completely dissolved. Continue heating, whisking constantly, until the custard thickens, about 10 minutes. When the custard coats the back of a wooden spoon or reaches 140°F on a candy thermometer, remove the pan from the heat. Do not allow the mixture to warm to over 140°F or the eggs will begin to cook.

Stir the extracts, spices, and salt into the ice cream mixture. Transfer to a bowl and place in the refrigerator to cool.

When cool, churn the ice cream mixture in an ice cream maker following the manufacturer's directions. Add the cookies to the ice cream while it is churning and after it has begun to freeze, but while the ice cream is still soft. Continue churning until it reaches your desired consistency.

Store leftovers in the freezer. When frozen, this ice cream will harden to a solid state. Allow to thaw at room temperature for about 10 minutes before enjoying.

tip

The type of sweetener used makes a huge difference in the texture of the ice cream. For the best texture, use allulose or xylitol; remember that each sweetener has different characteristics (see pages 19 and 20). Use the sweetener that you prefer and that does not impact your blood glucose.

CALORIES: 219 | FAT: 11.2g | PROTEIN: 14.5g | CARBS: 3g | FIBER: 0.4g | ERYTHRITOL: 20.1g | OAT FIBER: 5.6g

White Christmas Mojito

makes
4 servings

Make up a pitcher of these festive mojitos for a little extra jolly at your holiday parties! Even without the rum, this makes a great holiday drink. The cream soda, black cherry, and lemon-lime flavors blend well with the mint. The heavy cream adds just enough creaminess to make this feel like a treat. When I make this mojito, I use Zevia sugar-free sodas sweetened with stevia. If you use a different brand, make sure it is truly sugar-free.

6 ounces white rum

¼ cup lime juice

½ cup fresh mint

8 ounces black cherry soda

8 ounces cream soda

8 ounces lemon-lime soda

1 cup heavy cream (or coconut milk for dairy-free)

FOR GARNISH:

4 lime slices

Handful of fresh cranberries

4 fresh mint sprigs

In a small bowl, mix together the rum and lime juice. Add the mint.

Use a muddler or the handle of a wooden spoon to muddle the mint in the rum and lime juice mixture; bruise the leaves, being careful not to shred them.

In a large pitcher or punch bowl, combine the sodas, heavy cream, and rum mixture. Stir and serve over ice. Garnish with a lime slice, a few cranberries, and a sprig of mint.

CALORIES: 205 | FAT: 0.9g | PROTEIN: 10.8g | CARBS: 3.1g | FIBER: 3g

Christmas Morning

Breakfast Strata · 310

French Toast Casserole · 312

Breakfast Strata

makes
8 servings

By Christmas morning, my family is usually ready to spend the entire day in pajamas. It's truly my favorite day of the season because we traditionally spend at least the first half of the day at home. The children wake early to see what Santa left for them. David and I share their excitement but no longer pretend to be surprised. We take turns pulling goodies from our stockings before we exchange gifts. By the time we finish unwrapping, we're all hungry. I never want to miss out on any of that special time to cook, so I look for breakfast dishes that can be prepped ahead of time. This filling casserole is perfect for that purpose. It can be assembled the day before and baked in the morning so that it is fresh and hot. Alternatively, it can be baked ahead of time and then reheated in a 300°F oven until warmed through. Either way, this casserole is full of classic breakfast ingredients. You can dress it up by adding ½ cup of sautéed chopped mushrooms or asparagus or 1½ cups of fresh spinach when you combine the bread, meats, and cheese.

¼ cup (½ stick) unsalted butter, softened

3 cups cubed Modified Soul Bread (page 342)

8 slices bacon, chopped

8 ounces mild breakfast sausage, cooked and crumbled

8 ounces cheddar cheese, shredded and divided (about 2 cups)

8 large eggs

1¼ cups heavy cream

1 teaspoon mustard powder

1 teaspoon fresh thyme leaves, or ¼ teaspoon dried thyme

½ teaspoon ground black pepper

Preheat the oven to 350°F. Liberally grease a 9 by 13-inch baking dish with the butter.

Add the bread, bacon, sausage, and 6 ounces of the cheese to the prepared baking dish. Toss to combine and set aside.

In a large bowl, whisk together the eggs, heavy cream, mustard powder, thyme, and pepper. Pour the egg mixture over the bread mixture. Top with the remaining 2 ounces of cheese.

Cover the strata with foil and bake for 25 to 30 minutes, until the cheese is melted and the eggs are starting to set. Uncover and bake for an additional 15 to 20 minutes, until the top is lightly browned.

Let sit for at least 10 minutes before serving.

CALORIES: 549 | FAT: 44.5g | PROTEIN: 25.3g | CARBS: 2.9g | FIBER: 0.1g | OAT FIBER: 10.5g

French Toast Casserole

makes
8 servings

This recipe is easy to make ahead of time, so it is convenient to serve on Christmas morning if your family prefers a sweet breakfast. Like the strata (page 310), it can be assembled a day or two in advance and then baked just before serving, or it can be fully prepared in advance and reheated just before serving. I prefer to bake it just before serving because it makes the house smell amazing! It's also hard to resist just out of the oven. I like to serve it with sausage and/or bacon.

4 cups Cinnamon Soul Bread (page 138), crumbled or cut into 1-inch cubes

6 ounces cream cheese (¾ cup), softened

⅓ cup powdered sweetener

1 teaspoon vanilla extract

8 large eggs

½ cup heavy cream

4 drops liquid sweetener

¼ teaspoon ground cinnamon

STREUSEL TOPPING:

1 tablespoon unsalted butter, softened

½ cup chopped pecans

⅓ cup brown sugar substitute

3 tablespoons oat fiber

½ teaspoon ground cinnamon

⅛ teaspoon salt

Preheat the oven to 350°F. Butter a 9 by 13-inch baking dish.

Place the bread pieces in the prepared baking dish.

In a bowl, mix together the cream cheese, powdered sweetener, and vanilla extract until smooth and creamy. Dollop the cream cheese mixture over the bread.

Use a blender to combine the eggs, heavy cream, liquid sweetener, and cinnamon. Pour the egg mixture over the bread and cream cheese, making sure to cover all of the bread and cream cheese.

Make the topping: In a bowl, mix together the Streusel Topping ingredients. Sprinkle the topping over the casserole.

Bake for 35 to 45 minutes, until the center is set. Let cool for at least 5 minutes before serving.

CALORIES: 396 | FAT: 35.5g | PROTEIN: 13.5g | CARBS: 4.2g | FIBER: 1.5g | ERYTHRITOL: 12g | OAT FIBER: 12.8g

Holiday Dinner

Perfect Beef Tenderloin · 316

Baked Macaroni and Cheese with Crab Meat · 318

Grandmother's Christmas Coconut Cream Cake · 320

Black Forest Cheesecake · 322

Perfect Beef Tenderloin

makes
6 to 9 servings

Because of the price, beef tenderloin is a once-a-year treat for my family, and what better time to serve something special than on Christmas Day? Truly, this is a simple recipe with fantastic results. I don't trim the fat from my beef tenderloin, but I do trim the silverskin, which is a tough membrane that often runs the length of the roast. You can ask the butcher to do this step for you. You can also request a center-cut tenderloin so that the thickness of the roast is more uniform. If you happen to get a tenderloin with a thinner "tail," either fold in the tail toward the thicker part and tie it with butcher string; slice it off and cook it separately; or cook the whole tenderloin as is, understanding that the thinner portion may be well done while the thicker part will be more rare. That solution works well for my family because the kids like their meat well done, while David and I prefer it medium-rare.

2 to 3 pounds beef tenderloin, silverskin removed

3 tablespoons unsalted butter, softened

1 tablespoon coarse sea salt

1½ teaspoons chopped fresh rosemary

1 teaspoon ground black pepper

Let the roast sit at room temperature for up to 1 hour before roasting.

Preheat the oven to 475°F.

Rub the butter into the beef tenderloin with your fingers, making sure to coat all sides well. Sprinkle the coarse salt, rosemary, and pepper over the roast and rub in the seasonings to form a thick crust. Use more butter and seasonings if necessary to cover the entire tenderloin.

Place the roast in an oven-safe skillet or a roasting pan. Bake for 20 to 25 minutes, until the temperature reaches your desired doneness. Use the chart at left to know when to remove the roast from the oven.

Wrap the roast tightly in foil and let it rest for about 20 minutes before slicing and serving.

165°F	Well-done
155°F	Medium
140°F	Medium-rare
135°F	Rare

CALORIES: 277 | FAT: 8.7g | PROTEIN: 40.7g | CARBS: 0g | FIBER: 0g

Baked Macaroni and Cheese with Crab Meat

makes
12 servings

This dish inserts a little more special into a special family treat. My daughter has always loved macaroni and cheese, and so have I. While neither of us used to turn down the boxed version, it was the old-fashioned baked version that I preferred and that we ate on special occasions. When I began using shirataki noodles made from konjac, I wondered if I could create a keto-friendly version of my favorite baked macaroni. After all, the baked version includes a lot of butter, cheese, and milk—all ingredients that we enjoy as part of our low-carb diet. The answer is yes! And it is delicious. Adding crab meat makes this a truly celebratory dish. If you don't like the shirataki noodles or can't find them, then you can use cabbage noodles, chopped zucchini, or chopped cauliflower instead. Just be sure to blanch or steam the veggies and remove as much moisture as possible before adding them to the sauce mixture and baking.

½ cup (1 stick) plus 2 tablespoons unsalted butter

3 ounces cream cheese (¼ cup plus 2 tablespoons)

1 cup heavy cream

½ cup sour cream

2 large eggs, beaten

1 teaspoon salt

½ teaspoon garlic powder

¼ teaspoon cayenne pepper (optional)

4 (7-ounce) packages shirataki fettuccine noodles, cut into 1-inch lengths

8 ounces crab meat, cartilage removed

8 ounces mild cheddar cheese, shredded (about 2 cups)

8 ounces sharp cheddar cheese, shredded (about 2 cups)

TOPPING:

2½ tablespoons unsalted butter, softened

⅓ cup pork dust (ground pork rinds)

1 ounce Parmesan cheese, grated (about ⅓ cup)

¼ cup oat fiber

Preheat the oven to 325°F. Grease a 9 by 13-inch glass baking dish.

Melt the butter and cream cheese in a large saucepan over low heat. When melted, whisk in the heavy cream, sour cream, and beaten eggs. Continue to cook over low heat, whisking constantly, until the mixture thickens and is creamy and smooth. Add the salt, garlic powder, and cayenne, if using.

Remove from the heat and stir in the shirataki noodles, crab meat, and cheddar cheeses until thoroughly combined. Pour the mixture into the prepared baking dish.

Make the topping: Mix together the butter, pork dust, Parmesan cheese, and oat fiber. The mixture should be coarse like sand. Sprinkle the topping over the casserole.

Bake for 30 to 35 minutes, until golden brown and bubbling. Let cool for 10 minutes before serving.

CALORIES: 387 | FAT: 35.2g | PROTEIN: 16.1g | CARBS: 2.2g | FIBER: 0g | OAT FIBER: 3.8g

Grandmother's Christmas Coconut Cream Cake

makes
16 servings

Unashamedly I will confess that one bite of this low-carb coconut cake made me cry. My grandmother made this dessert only at Christmas. Often she made two cakes because she had promised each of her "most special" 15 grandchildren a slice or two. Her coconut cake was moist and sweet, and my mother and one of her sisters often helped her make it. Grandmother insisted that the cake needed to sit overnight before serving, and I'm sure that step is what made it taste so amazing. My daughter, Grace, never got to try her great-grandmother's cake, but when she taste-tested this version for me, her face lit up and she said, "Mom, is it bad that I don't want to share this with anyone else?" No, baby girl, I feel the same way! Now that we have this recipe, created just for this book, it will become a new holiday tradition for the two of us. We are thankful that Grace's daddy doesn't like coconut so we don't have to share.

⅔ cup coconut flour

½ cup oat fiber

¼ cup whey protein isolate

2 teaspoons baking powder

½ teaspoon salt

½ cup (1 stick) unsalted butter, softened

1 cup granulated sweetener

8 large eggs

1 cup heavy cream

1 tablespoon vanilla extract

1½ teaspoons coconut extract

4 large egg whites

5 or 6 drops liquid sweetener, to taste

COCONUT ICING:

2¼ cups heavy cream

2½ cups sour cream, room temperature

¾ cup powdered sweetener

Preheat the oven to 350°F. Liberally grease two 9-inch round cake pans and line the pans with parchment paper.

Make the cake batter: In a large bowl, whisk together the coconut flour, oat fiber, protein isolate, baking powder, and salt; set aside.

In a separate large bowl, use a hand mixer or stand mixer to whip the butter and granulated sweetener. Add the whole eggs, one at a time, beating well after each addition. Stir in the heavy cream and extracts by hand. Add the dry ingredients and mix by hand until just incorporated.

In a third bowl, use the mixer to whip the egg whites until stiff peaks form. Fold the whipped whites into the batter, being careful to not overmix. Add the liquid sweetener.

Divide the batter evenly between the prepared cake pans. Bake for 18 to 22 minutes, until the cakes are lightly springy to the touch or a toothpick inserted in the center of a cake comes out clean. Let the cakes cool in the pans for about 15 minutes before removing from the pans and transferring to a cooling rack to cool completely.

While the cakes are cooling, make the icing: Use the mixer to whip the heavy cream. When the cream holds stiff peaks, beat in the sour cream, sweetener, and coconut extract. Mix in the shredded coconut by hand.

CALORIES: 319 | FAT: 19.1g | PROTEIN: 22.8g | CARBS: 7g | FIBER: 5.3g | ERYTHRITOL: 18.8

1½ teaspoons coconut extract

8 ounces unsweetened shredded coconut

2 ounces unsweetened shredded coconut, for garnish

To assemble, slice each cake in half horizontally. Place one layer on a cake plate and spread about ⅓ cup of the icing on top. Add another layer of cake, followed by another layer of icing; continue until all four layers are assembled. Cover the top and sides of the assembled cake with the remaining icing. Sprinkle the shredded coconut over the top.

Refrigerate for at least 6 hours or overnight before serving. Store leftovers in the refrigerator for up to 5 days.

Black Forest Cheesecake

makes
16 servings

This dessert falls under the category of "You've got to be kidding me! This is low-carb?" Yes. I promise that it is, even though cherries are not typically considered a low-carb fruit. The entire recipe uses just 2 ounces of pitted cherries, then uses some cherry extract to extend the cherry flavor without adding more carbs. If you're uncomfortable using cherries, you can substitute raspberries or strawberries, which are naturally lower in carbs than cherries. The chocolate cheesecake is rich and dense, and the fruit adds a nice pop of flavor. Garnished with shaved chocolate, freshly whipped cream, and a few chopped cherries, this dessert looks impressive on a buffet table.

CALORIES: 341 | FAT: 32.8g | PROTEIN: 7.6g | CARBS: 4.7g | FIBER: 5.6g | ERYTHRITOL: 14.6g

CHERRY SAUCE:

2 ounces pitted fresh Bing cherries, chopped

2 tablespoons powdered sweetener

¾ cup water, divided

1½ teaspoons unflavored gelatin

1½ teaspoons cherry extract

½ teaspoon vanilla extract

CRUST:

⅓ cup blanched almond flour

⅓ cup hazelnut flour

⅓ cup oat fiber

3 tablespoons unsweetened cocoa powder

⅛ teaspoon ground cinnamon

5 tablespoons unsalted butter, softened

2 tablespoons granulated sweetener

½ teaspoon vanilla extract

6 drops liquid sweetener

CHEESECAKE BATTER:

3 (8-ounce) packages cream cheese, softened

1 cup granulated sweetener

5 large eggs

3 ounces unsweetened baking chocolate, melted but not hot

⅓ cup heavy cream

1½ teaspoons vanilla extract

1 teaspoon cherry extract

4 drops liquid sweetener

FOR GARNISH:

Chocolate curls

Chopped Bing cherries

Whipped cream

Make the cherry sauce: In a small saucepan over low heat, bring the cherries, sweetener, and ½ cup of the water to a simmer. Allow to simmer for about 10 minutes, until the cherries have softened.

In a small bowl, dissolve the gelatin in the remaining ¼ cup of water.

When the cherries have softened, stir in the dissolved gelatin until it is thoroughly incorporated. Remove from the heat and add the extracts. Stir well and set aside to cool and thicken. It may take 1 hour or more for the sauce to thicken.

Make the crust: Mix all the crust ingredients by hand or in a food processor. Line a 9-inch springform pan with parchment paper. Press the crust into the bottom and ¼ inch up the sides of the pan. Set aside.

Preheat the oven to 325°F.

Make the cheesecake batter: In a large bowl, use a hand mixer or stand mixer to whip the cream cheese and granulated sweetener until creamy. Add the eggs one at a time, beating well after each addition. Pour in the melted chocolate, stirring as you add it. Stir in the heavy cream, extracts, and liquid sweetener.

To assemble, pour half of the cheesecake batter over the prepared crust. Top with the cherry sauce. Cover with the remaining cheesecake batter.

Bake for 1 hour 15 minutes to 1 hour 25 minutes, until just set. The center may still be slightly soft. Turn off the oven and leave the cheesecake in the oven with the door ajar for 1 hour before removing. Let cool completely. Remove the outer ring from the springform pan, wrap the cheesecake in plastic wrap, and refrigerate for at least 6 hours or overnight before serving.

Garnish with chocolate curls, a few chopped cherries, and freshly whipped cream.

Holiday Party

Cheese Straws

makes
12 servings

High-carb cheese straws were always one of my favorite snacks to serve at parties. I also ate ridiculous amounts of them myself. As I became a more experienced baker, I wondered if I might be able to make them low-carb. I did! This was one of those recipes that I made and then began texting photos to others. Even though I tried three different versions, the first batch I made was the favorite, and that's the version I'm excited to share with you here. You'll need a cookie press with a star-shaped tip to make these nibbles look like the ones pictured.

6 ounces cheddar cheese, shredded (about 1½ cups)

3 ounces cream cheese (¼ cup plus 2 tablespoons), softened

3 tablespoons unsalted butter, softened

⅔ cup oat fiber

1 tablespoon whey protein isolate

1 teaspoon baking powder

¼ teaspoon salt

¼ teaspoon cayenne pepper

1 large egg

SPECIAL EQUIPMENT:

Cookie press with star-shaped tip

Preheat the oven to 350°F. Line a baking sheet with parchment paper.

Place the cheddar cheese, cream cheese, and butter in a food processor and process until thoroughly mixed. Add the oat fiber, protein isolate, baking powder, salt, cayenne, and egg and continue processing until a thick dough forms.

Transfer the dough to a cookie press. Using a star-shaped tip, pipe 2½-inch strips of dough onto the prepared baking sheet. If the dough is too soft to work with, refrigerate for 1 to 2 hours before piping the cheese straws.

Bake for 6 to 10 minutes, until lightly browned and set. Transfer to a cooling rack and let sit for 2 to 3 hours to become crisp. You can also place the cheese straws on the cooling rack in the oven with the oven light on and the door ajar, which results in crispier cheese straws.

CALORIES: 124 | FAT: 11.3g | PROTEIN: 5g | CARBS: 0.7g | FIBER: 0g | OAT FIBER: 10g

Sausage Balls

makes
24 sausage balls
(2 per serving)

Before going keto, I loved sausage balls, especially if my grandmother made them. I was married with two kids before I tried making them myself. My husband won't let me forget that I was working to make them look right when his mother called. Because I knew she made great sausage balls, I complained to her that I couldn't get mine to stick together. As we talked, she figured out that I had cooked and drained the sausage before trying to combine it with the other ingredients! What I had coaxed into balls and baked were extremely dry. Because company was coming, I made a dip for them and kept right on going. Take it from someone who has learned an important lesson: don't cook the sausage before making the sausage balls! This low-carb version has passed the carbivore test. If you don't tell your guests that these are keto, they won't know.

½ **cup blanched almond flour**

½ **cup oat fiber**

1 **teaspoon baking powder**

½ **teaspoon salt**

1½ **ounces cream cheese
(3 tablespoons), softened**

1 **pound bulk pork sausage**

8 **ounces cheddar cheese,
shredded (about 2 cups)**

Preheat the oven to 350°F. Line a baking sheet with parchment paper.

In a large bowl, use a hand mixer or stand mixer to thoroughly combine all the ingredients. Shape the mixture into twenty-four 1-inch balls and place on the prepared baking sheet.

Bake the sausage balls for 12 to 15 minutes, until browned and cooked through. Serve warm.

CALORIES: 143 | FAT: 16.9g | PROTEIN: 8.5g | CARBS: 1.6g | FIBER: 0.5g | OAT FIBER: 7.6g

Gingerbread Cookies

makes
12 cookies
(1 per serving)

As if you needed additional evidence that you can enjoy traditional holiday favorites and stay on plan, here's one more recipe to convince you that you won't miss a thing. Like most cookie recipes, this one is simple. Although the dough is more fragile than a traditional dough made with all-purpose flour, you can roll it and cut it into shapes. Be sure to refrigerate the dough to make it easier to handle. If it becomes too warm, simply refrigerate it for another 30 to 45 minutes. Even though we like eating gingerbread cookies, I believe that making and decorating the cookies together is the best part.

¾ cup blanched almond flour or hazelnut flour (see Tips)

¾ cup oat fiber

½ cup brown sugar substitute

½ teaspoon salt

1 teaspoon baking powder

1½ teaspoons ginger powder

1 teaspoon ground cinnamon

¼ teaspoon ground cloves

1 large egg

1 large egg white

6 tablespoons (¾ stick) unsalted butter, softened

1 tablespoon refined coconut oil

1 teaspoon vanilla extract

ICING:

¼ cup powdered sweetener

1 tablespoon heavy cream

2 drops vanilla extract

Place the flour, oat fiber, brown sugar substitute, salt, baking powder, ginger, cinnamon, and cloves in a food processor and process until it is well mixed. Add the egg, egg white, butter, coconut oil, and vanilla extract; process until a dough forms. Place the dough in the refrigerator to chill for 45 minutes to 1 hour.

When ready to bake, preheat the oven to 325°F. Line a cookie sheet with parchment paper.

Roll the chilled dough to a ¼-inch thickness between two pieces of parchment paper. If you find the dough too sticky, sprinkle it with oat fiber to make it easier to handle.

Cut the rolled dough into shapes and place on the prepared cookie sheet. Bake for 9 to 11 minutes, until slightly browned and set. Carefully remove the cookies to a cooling rack to cool. They will be soft when they first come out of the oven but will crisp up as they cool.

While the cookies are cooling, make the icing: In a small bowl, mix all the icing ingredients well. Decorate the cookies with the icing as desired.

tips

I like to use hazelnut flour rather than almond flour in this recipe because it provides more flavor and fewer carbs.

If you don't want to roll out the dough and cut it into shapes, you can roll the dough into 1-inch balls and then flatten them before baking.

CALORIES: 109 | FAT: 10.8g | PROTEIN: 1.7g | CARBS: 1.4g | FIBER: 0.5g | ERYTHRITOL: 24.3g | OAT FIBER: 11.3g

No-Bake Chocolate Cow Patty Cookies

makes
10 cookies
(1 per serving)

These were the easy cookies that my Aunt Jo made, and I adored them. I loved making them myself and craved them when I was pregnant with Grace. I never expected to develop a keto-friendly version, but when I discovered that hemp hearts make a good alternative to oatmeal, I was determined to give it a try. It took more than one attempt, but I'm really excited to share this recipe. The chocolate and peanut butter combination is perfect, and even though the texture is different from oatmeal, the hemp hearts are a very good, and very healthy, alternative as they are loaded with good omega-3 fats.

3 tablespoons unsalted butter

2 tablespoons chunky salted peanut butter

3 tablespoons powdered sweetener

2 drops liquid sweetener

1½ tablespoons unsweetened cocoa powder

1 tablespoon oat fiber

1 tablespoon peanut flour

¼ teaspoon instant coffee granules or espresso powder

⅛ teaspoon salt

1½ teaspoons vanilla extract

¼ cup hemp hearts (shelled hemp seeds)

Line a cookie sheet with parchment paper.

Melt the butter and peanut butter in a small saucepan over low heat. When fully melted, stir in the sweeteners, cocoa powder, oat fiber, peanut flour, coffee granules, salt, and vanilla extract. Mix until everything is smooth and the sweetener and coffee are fully dissolved. Remove from the heat and stir in the hemp hearts.

Let sit for at least 20 minutes before using a large spoon to drop the dough onto the prepared cookie sheet. The cookies will be very soft and may look too wet, but the hemp seeds will absorb the moisture. Place the cookies in the refrigerator until firm, 1½ to 2 hours.

Store in an airtight container in the refrigerator for up to a week.

CALORIES: 85 | FAT: 7.4g | PROTEIN: 2.6g | CARBS: 1.9g | FIBER: 1g | ERYTHRITOL: 2.7g | OAT FIBER: 1.1g

Shortbread Cookies

makes
24 cookies
(1 per serving)

These are some of the best shortbread cookies I have ever made. The dough is sturdy enough that, when cold, it could be used for cutout cookies. Just be sure to let the baked cookies cool before trying to decorate them. You could drizzle a little melted chocolate over the cookies if you're feeling fancy. If you're doing a holiday cookie exchange, you will definitely want these on your list.

1½ cups blanched almond flour

⅓ cup granulated sweetener

3 tablespoons oat fiber

¼ teaspoon salt

5 tablespoons unsalted butter, cold

2 large egg whites

1 teaspoon water

1½ teaspoons vanilla extract

Combine the flour, sweetener, oat fiber, salt, and butter in a food processor and pulse until the mixture has the texture of coarse crumbs. Add the egg whites, water, and vanilla extract and process until a thick dough forms.

Roll the dough into a 2-inch log. Wrap the log in plastic wrap or parchment paper and refrigerate for at least 1 hour.

When ready to bake, preheat the oven to 350°F. Line a cookie sheet with parchment paper.

Cut the dough into ⅛-inch slices. Place the slices on the prepared cookie sheet.

Bake for 6 to 8 minutes, until just golden brown. Remove the cookies to a cooling rack and let cool for up to 4 hours. The cookies will be soft when removed from the oven but will firm up as they cool. The longer they sit on the cooling rack, the more crisp they will be.

Store in an airtight container in the refrigerator for up to a week.

CALORIES: 60 | FAT: 3.5g | PROTEIN: 3.8g | CARBS: 1.5g | FIBER: 0.8g | ERYTHRITOL: 2.7g | OAT FIBER: 1.4g

Little Black Dress Recipes

From time to time, events call for a classic Little Black Dress (LBD). The best LBDs can be dressed up with pearls or made more casual with a pair of flats. The recipes in this chapter, like an LBD, are classics that pair well with a variety of other recipes for any occasion. I have included them because they serve as components of other recipes in this book, and so that you can add them to your repertoire of kitchen basics. These recipes are adaptable and versatile, and you may find many more occasions to use them.

Kristie's Ketchup

makes
about 1 cup
(2 tablespoons
per serving)

Yes, there are "low-carb" commercial ketchups. I used to use them, but when I started paying attention to the quality of ingredients, I decided to make my own instead. Not only is making ketchup far less expensive than buying it, but the homemade version truly tastes better!

1 (8-ounce) can tomato sauce

2 tablespoons apple cider vinegar

⅓ cup brown sugar substitute or your preferred granulated sweetener

1 teaspoon garlic powder

1 teaspoon onion powder

⅛ teaspoon ground cinnamon

⅛ teaspoon ground cloves

⅛ teaspoon salt

In a small saucepan over low heat, combine all the ingredients. Simmer for 10 to 15 minutes, until thickened. Store in the refrigerator for up to 2 weeks.

CALORIES: 12 | FAT: 0g | PROTEIN: 0.6g | CARBS: 2.2g | FIBER: 0.6g | ERYTHRITOL: 2g

Dry Ranch Mix

makes
1¾ cups
(2 tablespoons
per serving)

I always have some of this seasoning mix made ahead so that I can whip up a batch of ranch dressing in no time! But don't feel as if dressing is your only option with this seasoning mix. You can also use it to season meats, vegetables, soups—even deviled eggs!

¾ cup dried parsley

⅓ cup garlic powder

⅓ cup onion powder

2 tablespoons salt

1 tablespoon dried dill weed

2 teaspoons ground black pepper

Place all the ingredients in a bowl and mix well. Store in an airtight container in the pantry for up to 6 weeks.

CALORIES: 40 | FAT: 0g | PROTEIN: 2g | CARBS: 5g | FIBER: 1g KETO *Gatherings*

Classic BBQ Sauce

makes
about 1¼ cups
(2 tablespoons
per serving)

If you're looking for a simple and versatile BBQ sauce to enjoy with barbecued or grilled meats, this is it! I use it on pulled pork, ribs, and wings. This classic tomato-based sauce is what I grew up eating in western North Carolina, but it's no longer just a regional style—it's the default BBQ sauce for most Americans. The addition of cinnamon and cloves is what really makes this sauce special. Maple extract and liquid smoke also kick this recipe up a notch or two. Be sure to make plenty to use as a dipping sauce at the table. Our non–low-carb family members and friends always ask for the recipe, and that's high praise!

1 tablespoon bacon fat

1 (8-ounce) can tomato sauce

2 tablespoons apple cider vinegar

1 tablespoon prepared yellow mustard

1 tablespoon Worcestershire sauce

½ teaspoon maple extract

¼ teaspoon liquid smoke (optional)

1 teaspoon garlic powder

1 teaspoon onion powder

½ teaspoon mustard powder

½ teaspoon salt

¼ teaspoon cayenne pepper (optional)

⅛ teaspoon ground cinnamon

⅛ teaspoon ground cloves

Sweetener, to taste

Melt the bacon fat in a small saucepan over low heat. Add the tomato sauce, vinegar, mustard, and Worcestershire sauce and bring to a low simmer. Simmer for about 5 minutes.

Add the remaining ingredients and continue to simmer over very low heat for 10 to 15 minutes to allow the sauce to thicken. It keeps well in the refrigerator for at least 2 weeks.

CALORIES: 14 | FAT: 0.8g | PROTEIN: 0.3g | CARBS: 1.2g | FIBER: 0.3g

Eastern NC BBQ Sauce

makes
about 1 cup
(2 tablespoons
per serving)

I often tell people that David and I have a mixed marriage. While he grew up in eastern North Carolina, I grew up in western North Carolina, where BBQ sauce is supposed to be red, like a classic tomato-based BBQ sauce. He grew up in a land where BBQ sauce is white and vinegar based. Somehow we make it work! That's because we often compromise and have a little bit of everything on the table. I used to buy his favorite bottled vinegar-based barbecue sauce, but those eastern North Carolina folks are prone to slipping a little sugar into the bottle. We've found that this homemade sauce is equally tasty with no sugar added, but you can add sweetener if you like.

This vinegar-based sauce is lower in carbs than a traditional tomato-based sauce but packs a lot of great flavor. It should be made at least 12 hours in advance to allow the spices to flavor the vinegar.

1 cup white vinegar

1 tablespoon salt

2 teaspoons granulated sweetener, or 2 drops liquid sweetener (optional)

1 teaspoon hot sauce

1 teaspoon ground black pepper

1 teaspoon red pepper flakes

1 teaspoon smoked paprika

Mix all the ingredients in a jar or bottle with a tight-fitting lid. Store in the refrigerator for up to 3 weeks. Shake well before using.

CALORIES: 0 | FAT: 0g | PROTEIN: 0g | CARBS: 0g | FIBER: 0g KETO *Gatherings*

Modified Soul Bread

makes
18 servings

Arguably there is no perfect substitute for "real" bread, but this is the best low-carb bread substitute I have found. I love the texture of this bread, and it is excellent toasted, grilled, or used in recipes. More than that, it is truly low-carb. The texture does change over time and improves the day after baking. You can experiment by adding various spices or seasonings, but be careful of which brand of whey protein isolate you use, as different products can change the flavor and texture of the bread. My preferred brand is Isopure Zero Carb whey protein isolate.

1¼ cups whey protein isolate

½ cup oat fiber

2½ teaspoons baking powder

1 (1¼-ounce) packet active dry yeast

1 teaspoon xanthan gum

¼ teaspoon baking soda

¼ teaspoon cream of tartar

¼ teaspoon salt

12 ounces cream cheese (1½ cups), softened

4 large eggs

¼ cup heavy cream

¼ cup (½ stick) unsalted butter, melted but not hot

¼ cup bacon fat or coconut oil, melted but not hot

2 tablespoons apple cider vinegar

Preheat the oven to 325°F. Liberally grease a 9 by 5-inch loaf pan.

In a large bowl, whisk together the protein isolate, oat fiber, baking powder, yeast, xanthan gum, baking soda, cream of tartar, and salt; set aside.

In a separate bowl, using a hand mixer or stand mixer, combine the cream cheese, eggs, heavy cream, butter, bacon fat, and vinegar.

Use a sieve or sifter to sift the dry ingredients into the wet ingredients. Lightly stir by hand to combine. Do not overmix.

Pour the batter into the prepared loaf pan and bake for 45 minutes, until the loaf is golden brown and a toothpick inserted in the middle comes out clean. Don't underbake or the bread will sink as it cools. Let cool for at least 15 minutes before slicing with a serrated knife. Store in the refrigerator for up to a week.

variation ——————————————————

Soul Bread Crumbs. Cube or crumble the cooled bread into small pieces slightly larger than pebbles. Spread the pieces out on a rimmed baking sheet and let sit in the oven with the oven light on to dry out overnight.

Yogurt

makes
1¼ cups
(2 servings)

Few people think of yogurt as an unhealthy breakfast choice. On a ketogenic diet, however, commercial yogurt is often too high in sugar and carbs. Because low-carb yogurt is hard to find, I have developed an excellent low-carb alternative.

¾ **cup mascarpone**

½ **cup crème fraîche**

4 drops liquid sweetener

Use a rubber spatula or whisk to lightly mix all the ingredients. Do not overmix.

tip

You can substitute an equal amount of sour cream for the crème fraîche and mascarpone.

CALORIES: 321 | FAT: 33.5g | PROTEIN: 3.4g | CARBS: 2.4g | FIBER: 0g

Strawberry Sauce

makes
2½ cups (¼ cup per serving)

While you have to be careful with the carbs in fruit, this strawberry sauce is included to be used with Strawberry Shortcake on page 108. You can also spoon it over Creamy Vanilla Ice Cream (page 348) or Cinnamon Soul Bread (page 138) or mix it with a little cream cheese for a sweet treat at the end of a long day.

2 cups fresh strawberries, sliced

⅓ cup powdered sweetener

½ cup water, divided

¼ teaspoon unflavored gelatin

1 teaspoon strawberry extract

In a small saucepan over low heat, mix the strawberries, sweetener, and ¼ cup of the water. Cook for 5 to 7 minutes, until the berries have cooked down into a soft sauce.

Meanwhile, in a small bowl, sprinkle the gelatin over the remaining ¼ cup of water and stir until dissolved. Let sit for 3 to 5 minutes.

Stir the dissolved gelatin and strawberry extract into the cooked-down berries. Remove from the heat and let cool for 20 to 30 minutes. Store leftovers in the refrigerator for up to 4 days.

CALORIES: 10 | FAT: 0g | PROTEIN: 0.2g | CARBS: 2.4g | FIBER: 0.6g | ERYTHRITOL: 4.8g   KETO *Gatherings*

Chocolate Ganache

makes
1 cup
(1 tablespoon
per serving)

Can you name one thing that is not made better when covered in chocolate? Few things come to my mind. This simple chocolate sauce lends an elegant finish to the humble Peanut Butter Bundt Cake (page 88).

¾ **cup heavy cream**

2 ounces unsweetened baking chocolate, finely chopped

2 tablespoons unsalted butter

⅓ **cup powdered sweetener**

1 teaspoon vanilla extract

In a double boiler or small saucepan over very low heat, melt the heavy cream, chocolate, and butter. Whisk until smooth.

Whisk in the sweetener and vanilla extract; continue whisking until the sweetener is dissolved. Remove from the heat and allow to cool slightly before using.

CALORIES: 50 | FAT: 5g | PROTEIN: 0.8g | CARBS: 1.1g | FIBER: 0.6g | ERYTHRITOL: 3g

Hot Fudge Sauce

**makes
about 3 cups**
(¼ cup per
serving)

Unlike Chocolate Ganache, which firms up at room temperature and is perfect for pouring over cakes or drizzling over cookies, hot fudge sauce is a bit creamier. It works well on puddings and makes a decadent topping for ice cream. We love it over the Hot Fudge Cake on page 174.

½ cup (1 stick) unsalted butter

4 ounces unsweetened baking chocolate

1 cup heavy cream

1 cup powdered sweetener

⅓ cup unsweetened cocoa powder

½ cup unsweetened almond milk or coconut milk

2 teaspoons vanilla extract

¼ teaspoon salt

Melt the butter and chocolate in a medium saucepan over low heat. Whisk in the heavy cream, sweetener, and cocoa powder. After the mixture comes to a simmer, whisk in the almond milk, vanilla extract, and salt; remove from the heat. Use while warm.

Store leftovers in the refrigerator for up to a week. Rewarm in a small saucepan over low heat or in 15-second increments in the microwave, stirring well after each increment.

Creamy Vanilla Ice Cream

makes
about 2 cups
(⅓ cup per
serving)

I used to think that those who ate plain vanilla lacked any bit of adventure, but that was before I enjoyed this vanilla ice cream. Using real cream and fresh egg yolks creates a flavorful treat that is anything but boring. I have included it here to be used in the Hot Fudge Cake recipe (page 174), but this classic can be enjoyed on its own.

2½ cups heavy cream

¼ cup (½ stick) salted butter

6 large egg yolks

½ cup powdered sweetener
(see Tip)

2 teaspoons vanilla extract

¼ teaspoon salt

SPECIAL EQUIPMENT:
Ice cream maker

In a heavy saucepan over low heat, heat the heavy cream and butter, stirring with a whisk until the butter is melted. Add the egg yolks and continue whisking until just warmed. Add the sweetener and whisk until completely dissolved. Continue heating, whisking constantly, until the custard thickens, about 10 minutes.

When the custard coats the back of a wooden spoon or reaches 140°F on a candy thermometer, remove the pan from the heat. Do not allow the mixture to warm to over 140°F or the eggs will begin to cook.

Stir in the vanilla extract and salt. Transfer the mixture to a bowl and place in the refrigerator to cool.

When cool, churn the ice cream mixture in an ice cream maker following the manufacturer's directions until it reaches your desired consistency.

Store leftovers in the freezer. When frozen, this ice cream will harden to a solid state. Allow to thaw at room temperature for about 10 minutes before enjoying.

tip
The type of sweetener used makes a huge difference in the texture of the ice cream. For the best texture, use allulose or xylitol; remember that each sweetener has different characteristics (see pages 19 and 20 for details). Use the sweetener that you prefer and that does not impact your blood glucose.

Chocolate Ice Cream

makes
about 2 cups
(⅓ cup per
serving)

My husband says this ice cream is "too chocolatey." He even believes that! You can reduce the amount of chocolate to 4 ounces, which is what I do for him, but if you're a true chocolate lover as I am, more chocolate is certainly not a problem.

2½ cups heavy cream

6 ounces unsweetened baking chocolate, chopped

6 large egg yolks

1 cup powdered sweetener (see Tip)

2 teaspoons vanilla extract

½ teaspoon salt

SPECIAL EQUIPMENT:

Ice cream maker

In a heavy saucepan over low heat, heat the heavy cream, stirring with a whisk. Add the chocolate and continue stirring until the chocolate has melted. Add the egg yolks. Continue whisking on low heat until just warmed. Add the powdered sweetener and whisk until completely dissolved. Continue heating, whisking constantly, until the custard thickens, about 10 minutes.

When the custard coats the back of a wooden spoon or reaches 140°F on a candy thermometer, remove the pan from the heat. Do not allow the mixture to warm to over 140°F or the eggs will begin to cook.

Stir in the vanilla extract and salt. Transfer the mixture to a bowl and place in the refrigerator to cool.

When cool, churn the ice cream mixture in an ice cream maker following the manufacturer's directions until it reaches your desired consistency.

Store leftovers in the freezer. When frozen, this ice cream will harden to a solid state. Allow to thaw at room temperature for about 10 minutes before enjoying.

tip

The type of sweetener used makes a huge difference in the texture of the ice cream. For the best texture, use allulose or xylitol; remember that each sweetener has different characteristics (see pages 19 and 20 for details). Use the sweetener that you prefer and that does not impact your blood glucose.

Iced Tea

makes
1 gallon
(8 ounces per
serving)

While it may seem silly to include a recipe for unsweetened iced tea, the art of brewing good tea is lost on those who actually boil tea bags! We have to teach them better. Whether you used this tea as your Thanksgiving table wine or use it to make the Spiked Arnold Palmer (page 162), you need the mellow sunshiny taste of real brewed tea that isn't bitter and won't disappoint.

4 cups water

6 tea bags

Additional cold water, as needed

In a pot over high heat, bring the water to a rolling boil. After the water boils, remove the pot from the heat and let sit for 1 full minute, then add the tea bags. Place the lid on the pot and set aside to steep for at least 1 hour.

After the tea has steeped, pour the concentrated tea into a gallon-sized pitcher. The tea will not fill the pitcher, so use additional cold water to fill it. Refrigerate any leftovers for up to a week.

CALORIES: 0 | FAT: 0g | PROTEIN: 0g | CARBS: 0g | FIBER: 0g

With Gratitude

This book includes my very favorite recipes shared with friends and family. I am grateful for their love and friendship. I am especially grateful for the love and support of my family. David, Grace, and Jonathan have tasted and tested the best and the worst as Mom dragged them along on her uncertain journey. They have washed dishes, helped with food photos, endured family photographs, and rolled their eyes, but every day they have given me their love and support. My extended family has also served as inspiration and guinea pigs through the trials that have resulted in some new family favorites. Their enthusiasm and willingness to try apples that are not apples, oatmeal that is not oatmeal, and noodles that are not quite noodles has helped make each of these recipes better. For my friends who loved me even when I put raw broccoli in a casserole and failed to dissolve the instant coffee into the mocha torte (Gwen, Sean, Allison, and Susan), your lifelong friendship has saved me more than once. I love you all!

To my online friends who bravely tested recipes, provided feedback, and tested again, many, many thanks. You have made many of these recipes better, and for that we are all grateful! Your kind support of me and your commitment to this way of eating never ceases to amaze me. In addition to the recipe testers, I continue to be deeply indebted to the admins and moderators of my Facebook group. You incredible folks are working every day to support total strangers as they reclaim their health. You give selflessly of your time and attention because you, too, know the struggle. My work would not be possible without your commitment.

To the team at Victory Belt, you did it again! Pam is the editor who thinks of everything! You never cease to amaze me with how efficient you are. Bill and Haley created the most gorgeous cover I have ever seen—one that I could not wait to share with others. Thank you! Thanks also to the designers who took all of the pieces and brought this book to life in a way that is functional and beautiful. Your skill and vision inspire me! Lance, thanks for you leadership on this project. I've appreciated the guidance. Susan, thanks for entertaining my ideas and helping me to share this book. Erich, thanks for believing in me for one more project.

To Kim and John Varga, thank you for taking on this project, sticking with it through the challenges, and producing some really great photos. To Jenny Lowder, thank you for your hard work with the additional photos and two marathon days of shooting. We have once again bonded over melting ice cream, unphotogenic casseroles, and cookies that were way too busy! Thank you for becoming my friend and my local photographer. To Mary Bridsgche, thank you for pitching in on one of those marathon photography days. Your servant leadership has always made me admire you and is what makes you so beloved by so many. We could not have completed the photos without your help that day.

I am grateful to the low-carb and keto community who believe in me enough not only to purchase my books, but to gift them or recommend them to others. It is your trust in my recipes and my guidance that touches me most and keeps me striving to make great recipes that can help all of us enjoy better health as we sustain a lifestyle that many consider unsustainable. Thank you for being part of my journey.

Sukrin USA graciously provided sweetener for the recipes in this book. The Sukrin Melis (powdered sweetener), Sukrin:1 granulated sweetener, and Sukrin Gold granulated sweetener were used to test and photograph these recipes. I am so grateful for their exceptional products and for their kind support as I develop recipes.

KRISTIE H. SULLIVAN, PhD

Recipe Index

January

February

March

86
Savory Breakfast Muffins

88
Peanut Butter Bundt Cake

90
Pistachio Ice Cream

92
Old-Fashioned Whiskey Sour

SAINT PATRICK'S DAY

94
Homemade Corned Beef

96
Easy Weeknight Reuben Casserole

98
Delicious Faux-tato Cakes (Cauli Fritters)

100
Traditional Angel Food Cake

102
Taste of Summer Lemon Curd

April

106
Lemon Poppyseed Muffins

108
Strawberry Shortcake

110
Old-Fashioned Strawberry Ice Cream

112
Lemon Drop Martini

EASTER

114
Miracle Ham Biscuits with Herbed Butter

116
Quick and Easy Sautéed Asparagus

118
Jalapeño Popper Deviled Eggs

120
Saucy Shrimp Scampi

122
Kristie's Carrot Cake Cheesecake

124
Healthy Peanut Butter Cups

May

128
Everyone's Favorite Blueberry Cream Cheese Muffins

130
Classic Keto No-Nana Pudding

132
Peanut Butter Cup Ice Cream

134
Margarita

MOTHER'S DAY

136
Cream-Filled Crêpes with Blueberry Sauce

138
Cinnamon Soul Bread

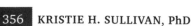

140

Faux Yogurt
Parfaits

CINCO DE MAYO

142

Slow Cooker
Barbacoa

144

Al Pastor
(Mexican Pork)

146

Wheat-Free
Tortillas

148

Cheese Taco Shells

150

Authentic
Salsa Verde

152

Jalapeño Cheddar
Bread

June

156

Just Like the Real
Thing Chocolate
Chip Muffins

158

Summer's Here
Strawberry
Layer Cake

160

Coffee Ice Cream

162

Spiked Arnold
Palmer

FATHER'S DAY

164

David's Favorite
Southwestern
Breakfast Casserole

166

Cinnamon Bagels

168

Shrimp Fra Diavolo

170

Creamy Parmesan
Lemon Chicken
with Artichokes

172

Sausage and
Cheese Stuffed
Mushrooms

174

Hot Fudge Cake

July

178

Lime in the
Coconut Muffins

180

Grace's Epic
Banana Split
Ice Cream Cake

182

Cookies and Cream
Ice Cream

184

Kristie's Mojito
Muy Bueno

FOURTH OF JULY

186

Summertime
Citrusy Shrimp

188

Kristie's Southern
Summer
Tomato Pie

190
Mediterranean
Marinated Cheese

192
Seven-Layer Salad

194
Jerk Chicken
Thighs

196
Private Island
Key Lime Pie

August

200
Peanut Butter
No-Nana Muffins

202
Perfect Pound Cake

204
Mint Chocolate
Chip Ice Cream

206
Piña Colada

FAREWELL TO
SUMMER

208
Tony's Favorite
Cold Veggie Pizza

210
Best of Summer
Seafood Casserole

212
Classic Caesar
Salad

BACK TO SCHOOL

214
Orange Danish
Pull-Apart Bread

216
Simple Flatbread

218
Jonathan's Favorite
Vegetable Beef
Stew

220
Grilled Ham and
Cheese with
Red Pepper Strips

222
K-E-T-O Chocolate
Sandwich Cookies

September

226
Perfect Pumpkin
Spice Muffins

228
Chocolate Éclair
Cake

230
Pumpkin Spice
Ice Cream

232
Pumpkin Spice
Margarita

THE FIFTH SEASON:
PUMPKIN SPICE

234
Pumpkin Spice
Fudge

236
Creamy Pumpkin
Spice Coffee

TAILGATING

238
Faux Apple Danish

240
Glazed Maple
Cinnamon Donuts

242
Mason Jar Chili
and Cornbread

244
Mexican Meatballs

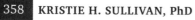

October

248
No-Apple Spice Muffins

250
Peanut Butter Pie

252
Brownie Ice Cream

254
Hot Buttered Rum

COZY FALL FOODS

256
Baked Cinnamon Faux Apple Oatmeal

258
Cinnamon Roll Pull-Apart Bread

260
Korean Short Ribs

262
Smoked Gouda Cauli Mash

PRE–TRICK-OR-TREATING

264
Brunswick Stew

266
Zuppa Toscana (Sausage and Kale Soup)

268
Jalapeño Cheddar Cornbread

November

274
Cinnamon Pecan Muffins

276
Cherry Yum-Yum

278
Butter Pecan Ice Cream

280
Mint Julep

THANKSGIVING

282
Sausage Stuffing

284
Green Bean Casserole

286
Harvest Squash Casserole

288
Keto-Friendly Cranberry Sauce

290
Perfect Keto Pecan Pie

292
Pumpkin Pie Cheesecake

294
Italian Cream Cake

296
Leftover Turkey Pot Pie

December

302
Sparkling Orange Cranberry Muffins

304
Mocha Brownie Torte

306
Gingerbread Ice Cream

308
White Christmas Mojito

CHRISTMAS MORNING

310
Breakfast Strata

312
French Toast Casserole

HOLIDAY DINNER

316
Perfect Beef Tenderloin

318
Baked Macaroni and Cheese with Crab Meat

320
Grandmother's Christmas Coconut Cream Cake

322
Black Forest Cheesecake

HOLIDAY PARTY

326
Cheese Straws

328
Sausage Balls

330
Gingerbread Cookies

332
No-Bake Chocolate Cow Patty Cookies

334
Shortbread Cookies

Little Black Dress Recipes

338
Kristie's Ketchup

339
Dry Ranch Mix

340
Classic BBQ Sauce

341
Eastern NC BBQ Sauce

342
Modified Soul Bread

344
Yogurt

345
Strawberry Sauce

346
Chocolate Ganache

347
Hot Fudge Sauce

348
Creamy Vanilla Ice Cream

350
Chocolate Ice Cream

352
Iced Tea

General Index